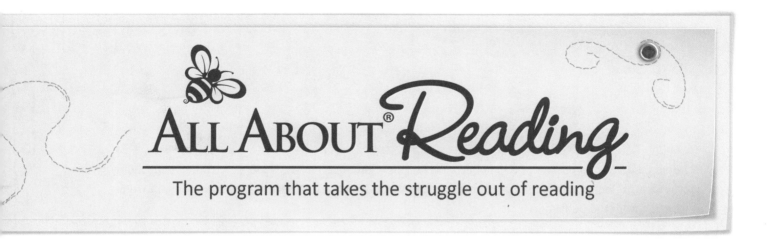

All About® Reading

The program that takes the struggle out of reading

Level 1

Color Edition

by Marie Rippel

Copyright © 2019 by All About® Learning Press, Inc.
Previous editions copyright © 2011-2018
Printed in the United States of America

Color Edition
v.2.1.0

All About® Learning Press, Inc.
615 Commerce Loop
Eagle River, WI 54521

ISBN 978-1-935197-78-2

Editor: Renée LaTulippe
Cover Illustrations and Design: Dave LaTulippe
Graphics: Shanna Behrens, Donna Goeddaeus, Emily F. Johnson, Dave LaTulippe

The *All About Reading* Level 1 Teacher's Manual is part of the *All About® Reading* program.

For more books in this series, go to www.AllAboutReading.com.

Contents

1 Preparing for Level 1

Let Us Show You!... 7
What Do You Need?.. 9
What You Should Know about This Program.................................. 11
Is Your Student in the Right Level?.. 13
Preview the Teacher's Manual.. 15
Preview the Activity Book.. 17
Preview the Readers.. 21
Prepare Your Reading Review Box.. 23
Set Up the Letter Tiles.. 25
Preview the Letter Sounds.. 29
How Much Time Should I Spend on Reading?............................... 31

2 Complete Step-by-Step Lesson Plans

Lesson 1: Letters M, S, P, and A.. 35
Lesson 2: Letters N, T, B, and J.. 45
Lesson 3: Read "Bam!"... 55
Lesson 4: Letters G, D, C, and Y.. 61
Lesson 5: Read "The Cat".. 69
Lesson 6: Letters H, K, and R.. 73
Lesson 7: Read "Jam" and "A Hat".. 81
Lesson 8: Letters I, V, F, and Z... 87
Lesson 9: Read "Hit the Gas" and "The Bad Rat"...................... 95
Lesson 10: Letters O, L, and W.. 101
Lesson 11: Read "Jan Did It" and "The Job".............................. 109
Lesson 12: Letter U and the Second Sound of S........................ 115
Lesson 13: Read "Run, Bug, Run!" and "Kip the Pup"................. 123
Lesson 14: Letter E.. 129
Lesson 15: Read "The Gum" and "The Sad Hog"......................... 135
Lesson 16: Letters QU and X.. 139
Lesson 17: Read "Pet Ox" and "Fox in a Box"............................. 145
Lesson 18: Consonant Team TH... 151
Lesson 19: Read "Get Them!" and "The Red Pen"....................... 157
Lesson 20: Consonant Team SH... 163
Lesson 21: Read "Run!" and "Six Fish"....................................... 169
Lesson 22: Consonant Team CH... 175
Lesson 23: Read "The Tub" and "Get the Moth, Meg!"................ 181
Lesson 24: Words with Final Blends... 187
Lesson 25: Read "Tin Raft" and "Lost in the Bog"...................... 193
Lesson 26: Words with Initial Blends... 197
Lesson 27: Read "Lunch" and "The Big Top".............................. 203
Lesson 28: Read "Slim Went West" and "The Hit"...................... 209
Lesson 29: FF, LL, and SS... 215

Lesson 30: Read "Mud Milk" and "The Ant Hill" 221

Lesson 31: Three Leap Words 227

Lesson 32: Read "The Plan" and "The Big Mess" 231

Lesson 33: Read "The Runt Pig" and "Fish Class" 237

Lesson 34: Consonant Team CK 243

Lesson 35: Read "The Pet Duck" and "Fun at the Pond" 249

Lesson 36: Consonant Team NG 255

Lesson 37: Read "The Bat and King Sam" and "The Long Nap" 263

Lesson 38: Consonant Team NK 269

Lesson 39: Read "Frank Shrank" and "At Camp" 275

Lesson 40: Compound Words 281

Lesson 41: Read "Cobweb the Cat" and "Yuck!" 287

Lesson 42: Plural Words 293

Lesson 43: Read "Ten Wishes" and "Fast Fun" 299

Lesson 44: Additional Sounds for A, I, and C 305

Lesson 45: Read "The Lost List" and "No Mud for Max" 309

Lesson 46: Additional Sounds for O and G 313

Lesson 47: Read "Pip the Milkman" and "The Duck Egg" 317

Lesson 48: Additional Sounds for E, U, Y, and CH 323

Lesson 49: Read "The Sled" and "Ducks in a Truck" 327

Lesson 50: Short Vowels and Counting Syllables 333

Lesson 51: Read "Biff and the Bathtub" and "The Wind on the Hill" 337

Lesson 52: Open and Closed Syllables 343

Lesson 53: Read "Gus and Hal Go on a Trip" and "The Best Lunch" 349

3 Appendices

Appendix A: Scope and Sequence of Level 1 357

Appendix B: Phonograms Taught in Levels 1-4 359

Appendix C: Blending Procedure 363

Appendix D: Solving Letter Reversal Problems 365

Appendix E: How to Assemble Word Flippers 369

Appendix F: Tips and Activities for Using the Practice Sheets 371

Appendix G: Activities for Reviewing Phonograms 381

Appendix H: Activities for Reviewing Word Cards 383

Appendix I: List of Comprehension Activities 385

Appendix J: If Your Student Struggles with the Stories.. 387

Appendix K: Methods for Counting Syllables 389

Appendix L: Magnet Board Setup at the End of Level 1 391

Appendix M: Leap Words Taught in Level 1 393

Appendix N: Words Taught in Level 1 395

1

Preparing for Level 1

Let Us Show You!

If you prefer, you can skip the reading in Part 1 (pages 9-31) and let us show you instead! For a complete overview of how to prepare for *All About Reading*, check out our short videos.

Just follow these three easy steps.

 Grab a cup of coffee or tea.

 Access www.aalp.tv/reading-level-1 on your phone, tablet, or computer.

 Let us show you how to get set up for success!

You will only need to do this once, and then you and your student will be all set for the best teaching and learning experience you've ever had!

After watching the videos, rejoin us on page 35 of this Teacher's Manual to start teaching the first lesson.

What Do You Need?

In addition to this Teacher's Manual, you will need the following items:

1. Student Packet

The Student Packet contains:
- *Blast Off to Reading!* activity book
- Phonogram Cards and Word Cards
- Viewfinder Bookmark
- Stickers for the Progress Chart

2. Interactive Kit

The Interactive Kit contains:
- Letter Tiles
- Divider Cards
- Phonogram Sounds app
- Reading Review Box (Deluxe Kit)
- Tote Bag (Deluxe Kit)

(If you did not purchase the Reading Review Box, you will need an index card box.)

3. Readers
- *Run, Bug, Run!*
- *The Runt Pig*
- *Cobweb the Cat*

(This Teacher's Manual must be used with the Second Edition or Color Edition readers.)

4. Letter Tiles App or 2' x 3' Magnetic White Board

Our Letter Tiles app makes building words fun and easy. Go to www.allaboutlearningpress.com/letter-tiles-app/ to download. If you prefer working with physical letter tiles, then a magnetic white board is highly recommended.

5. Common Craft Materials
- Scissors
- Stapler
- Two small baggies (if you are using the physical letter tiles)

What You Should Know about This Program

First of all, you can do this! *All About Reading* is a scripted, open-and-go program developed for busy parents, teachers, and tutors who want to teach reading in the most effective way possible. This program doesn't require long periods of study, you don't have to develop your own lesson plans, and you don't have to stress over what to teach next—because everything is laid out for you, step by step. You'll get solid grounding in how to teach reading without being overwhelmed.

Your student will be actively involved in the learning process. This is a truly multisensory program; your student will learn through sight, sound, and touch. Everything is taught in context and your student will apply what he has learned right away. Your student will be engaged in thinking, processing, comparing, and learning.

Students who use the *All About Reading* method tend to feel a sense of excitement in learning. And they should! They are learning how to think, explore, and grow in their abilities. They feel successful as they see continual progress.

There are no gaps in this program. Your student will be taught everything he or she needs to know about reading, so no guessing is required. Each new concept builds upon the previous one, and no steps are skipped.

There are five key components of reading—and our program teaches all of them thoroughly. These five components are:

1. Phonological Awareness
2. Phonics and Decoding
3. Fluency
4. Vocabulary
5. Comprehension

All About Reading **is a mastery-based program.** As such, the levels don't correspond to grade levels. In mastery-based learning, students master one concept before moving on to a more advanced concept, regardless of age or grade level.

Most importantly, *All About Reading* **is committed to results.** The *All About Reading* program has a very focused mission: to enable you to teach your student to read while guaranteeing retention and enjoyment. Our approach to reading focuses on enabling students to become confident, fluent readers who can absorb and retain new information.

If you ever have a question as you are teaching, please feel free to contact us at support@allaboutlearningpress.com or 715-477-1976. We're here to help!

Is Your Student in the Right Level?

Starting Level 1 of *All About Reading* is an exciting time for you and your student. Together, you'll explore fascinating new concepts—including phonograms, counting syllables, and reading stories—and begin to establish a firm foundation for a lifetime of reading. But before your student begins Level 1, be sure he or she is comfortable with these vital prerequisite concepts.

Your student should display **letter knowledge**.

☐ Your student can recite the alphabet song.

☐ Your student recognizes the capital letters. If you ask your student to point to an <u>M</u>, he can do it.

☐ Your student recognizes the lowercase letters. If you ask your student to point to an <u>r</u>, he can do it.

Your student should display **print awareness**.

☐ Your student knows the proper way to hold a book.

☐ Your student understands that books are read from front to back.

☐ Your student understands that sentences are read from left to right.

☐ Your student knows that words on the page can be read.

Your student should display **listening comprehension**.

☐ Your student is able to retell a familiar story in his own words.

☐ Your student can answer simple questions about a story.

☐ Your student asks questions (*Why did the elephant laugh?*) during read-alouds.

Your student should display **phonological awareness**.

☐ Your student can rhyme. If you say *bat*, your student can come up with a rhyming word like *hat*.

☐ Your student understands word boundaries. If you say the sentence *Don't let the cat out*, your student is able to separate the sentence into five individual words.

☐ Your student can clap syllables. If you say *dog*, your student knows to clap once. If you say *umbrella*, your student knows to clap three times.

☐ Your student can blend sounds to make a word. If you say the sounds *sh...eep*, your student responds with the word *sheep*.

☐ Your student can identify the beginning sound in a word. If you ask your student to say the first sound in *pig*, your student is able to respond with the sound /p/.

☐ Your student can identify the ending sound in a word. If you ask your student to say the last sound in the word *jam*, your student is able to respond with the sound /m/.

Your student should display **motivation to read**.

Use your intuition to understand if your student is motivated to begin reading. The following are all signs that your student is motivated to read and has achieved the understanding that reading is fun.

☐ Does your student enjoy being read to, at least for short periods of time?

☐ Does your student pretend to read or write?

☐ Does your student frequently request read-aloud time and show a general enthusiasm for books?

How did your student do?

- If all or most of the boxes are checked, then your student is ready for *All About Reading* Level 1!

- If there are some missing checkmarks, then you've identified the areas that you should work on with your student.

- It is surprisingly easy to fill in these gaps in an engaging way with the *All About Reading* Pre-reading program.

Preview the Teacher's Manual

As you flip through the Teacher's Manual, you'll notice that all the lessons are laid out for you, step by step. You'll also notice that there are two types of lessons.

"New concept" lessons. In these lessons, your student will learn new phonograms and new words. You can see an example of a typical "new concept" lesson in Lesson 1 on page 35.

"Read a story" lessons. In these lessons, your student will practice the new concepts taught in the previous lesson by reading a story. Vocabulary and comprehension strategies are emphasized. You can see an example of a typical "read a story" lesson in Lesson 3 on page 55.

The lessons consist of five parts:

1. **Before You Begin.** This cream-colored box contains an overview of the lesson and is meant only for you, the teacher. It never takes more than a few minutes to read it, after which you will be well equipped to teach the lesson confidently.

2. **Review.** Beginning with Lesson 2, you'll give your student a quick review of previously taught concepts. You will need your student's Reading Review Box for this part of the lesson.

3. **New Teaching.** This is the hands-on portion of the lesson. Your student will work with the letter tiles and activity sheets while completing comprehension, vocabulary, and fluency exercises.

4. **Read-Aloud Time.** This section is a friendly reminder to fit in twenty minutes of read-aloud time every day.

5. **Track Your Progress.** At the end of each lesson, you'll record your student's progress on the Progress Chart.

If you are working with a younger student, you may only complete part of a lesson at a time. That's okay! Simply mark your place in the lesson plan. The next day, start your lesson with a quick review and then pick up where you left off.

Don't feel like you must push through an entire lesson in one sitting if your student isn't ready. Do what is best for your student.

Preview the Activity Book

The *Blast Off to Reading!* activity book contains:

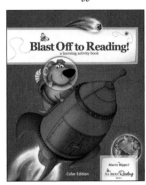

- Progress Chart
- Read-Aloud Record
- Activity Sheets
- Warm-Up Sheets
- Practice Sheets
- Certificate of Achievement

The lesson plans in the Teacher's Manual will tell you which pages you need for each lesson. The pages in the activity book are perforated for easy removal.

Let's take a quick look at each part of the activity book.

Progress Chart

The Progress Chart can be found on page 5 of the activity book.

This chart is a motivating part of the lessons for many students because it is a visual reminder of the progress they have made toward reading independently.

Remove the chart on the perforation and decide where to place it. Choose a prominent place like a bulletin board, the refrigerator, the back of a door, or another easily accessible area.

After each lesson has been completed, have your student color in or place a sticker over the next star on the chart.

Read-Aloud Record

The Read-Aloud Record can be found on page 7 of the activity book.

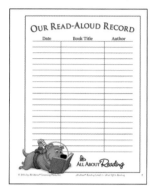

This chart is simply a place to record the books that you read aloud to your student. Toward the end of each lesson, you will be prompted to read to your student for twenty minutes. The daily read-aloud time may seem like a simple part of the reading lessons, but it's actually one of the most important components.

While your student is listening to good books, he'll also be
- gaining important background knowledge on a wide variety of subjects;
- developing a larger vocabulary; and
- hearing a variety of language patterns.

Your student's reading comprehension will be much higher because you've given him these huge benefits through daily read-aloud time.

This list is more for your use than for your student's. Not only is it a reminder of the many books that you enjoyed with your student, it is also great for accountability. If you skip read-aloud time, it will be obvious because of the short list! Aim for a long and varied list of books by the end of Level 1.

Here are some things to think about as you plan ahead for read-aloud time:

- **Figure out the best time of day for your read-aloud time.**
  You might find it easiest to connect read-aloud time to something else that you already do every day. It often works well to schedule it after lunch, recess, or a specific class. If you are a parent, bedtime is a natural time for enjoying books together.

- **Gather a variety of books, both fiction and non-fiction.**
  To keep interest high, look for books related to your student's specific interests and hobbies. You can also stimulate new interests by choosing read-alouds on topics that are completely new to your student.

- **Decide how you will minimize distractions.**
  At home, turn off the TV, computer, and telephone. Clear away competing toys and games. If you have a wiggly student, you can help him concentrate on the story by allowing him to play quietly while you read. Some students will be fine just holding a toy, while others might prefer to build with blocks, knead clay, or color quietly. For some students, it is easier to stay in one place and pay attention to what you are reading if they don't have to remain perfectly still.

Activity Sheets

The activity sheets are very motivating for most kids. They provide a variety of ways to practice the new concepts taught in the lessons. Flashcards and word banks have their place, but it is nice to break out of the "serious" learning and have a little fun applying it!

Take a look at the activity called "Word Match" on page 9 of the activity book. When you get to Lesson 1, the lesson plans will prompt you to cut out the word cards from the bottom of the page. You'll place the word cards in a pile, and your student will choose a card and place it under the matching picture with the word facing up. He will then answer a couple of comprehension questions about the words.

If you are working with an older student who doesn't need the additional practice for a certain concept, or who doesn't want to do "kid" activities, feel free to skip that particular activity sheet. But you may find that even adult learners enjoy the mental break that the activity sheets provide.

For the activity sheets, you will just need scissors and a stapler.

Warm-Up Sheets

You can find an example of a Warm-Up Sheet on page 19 of the activity book.

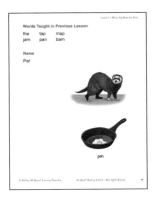

The Warm-Up Sheets are used just before reading a new story and contain words and phrases your student is about to encounter. Although all the words in the stories are completely decodable, these warm-up exercises give your student a little extra practice so he doesn't start reading "cold." Just as warming up our muscles before exercising is beneficial, warming up the brain before jumping right into a story helps your student be more successful.

The illustrations on the Warm-Up Sheets are used during short, pre-reading vocabulary discussions.

Practice Sheets

Take a look at the first Practice Sheet on page 15 of the activity book.

The Practice Sheets give your student practice reading words that reflect newly learned concepts. Most of the Practice Sheets contain three sections: New Words, Phrases, and Sentences.

The Sentences section includes short phrases like *Bob got*, and longer sentences like *Bob got the mop*.

This type of practice is called *phrased reading*. Phrasing is important for fluency; fluent readers are able to phrase, or break text into meaningful chunks.

If your student does not need practice with phrasing, feel free to skip the shorter phrases and have your student read just the full sentences.

Over time, the Practice Sheets will help your student move from sounding out words letter by letter to instant recognition of words. This change usually happens gradually, so don't expect perfection at first.

Here are some tips to help you get the most benefit out of the Practice Sheets:

1. **Place the sheet directly in front of your student.**

2. **Read across the page from left to right** to reinforce proper eye movements. Don't read down the columns.

3. **Stop before your student fatigues.** You might not complete the Practice Sheet all in one day, depending on your student's age and attention span.

4. **Would your student benefit from reviewing the Practice Sheet several times?** If so, repeat the exercise several days in a row.

5. **On the other hand, don't overwhelm your student with *too* much practice.** It is important to find the right balance for your individual student. Some students desperately need the practice provided, while others (especially younger students) are better served by reading every other line or every third line.

Preview the Readers

All About Reading Level 1 includes three readers that are 100% decodable.

 Run, Bug, Run!
First used in
Lesson 3

 The Runt Pig
First used in
Lesson 25

 Cobweb the Cat
First used in
Lesson 41

Your student will read one or two stories approximately every other lesson.

The first time a student reads a story is called a "cold reading." The student may read choppily, one word at a time. This is normal because the student is working very hard at decoding many of the individual words. Don't expect smooth reading during the cold reading.

Most students benefit from repeated readings—that is, reading the story a second or even third time. You'll find that during the repeated reading, your student will read more fluently and with better understanding. Since every student's needs will vary, these repeated readings are not scheduled in the lesson plans. Be sure to make time for them!

The Teacher's Manual provides comprehension questions and activity sheets for each story. If you feel your student would benefit from further activities, refer to Appendix I: List of Comprehension Activities.

If your student is having difficulty reading the stories, refer to Appendix J: If Your Student Struggles with the Stories.

Prepare Your Reading Review Box

The Reading Review Box organizes your flashcards so review time can be productive for your student. Every lesson, except the first one, starts with review. Whether you use our custom Reading Review Box or your own index card box, follow the instructions below to set it up.

1. **Place the divider cards in your box.** The divider cards are numbered 1-6 so you can be sure to get them in the correct order. Foam spacers are also provided to allow the cards to stand upright. As you need more room for cards, simply remove a foam spacer.

2. **Locate the yellow Phonogram Cards** in the Student Packet. Separate the perforated cards and place them behind the yellow tabbed divider called *Phonogram Cards–Future Lessons*.

3. **Locate the green Word Cards** in the Student Packet. Separate the perforated cards and place them behind the green tabbed divider called *Word Cards–Future Lessons*.

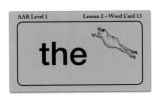

4. **Preview the Leap Word Cards.** Take a look at Word Card 13. See the frog?

   We use the frog graphic to indicate high-frequency words that either don't follow the normal rules or that contain phonograms that your student hasn't practiced yet. Your student will be "leaping ahead" to learn these words as sight words.

There are eleven Leap Words in Level 1, and the first one is taught in Lesson 2. Several techniques will be used to help your student remember these Leap Words:

- The frog graphic acts as a visual reminder to your student that the word is being treated as a sight word.

- Leap Word Cards are kept behind the Review divider in your student's Reading Review Box until your student has achieved instant recognition of the word.

- Leap Words frequently appear on the Practice Sheets.

- Leap Words are used frequently in the readers.

- If a Leap Word causes your student trouble, have your student use a light-colored crayon to circle the part of the word that doesn't say what the student expects it to say. Help your student see that Leap Words generally have just one or two letters that are troublesome, while the rest of the letters say their regular sounds and follow normal patterns.

For the complete list of Leap Words taught in Level 1, see Appendix M.

Set Up the Letter Tiles

Letter tiles are used in every "new concept" lesson to help your student quickly and easily grasp new concepts.

You have the option to use either the Letter Tiles app or the physical letter tiles. Here are some considerations to help you decide between the two formats.

With the Letter Tiles app:

- It's easy to capitalize words.
- You can hear the sounds of the phonograms as you teach.
- No more worries about lost letter tiles.
- Lessons are easy to teach "on the go."
- It's easy to switch between students. Simply select your current lesson in *All About Reading* or *All About Spelling* and you're ready to begin.

The Letter Tiles app has been our most requested product of all time, but the physical letter tiles have devoted fans as well.

With the physical letter tiles:

- No tablet is required to complete the lessons.
- Larger tiles are easy to read.
- It's easy to incorporate hands-on alphabetizing practice.
- Timeless and traditional educational tool.

Can't decide which tool to use? Consider which one would be most engaging for your student based on his current preferences. For example, does your student prefer colored pencils, or does she like video games? Is your student used to using technology for learning, or is he more comfortable with traditional methods of learning? Does she prefer e-books or paper books?

And don't forget to consider *your* preferences as well. Do you like the larger format of the magnetic white board and physical tiles? Or do you like the more compact nature of the app?

You really can't go wrong with either the app or the physical letter tiles since they both make reading concepts more concrete for your student. Choose one (or both) methods for working with letter tiles.

If You Choose the Letter Tiles App

Visit www.allaboutlearningpress.com/letter-tiles-app to purchase the app for your tablet.

Two short tutorial videos are available in the app menu to show you everything you need to know about using the app in your lessons.

If You Choose the Physical Letter Tiles

Take out the laminated Letter Tiles sheets. Separate the letter tiles and labels on the perforations.

Apply the magnets to the back of the letter tiles. Stick one magnet on the back of each letter tile and two magnets on the back of each label. (Skip this step if you will be using the letter tiles on a tabletop instead of a magnetic white board.)

Place one row of letter tiles on your magnetic white board. Include the letters <u>a</u> to <u>z</u>, plus a second <u>y</u>, as shown below. (Skip this step if you will be using the letter tiles on a tabletop.)

Prepare two small plastic baggies. Label one bag Level 1 and the other bag Levels 2-4. Place the following tiles and labels in your Level 1 baggie:

- remaining set of letters <u>a</u> to <u>z</u>
- letter tiles <u>th</u>, <u>sh</u>, <u>ch</u>, <u>ck</u>, <u>ng</u>, <u>nk</u>, and third <u>s</u>
- hyphen tile
- Consonant Teams label
- Other Tiles label

Put the remaining tiles and labels, including the blank ones, in the Levels 2-4 baggie. Store the baggie in your *All About Reading* tote bag or another safe place.

Answers to Common Questions about Letter Tiles

What do the different colors mean?

b   Blue tiles are consonants and consonant teams.

u   Red tiles are vowels and vowel teams.

er   Purple tiles are for the sound of /er/.

or   Yellow tiles are for Bossy R combinations that don't say /er/.

ci   Green tiles are for alternate spellings of /sh/: <u>ti</u>, <u>ci</u>, <u>si</u>.

ed   Orange tiles are for miscellaneous symbols and letters.

You'll learn about each category when you get to it in the lessons.

Why are there two different y's?
- <u>Y</u> can be a consonant or a vowel, depending on the word.
- When it is a consonant, it says /y/.
- When it is a vowel, it can say /ĭ/, /ī/, or /ē/.

Why are q and u together on a tile?
Since <u>q</u> is always followed by a <u>u</u> in English words, they are placed together on a single tile.

What will happen with the other letter tiles that are left in my Level 1 baggie?
- Starting in Lesson 18, we will gradually add the remaining letter tiles to the board.
- Keep the baggie in a safe place (such as your reading tote bag) until the tiles are needed.
- To see what the board will look like by the end of Level 1, see Appendix L.

What if I don't have a magnetic white board?
A magnetic white board makes it easier and faster to set up for your reading lessons, but if you don't have a magnetic white board, you can set up the letter tiles right on your table.

What do all these funny marks and symbols mean?
As a shorthand way to represent the sounds of letters in this Teacher's Manual, we use slashes. For example, /m/ stands for the spoken sound *mmm* as in *monkey*.

You will also see two other sound symbols:

- A straight line above a letter, as in /ā/, represents the long vowel sound. This symbol is called a *macron*.
- A "smile" above a letter, as in /ă/, represents the short vowel sound. This symbol is called a *breve*.

For a complete list of letter sounds and key words, see Appendix B.

Preview the Letter Sounds

Your student will learn the sounds of letters and letter combinations, called *phonograms*. For example, phonogram t says /t/ as in *tent*. Phonogram sh says /sh/ as in *ship*.

The lesson plans will prompt you to preview the sounds of new phonograms before you teach them to your student. There are three ways you can preview the sounds:

1. **Phonogram Sounds app.** This free app can be used on your computer, tablet, or phone. Go to www.allaboutlearningpress.com/phonogram-sounds-app to download. Simply tap the phonogram to hear the sound.

2. **Letter Tiles app.** If you own the Letter Tiles app, "long hold" on a letter tile to hear the sound(s). (As discussed on page 25, this app has many other features as well, including moveable letter tiles.)

3. **Chart in Appendix B.** Key words are given for each phonogram.

Using the method you prefer, take a moment to preview the first two phonograms taught in Lesson 1: m and s. You'll discover that m has one sound (/m/), while s has two sounds (/s/ and /z/). In Lesson 1, you will only be teaching the first sound of s, /s/. Later, in Lesson 12, you will teach the second sound. The same is true for all of the letter tiles in Level 1 that have more than one sound: first we teach the most common sound, and within a short period of time, we teach the remaining sounds.

For letters with more than one sound, you may choose to teach all the sounds up front, and that is perfectly acceptable. Simply teach the multiple sounds and then let your student know that you will be working with the first sound for the rest of the lesson. You'll work with the remaining sounds in future lessons.

How Much Time Should I Spend on Reading?

All About Reading lessons are designed so that you can work at your student's pace. Following are general guidelines.

Spend 20 minutes per day teaching reading.

We recommend spending about 20 minutes per day, five days a week, on reading instruction, but you can adjust this if necessary for early readers or for older remedial students.

It can be helpful to set a timer. When 20 minutes are up, mark the spot in the lesson where you stopped. When you begin teaching the next day, briefly review some of the daily review cards, and then begin in the Teacher's Manual wherever you left off previously.

Short daily lessons are much more effective than longer, less frequent lessons. Your student's attention is less likely to wander, and you can accomplish more when your student is actively engaged in the lesson.

If you aren't done with the lesson when the 20 minutes are up, don't worry! This next tip is for you.

Lessons often take more than one day to complete.

Please know that the lessons in *All About Reading* are **not** meant to be completed in one day.

In fact, some lessons may take a week or more to finish. A number of variables including your student's age, attention span, prior experience, the difficulty of the concept being taught, and the length of the stories all play a part in how quickly a lesson can be completed.

And after the formal lesson, it will be time for some great read-alouds!

In addition to the lessons, read aloud to your student for 20 minutes per day.

Reading aloud to your student is one of the most important things you can do to promote future reading ability. In fact, this is such an important part of the program that it is actually added as a reminder at the end of every lesson.

Reading aloud for 20 minutes a day may not seem like a lot, but the cumulative effect cannot be overstated. By reading aloud for just 20 minutes a day over a five-year period, your student will have the advantage of 600 hours of read-alouds. That equates to huge gains in vocabulary, comprehension, and background information.

When you combine 20 minutes of direct reading instruction with 20 minutes of read-aloud time, you can rest assured that you are providing your student with the very best opportunity for long-term reading success.

Hello there, new friend!
My name is Rocket, and I'll be blasting
through the lessons with you,
giving you pep talks and helping you study
along the way.

So you better buckle up
and put on your spacesuit,
because it's time for ...

BLASTOFF!

2

Complete Step-by-Step Lesson Plans

Lesson 1   Letters M, S, P, and A

Objective

This lesson teaches words containing the letters <u>m</u>, <u>s</u>, <u>p</u>, and <u>a</u>. It also introduces the blending procedure and the terms *vowels* and *consonants*.

You Will Need

☐ Phonogram Cards 1-4   ☐ Word Cards 1-3

☐ *Blast Off to Reading!* page 9   ☐ Progress Chart

Before You Begin

At the beginning of each lesson, you will find a cream-colored "Before You Begin" section like this one. Review these instructions before you begin the lesson.

The actual lesson plan you will teach to your student begins *after* the "Before You Begin" section.

Preview the Sounds of the Letters

The four letters in this lesson were chosen because their sounds are easy for students to learn and can be used right away to form simple words.

m   The letter <u>m</u> says /m/ as in *moon*.

s   The letter <u>s</u> can say two sounds:

- /s/ as in *sun* (taught in this lesson)
- /z/ as in *has* (taught in Lesson 12)

p   The letter <u>p</u> says /p/ as in *pig*. Be sure that you and your student don't add /uh/ to the end of the sound, as in /puh/.

a   The letter <u>a</u> can say three sounds:

- /ă/ as in *apple*, known as the short sound (taught in this lesson)
- /ā/ as in *acorn*, known as the long sound (taught in Lesson 44)
- /ah/ as in *father* (taught in Lesson 44)

Refer to the Letter Tiles app or Phonogram Sounds app for a demonstration of the <u>m</u>, <u>s</u>, <u>p</u>, and <u>a</u> phonogram sounds.

Before You Begin
(continued)

Preview the Hand Motion for Letter A

 Note the hand on the card for <u>a</u>. This indicates that there is a hand motion that goes along with the sound. Your student will pretend to hold an apple in his hand as he says "/ă/–/ă/–apple."

Vowel sounds are often more difficult for students to learn. We make it easier by adding hand motions and teaching only one new vowel sound at a time.

To further cement this sound in your student's mind, take a bite out of the pretend apple with a loud crunch! The more dramatic you make this activity, the better your student will remember it.

Preview Vowels and Consonants

Your student will learn that the red tiles are vowels and the blue tiles are consonants.

If you are using a magnetic white board instead of the Letter Tiles app, set up the letter tiles in alphabetical order before the start of the lesson.

Preview the Blending Procedure

Blending is the technical term for *sounding out a word*. You say each sound in the word slowly (*s…i…t*) and then say the sounds together more quickly to form a word (*sit*). The sounds blend together in normal speech.

Throughout Level 1, we'll be using a specific blending procedure. The scripted lessons will walk you through the blending procedure, but you might also refer to Appendix C for an overview.

Note that learning to blend can take time! Don't be concerned if it takes several lessons for your student to grasp the concept of blending. We'll review blending in each "new concept" lesson, so your student will get plenty of practice.

Now you are ready to teach the first lesson!

Teach New Letter Sounds

Hold up the Phonogram Card for the letter <u>m</u>.

"This letter says /m/."

"Now it's your turn. What does this letter say?" *Student says /m/.*

Hold up the Phonogram Card for the letter <u>s</u>.

"This letter says /s/."

"Your turn. What does this letter say?" *Student says /s/.*

Hold up the Phonogram Card for the letter <u>p</u>.

"This letter says /p/."

"Your turn." *Student says /p/.*

Hold up the Phonogram Card for the letter <u>a</u>.

"This letter says /ă/."

Cup your hand as if you are holding an apple. "When we say /ă/, let's pretend that we are holding an apple. Say the sound of <u>a</u> like this: /ă/–/ă/–apple." *Student pretends to hold an apple and says /ă/–/ă/–apple.*

Point to the hand symbol on the card. "This hand will remind you that there is a hand motion for <u>a</u>."

Shuffle the cards and review them several times.

For extra practice with the new phonograms, play the game "Swat the Phonograms." For instructions, look for this icon in Appendix G.

File the flashcards behind the **Phonogram Cards Review** divider in your student's Reading Review Box. The cards will be reviewed at the beginning of the next lesson.

New Teaching
(continued)

Now move these four letter tiles into the workspace and practice the same sounds using the tiles.

Point to each tile in random order and ask your student to tell you the sound that the letter makes. Practice until your student can say the sound of each letter accurately.

Demonstrate How to Blend Sounds

Be sure your student uses the pointer finger of his dominant hand for this exercise.

Build the word *map* with letter tiles.

"Watch while I show you how we sound out words."

"I touch under each letter tile in order and I say the sound of that letter."

Touch under the m̲ and say /m/.

Touch under the a̲ and say /ă/.

Touch under the p̲ and say /p/.

Now go back to the beginning of the word and blend the sounds together as follows.

Slide your finger under the letters m̲-a̲ and say /mă/.

Lesson 1: Letters M, S, P, and A

New Teaching

(continued)

Start at the beginning of the word again. Slide your finger under the letters m-a-p and say *map* slowly.

Finally, read the word *map* at a normal pace as we do when we speak.

When your student reads the word in this last step, you may need to prompt him to say the word "fast like we talk."

Using the same blending procedure, have your student sound out the word *Sam*.

Leave the word *Sam* in the workspace.

Play "Change the Word"

"I'm going to change the first letter of this word."

"What does this new word say?" Encourage your student to sound out the new word, *Pam*.

> You may wish to point out to your student that *Sam* and *Pam* are names, and when they are in print, they are capitalized. You might show your student the names at the bottom of page 9 in the *Blast Off* activity book or, if you are using the Letter Tiles app, long hold to capitalize the first letter of the name.

Build the word *sap*.

"Sound out this word." *Student sounds out the word.*

Change the first letter to form the word *map*.

"What does this new word say?" Encourage your student to sound out the new word, *map*.

Teach Vowels and Consonants

"You may have noticed that the letter <u>a</u> tile is red, while the <u>m</u>, <u>p</u>, and <u>s</u> tiles are blue."

> If you are using the Letter Tiles app, select "All Tiles" from the program selection menu.

Move the vowels and consonants shown below into the workspace.

"Say the names of the letters on the red tiles." *A, e, i, o, u, and y.*

"The red tiles are *vowels*: <u>a</u>, <u>e</u>, <u>i</u>, <u>o</u>, <u>u</u>, and sometimes <u>y</u>."

"The blue tiles are *consonants*. <u>C</u> is a consonant. <u>P</u> is a consonant." Point to the letter tiles as you mention them.

"Can you tell me some other consonants?" *Student names some consonants.*

Move the blue <u>y</u> next to the red <u>y</u>. Point to the two <u>y</u> tiles.

"The letter <u>y</u> can be a vowel or a consonant. That's why we have a red <u>y</u> and a blue <u>y</u>."

New Teaching

(continued)

Don't Forget! If you are working with an older student, feel free to skip any of the activity sheets that your student wouldn't enjoy.

Complete Activity Sheet

"Let's match some words to pictures."

Word Match

Remove page 9 from the *Blast Off* activity book.

Cut out the word cards from the bottom of the page.

Have your student place the appropriate card under the matching picture.

Explain that names start with a capital letter.

Ask the following questions.

1. "Which of these words are names?" *Pam and Sam.*
2. "Which of these words rhyme?" *Pam and Sam, map and sap.*

Practice Reading Words

Have your student practice reading the words on Word Cards 1-3.

If your student can't automatically read these words by sight, he shouldn't guess at them. Instead, encourage your student to decode words using the blending procedure taught in this lesson.

 File the flashcards behind the **Word Cards Review** divider in your student's Reading Review Box. The cards will be reviewed at the beginning of the next lesson.

Read a Story or Poem

Read aloud to your student for twenty minutes. You can keep track of your read-alouds on the Read-Aloud Record found on page 7 of the activity book.

Mark the Progress Chart

Have your student mark Lesson 1 on the Progress Chart.

Lesson 1: Letters M, S, P, and A

Well, wag my tail!
Look at that ... you're reading!
And it's a good thing you learned
the word MAP, because I could use a good
co-pilot on my rocket. I'm great at flying,
but not so much at sniffing out directions.

So what do you say?
If you're ready for Lesson 2,
let's pack up our gear
and head for the stars!

Lesson 2   Letters N, T, B, and J

Objective

This lesson teaches words containing the letters n̲, t̲, b̲, and j̲ and the Leap Word *the*.

You Will Need

☐ Phonogram Cards 5-8   ☐ Word Cards 4-13

☐ *Blast Off to Reading!* pages 11-15

Before You Begin

Preview the Sounds of the Letters

n The letter n̲ says /n/ as in *nest*. If your student has difficulty discriminating between the sounds of /n/ and /m/, have him watch your lips as you pronounce the sounds.

t The letter t̲ says /t/ as in *tent*. Be sure that you and your student don't add /uh/ to the end of the sound, as in /tuh/.

b The letter b̲ says /b/ as in *bat*. It is impossible to say /b/ in isolation without any trace of /uh/ at the end, but clip the /uh/ as short as possible.

j The letter j̲ says /j/ as in *jam*. Be sure that you and your student don't add /uh/ to the end of the sound, as in /juh/.

  Refer to the Letter Tiles app or Phonogram Sounds app for a demonstration of the n̲, t̲, b̲, and j̲ phonogram sounds.

Look Ahead to the Review Section

You'll see that each lesson starts with a Review section. Review covers two main areas: Phonogram Cards and Word Cards.

You'll use the Reading Review Box to keep track of what has been mastered and what still needs to be reviewed. If you feel that a card has been mastered, place it behind the **Mastered** divider. If the card has not yet been mastered, place it behind the **Review** divider so it can be reviewed again in the next lesson.

Before You Begin
(continued)

How do you know when your student has mastered a Phonogram Card?

If your student...

- says the pure, clipped sound without adding /uh/ at the end— for example, he says /p/, not /puh/;
- responds quickly and easily when you hold up the card;
- does not hesitate to think of the answer; and
- you have no doubt that your student knows the card thoroughly...

...then that Phonogram Card is mastered! Move it behind the Mastered divider.

How do you know when your student has mastered a Word Card?

If your student is able to read the word on the card without having to sound it out, then you can consider that Word Card as mastered.

Preview the Practice Sheets

Over time, using the Practice Sheets will help your student move from sounding out words letter by letter to being able to instantly recognize words. This change usually happens gradually, so don't expect perfection at first.

Here are some tips to help you get the most benefit out of the Practice Sheets:

1. **Place the sheet directly in front of your student.**

2. **Read across the page from left to right** to reinforce proper eye movements. Don't read down the columns.

3. **The Viewfinder Bookmark can help your student focus on individual words.** Either run the top edge of the bookmark under the line of text, or center the word or phrase in the cutout area.

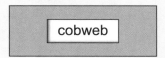

Lesson 2: Letters N, T, B, and J

Before You Begin
(continued)

4. **Stop before your student fatigues.** You might not complete the Practice Sheets all in one day, depending on your student's age and attention span.

5. **Would your student benefit from reviewing the Practice Sheets several times?** If so, repeat the exercise several days in a row.

6. **On the other hand, don't overwhelm your beginning reader with *too* much practice with the Practice Sheets.** It is important to find the right balance for your individual student. Some students desperately need the practice provided, while others (especially younger students) are better served by reading every other line or every third line.

See Appendix F for more tips on using the Practice Sheets.

Remember that this is hard work for most beginning readers, especially if they are still at the stage of sounding out each word. Reward effort with words of praise!

Review

 Review the Phonogram Cards that are behind the Review divider in your student's Reading Review Box. Show each card to your student and have him say the sound. If necessary, remind your student of the sound.

 Shuffle and review the Word Cards that are behind the Review divider in your student's Reading Review Box. If your student has difficulty reading a word, build the word with letter tiles and have your student sound it out using the blending procedure shown in Appendix C.

Ask your student to point to some vowels and some consonants.

Teach New Letter Sounds

 Hold up the Phonogram Card for the letter <u>n</u>.

"This letter says /n/."

"Now it's your turn. What does this letter say?" *Student says /n/.*

 Hold up the Phonogram Card for the letter <u>t</u>.

"This letter says /t/."

"Your turn. What does this letter say?" *Student says /t/.*

 Hold up the Phonogram Card for the letter <u>b</u>.

"This letter says /b/."

"Your turn." *Student says /b/.*

 Hold up the Phonogram Card for the letter <u>j</u>.

"This letter says /j/."

"Your turn." *Student says /j/.*

Now move these four letter tiles into the workspace and practice the same sounds using the tiles.

Point to each tile in random order and ask your student to tell you the sound that the letter makes. Practice until your student can say the sound of each letter accurately.

 Liven up practice with the new phonograms with the game "Phonogram Ball." For instructions, look for this icon in Appendix G.

New Teaching
(continued)

File the four new Phonogram Cards behind the **Review** divider and review them at the beginning of the next lesson. It often seems as if a student has mastered a new card during the reading lesson, but when you revisit that card in a day or two, it becomes obvious that he really hasn't.

It often takes multiple sessions to master a new phonogram.

Practice Commonly Confused Letters

Move the <u>m</u> and <u>n</u> tiles into the workspace.

Randomly dictate /m/ and /n/ to test whether your student can distinguish between the two sounds and choose the correct letter tile.

If your student has difficulty telling the difference between /m/ and /n/, have him watch your mouth as you say the sounds.

Blend Sounds with Letter Tiles

Build the word *pan* with letter tiles.

"I'll sound out this first word, and then you'll sound out the next word."

Touch under the <u>p</u> and say /*p*/.

Touch under the <u>a</u> and say /*ă*/.

Touch under the <u>n</u> and say /*n*/.

New Teaching
(continued)

Now go back to the beginning of the word and blend the sounds together as follows.

Slide your finger under the letters p-a and say /pă/.

Start at the beginning of the word again. Slide your finger under the letters p-a-n and say *pan* slowly.

Finally, read the word *pan* at a normal pace as we do when we speak.

Using the same blending procedure, have your student sound out the word *nap*.

> You may want to point out to your student that *pan* and *nap* contain the same letters, just in a different order. **Tip!**

Leave the word *nap* in the workspace.

Play "Change the Word"

"I'm going to change the first letter of this word."

"What does this new word say?" Encourage your student to sound out the new word, *tap*.

Continue to change one letter at a time to form the following words. Each time, have your student sound out the new word.

tap → tan → man → ban → an → at → bat → sat

New Teaching
(continued)

Complete Activity Sheets

"Let's match some words to pictures."

Word Match
Remove page 11 from the *Blast Off* activity book.

Cut out the word cards from the bottom of the page and have your student place the appropriate card under the matching picture.

Ask the following questions.

1. "Which picture starts with the sound /j/?" *Jam.*
2. "Which picture starts with the sound /m/?" *Man.*
3. "What is the first sound in the word *bat*?" */b/.*
4. "What is the first sound in the word *pan*?" */p/.*

"Good work! I think we deserve some ice cream now!"

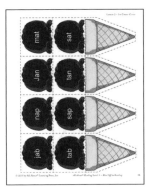

Ice Cream Cones
Remove page 13 from the activity book.

Cut out the ice cream scoops and cones.

Have your student read the words on each ice cream scoop. Put the rhyming words together to form ice cream desserts.

New Teaching
(continued)

Practice Reading Words

Have your student practice reading the words on Word Cards 4-12.

> The words *an* and *Ann* are homophones (words that sound alike but are spelled differently), as are *mat*, *Matt*, and *matte*. A sentence has been added to the Word Cards *an* and *mat*, and to all cards containing homophones in future lessons. Your student does not read these sentences—they are there for your reference in case you wish to discuss the correct word usage.

File the Word Cards behind the Review divider of the Reading Review Box.

Teach a Leap Word: *the*

For more information on Leap Words, see page 23.

Show Word Card 13 to your student.

"Most words follow the rules and say the sounds that we expect them to say. But there are a few words that do not. Here is one of those words."

"This word is *the*, as in *She has the balloons.*"

Point to the frog on the Word Card. "See this frog? This means that the word can't be sounded out. It is a Leap Word that you just need to remember."

"What is this word?" *The.*

Lesson 2: Letters N, T, B, and J

New Teaching
(continued)

> You may wish to explain that we usually pronounce this word as /thŭ/. Sometimes we do say /thē/, but for the purposes of the flashcard review, say the more common pronunciation: /thŭ/.

Review this Leap Word several times today and then file it behind the Review divider in the Reading Review Box.

Practice Fluency

Turn to page 15 in the activity book.

Point to a sentence that ends in a period. "This dot is a period. It is used to show the end of the sentence."

Point to a sentence that ends in an exclamation point. "This is an exclamation point. It is used to show emotion or excitement."

Model for your student the difference between reading a sentence with a period and reading a sentence with an exclamation point.

Have your student read from the Practice Sheet.

> Exclamation points are used in the story your student will read in the next lesson.

Read-Aloud Time

Read a Story or Poem

Read aloud to your student for twenty minutes.

Mark the Progress Chart

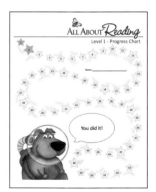

Have your student mark Lesson 2 on the Progress Chart.

Great job on Lesson 2!
And guess what?
Now you get to read your first story!

Go on!
There's a four-legged creature
(that's not me)
waiting to meet you
in Lesson 3.

Lesson 3   Read "Bam!"

Objective

In this lesson, students read a short story and practice reading sentences with periods and exclamation points.

You Will Need

☐ *Blast Off to Reading!* pages 17-19   ☐ optional: sticky notes

☐ *Run, Bug, Run!* book

Before You Begin

Preview the Story-Related Lessons

You've reached the first story-related lesson in Level 1! That means that your student will read a short story today. This is a great chance to practice newly learned decoding skills and learn comprehension strategies.

And of course we want to set your student up for success! To help her get the most out of this lesson, your student will do several warm-up activities before reading the story:

- **Completing an activity sheet** that introduces a new literary concept.
- **Reading a Warm-Up Sheet** to refresh her memory about words that have been explicitly taught in previous lessons.
- **Learning new vocabulary and activating prior knowledge** about story-specific topics through interesting pre-reading discussion.

During and after the story, we ask open-ended questions because we want students to relate to and put thought into what they're reading. We want them to contribute their ideas, test their predictions, and comprehend in a meaningful way. To encourage an active reading process, our reading comprehension strategies also focus on visualizing, questioning, summarizing, making predictions, and drawing conclusions.

Post-reading activities include discussing the main character or conflict, story sequencing, imagining alternate endings, and relating the story to your student's life. A complete list of reading comprehension activities can be found in Appendix I.

Together, these pre- and post-reading activities move your student toward the goal of reading with comprehension.

Before You Begin
(continued)

After completing the warm-up activities in this lesson, your student will read "Bam!" in the *Run, Bug, Run!* book. All the words in the story are decodable using previously taught concepts.

What should you expect when your student reads the stories?
It is normal if your student's reading is choppy at this very early stage. The first time she reads a story, she will probably read just one word at a time. Be patient and encouraging. Subsequent readings will be smoother and more fluent.

Review

Review the Phonogram Cards that are behind the Review divider in your student's Reading Review Box. Show each card to your student and have him say the sound. If necessary, remind your student of the sound.

Shuffle and review the Word Cards that are behind the Review divider in your student's Reading Review Box. If your student has difficulty reading a word, build the word with letter tiles and have your student sound it out using the blending procedure shown in Appendix C.

Test your student's Word Card memory with the game "Guess the Word." For instructions, look for this icon in Appendix H.

Remember: as your student masters the flashcards, move them behind the appropriate **Mastered** dividers.

How do you know when your student has mastered a card? Here are the signs:
- Your student responds quickly and easily when you hold up the card.
- You have no doubt that your student knows the card thoroughly.

Complete Activity Sheet

"In the last lesson you learned about periods and exclamation points, which you'll also see in today's short story. Let's see if you can help Rocket the Dog express his excitement with exclamation points."

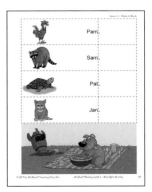

Down to Earth
Remove pages 17-18 from the *Blast Off* activity book.

Cut out the cards at the top of the sheet.

Tell your student that Rocket the Dog has just landed back on planet Earth and is excited to invite his friends to a picnic. Place a punctuation card (flipped to the "period" side) next to each name and read the names aloud. Then have your student help Rocket the Dog show his excitement by flipping the punctuation cards to reveal the exclamation points.

Read each name again with the exclamation point at the end.

Read the Warm-Up Sheet for "Bam!"

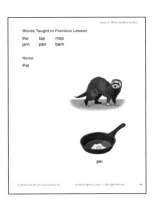

Turn to page 19 in the activity book.

Have your student practice reading words and phrases that will be encountered in "Bam!"

Teach Vocabulary and Activate Prior Knowledge

Point out the illustration of a ferret on the Warm-Up Sheet. "This is a *ferret*. Ferrets were once used in Europe to catch rats and rabbits, but now they are often kept as pets. Ferrets are quite playful, mischievous, and curious, like cats."

"What are some funny things that cats do? What kind of trouble can they get into?" Discuss your student's experience with and ideas about cats and their behavior.

"Ferrets can get into the same kind of trouble as cats. The story you are about to read is about a curious ferret that gets into a lot of mischief. Let's see what happens!"

Read "Bam!"

During the story, you will stop your student in several places to model important comprehension strategies. You'll model for your student how to stop and think about unfamiliar words or ideas. You'll also model the beginning stages of making predictions by thinking ahead to what might happen next.

If you wish, you can place a small sticky note at the bottom of pages 13 and 15 in the reader so you remember to stop after reading those pages.

"Turn to page 9 in your reader and read 'Bam!' aloud." Discuss your student's ideas for the questions below as you come to them.

After page 13: "Why do you think the ferret taps the bag?"

After page 15: "What do you think is going to happen to the pan?"

After reading: "What kind of trouble does the ferret get into?" Have your student skim the illustrations for answers.

Point Out *The End*

When your student gets to the last page of the story, read the phrase *The End* if your student doesn't already know it. Students generally catch on to this quickly because the phrase is at a predictable part of the story—the end!

Read-Aloud Time

Read a Story or Poem

Read aloud to your student for twenty minutes.

Read-Aloud Tip!

Why Read Aloud?
Reading aloud to your student is one of life's great joys, to be sure. But it's also one of the most important things you can do to promote your student's future reading ability. Reading aloud to children...
- creates a lifetime interest in reading
- extends their attention spans
- aids in language development
- strengthens their power of imagination
- builds reading comprehension
- creates a special one-on-one bond.

Track Your Progress

Mark the Progress Chart

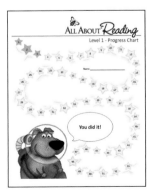

Have your student mark Lesson 3 on the Progress Chart.

Lesson 4   Letters G, D, C, and Y

Objective

This lesson teaches words containing the letters g, d̲, c̲, and y̲ and demonstrates that every word has a vowel.

You Will Need

☐ Phonogram Cards 9-12   ☐ Word Cards 14-23

☐ *Blast Off to Reading!* pages 21-25

Before You Begin

Preview the Sounds of the Letters

g The letter g can say two sounds:
- /g/ as in *goat*, known as hard g (taught in this lesson)
- /j/ as in *gem*, known as soft g (taught in Lesson 46)

d The letter d̲ says /d/ as in *deer*. Be sure that you and your student don't add /uh/ to the end of the sound, as in /duh/.

c The letter c̲ can say two sounds:
- /k/ as in *cat*, known as hard c̲ (taught in this lesson)
- /s/ as in *city*, known as soft c̲ (taught in Lesson 44)

y The letter y̲ can say four sounds:
- /y/ as in *yarn*, a consonant sound (taught in this lesson)
- /ĭ/ as in *gym*, a vowel sound (taught in Lesson 48)
- /ī/ as in *my*, a vowel sound (taught in Lesson 48)
- /ē/ as in *happy*, a vowel sound (taught in Lesson 48)

In the letter tile demonstrations in this lesson, you will be using the blue y̲ tile to represent the consonant sound of y̲. In Lesson 48, you will use the red y̲ tile to represent the vowel sounds of y̲.

The letter y̲ is unusual because it can represent either a consonant sound or a vowel sound.

Y̲ represents a consonant sound in approximately sixty words including *yarn*, *yellow*, and *beyond*. Much more often, in thousands of words, y̲ is a vowel, and it has the same three sounds that i̲ has: /ĭ/–/ī/–/ē/. Y̲ is also part of the vowel teams a̲y̲, o̲y̲, and e̲y̲.

Before You Begin
(continued)

Refer to the Letter Tiles app or Phonogram Sounds app for a demonstration of the g, d, c, and y phonogram sounds.

Preview Teaching Every Word Has a Vowel

Your student will learn that every word has a vowel. Later, when multisyllable words are taught, he will learn that every syllable has a vowel. This is helpful to know for decoding longer words.

Review Box Tip

Remember, as your student masters the flashcards, move them behind the appropriate **Mastered** dividers.

Here are the signs that your student has mastered a card:
• Your student responds quickly and easily when you hold up the card.
• You have no doubt that your student knows the card thoroughly.

Review

Review the Phonogram Cards that are behind the Review divider in your student's Reading Review Box. Show each card to your student and have him say the sound. If necessary, remind your student of the sound.

Shuffle and review the Word Cards that are behind the Review divider in your student's Reading Review Box. If your student has difficulty reading a word, build the word with letter tiles and have your student sound it out using the blending procedure shown in Appendix C.

Don't Forget!

Always shuffle the Word Cards before reviewing them. By doing so, your student will practice words with a variety of patterns.

Teach New Letter Sounds

Teach the Phonogram Cards for the letters g̲, d̲, c̲, and y̲.

For each card:
1. Hold up the Phonogram Card and demonstrate the sound.
2. Have your student repeat the sound.
3. Shuffle the new Phonogram Cards and do a mixed review.

File the Phonogram Cards behind the Review divider of the Reading Review Box.

Now move these four letter tiles into the workspace and practice the same sounds using the tiles.

Point to each tile in random order and ask your student to tell you the sound that the letter makes. Practice until your student can say the sound of each letter accurately.

 For extra practice with the new phonograms, play the game "Phonogram Snowball Fight." For instructions, look for this icon in Appendix G.

Practice Commonly Confused Letters

Move the b̲ and d̲ tiles into the workspace.

Randomly dictate /b/ and /d/ to test whether your student can distinguish between the two sounds and choose the correct letter tile.

If your student confuses the letters b̲ and d̲, see Appendix D for a multisensory solution. **Tip!**

Next, move the <u>b</u> and <u>p</u> tiles into the workspace.

Randomly dictate /b/ and /p/ to see if your student can distinguish between the two sounds and choose the correct letter tile.

If your student has difficulty with either pair of letters, have him watch your mouth as you say the sounds. Review several times, and then add a note to the Review section of the next several lessons so you remember to practice each day.

Blend Sounds with Letter Tiles

Build the word *cab* with letter tiles.

"I'll sound out this first word, and then you'll sound out the next word."

Touch under the <u>c</u> and say /k/.

Touch under the <u>a</u> and say /ă/.

Touch under the <u>b</u> and say /b/.

Now go back to the beginning of the word and blend the sounds together as follows.

Slide your finger under the letters <u>c</u>-<u>a</u> and say /kă/.

Lesson 4: Letters G, D, C, and Y

New Teaching
(continued)

Start at the beginning of the word again. Slide your finger under the letters <u>c</u>-<u>a</u>-<u>b</u> and say *cab* slowly.

Finally, read the word *cab* at a normal pace as we do when we speak.

Using the same blending procedure, have your student sound out the word *mad*.

Starting over at the beginning of the word is optional. Some students need the extra support provided by this step, while others do not.

Whenever you feel that your student is ready, blend all three letters without this additional step.

Leave the word *mad* in the workspace.

Play "Change the Word"

"I'm going to change the first letter of this word."

"What does this new word say?" Encourage your student to sound out the new word, *sad*.

Continue to change one letter at a time to form the following words. Each time, have your student sound out the new word.

sad → pad → pan → can → cap → gap → gas

Teach that Every Word Has a Vowel

"Did you notice that every word we made had a red tile—a vowel?"

Build several words to demonstrate this concept.

New Teaching
(continued)

Complete Activity Sheets

"Now it's time to feed the monster some bones."

Feed the Monster

Remove pages 21-22 from the *Blast Off* activity book.

Make a slit in the monster's mouth and cut out the bones.

Have your student read the words on the back of the bones. After reading a word correctly, he should feed the hungry monster by sticking the bone in the monster's mouth.

> The monster can be reused for future practice. Lots of kids like feeding the monster! **Tip!**

"Let's match some words and pictures."

Word Match

Remove page 23 from the activity book.

Cut out the word cards from the bottom of the page and have your student place the appropriate card under the matching picture.

Ask the following questions.

1. "Which picture ends with the sound /g/?" *Bag.*
2. "Which picture ends with the sound /d/?" *Sad.*
3. "What is the last sound in the word *gas*?" */s/.*
4. "What is the last sound in the word *cap*?" */p/.*

Lesson 4: Letters G, D, C, and Y

New Teaching
(continued)

Practice Reading Words

Have your student practice reading the words on Word Cards 14-23.

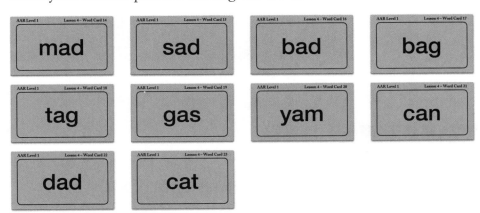

You may need to explain that a yam is a vegetable that tastes like a sweet potato. It grows undergound like a regular potato, and it is orange inside.

File the Word Cards behind the Review divider of the Reading Review Box.

Practice Fluency

Turn to page 25 in the activity book.

Have your student read from the Practice Sheet.

Don't Forget! Your beginning student isn't expected to read through the Practice Sheets in one sitting.

Many students will still be at the stage of sounding out many of the words, and that can be tiring mental work. Stop before your student fatigues. You can always continue tomorrow.

Read a Story or Poem

Read aloud to your student for twenty minutes.

Track Your Progress

Mark the Progress Chart

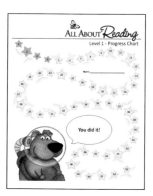

Have your student mark Lesson 4 on the Progress Chart.

Lesson 5   Read "The Cat"

Objective

In this lesson, students read a short story and learn words with multiple meanings.

You Will Need

☐ *Blast Off to Reading!* pages 27-29

☐ *Run, Bug, Run!* book

Before You Begin

Warm-Up Sheet Tip

As a general guideline, if your student was able to read the Practice Sheet in the previous lesson with no hesitation, you can skip these story-specific Warm-Up Sheets. These sheets provide a great warm-up for students who need extra practice before reading the story. Extra practice will enable students to read the story with greater fluency and comprehension.

Review

Review the Phonogram Cards that are behind the Review divider in your student's Reading Review Box. Show each card to your student and have him say the sound. If necessary, remind your student of the sound.

Shuffle and review the Word Cards that are behind the Review divider in your student's Reading Review Box. If your student has difficulty reading a word, build the word with letter tiles and have your student sound it out using the blending procedure shown in Appendix C.

Your student may enjoy reviewing Word Cards with the activity "Tell a Story." For instructions, look for this icon in Appendix H.

Complete Activity Sheet

"Some words can have more than one meaning, like *land*, which can mean *earth* or *to bring a plane to the ground*. Now we're going to play a game of tag with words that have two meanings."

Tag!
Remove page 27 from the *Blast Off* activity book.

Cut out the word cards and lay them face up on the table in front of your student.

Tell your student that you will read some sentences that go with the drawings on the activity sheet. After each sentence, your student should choose the appropriate word card and place it in the box next to the drawing it matches.

Read the double-meaning word first, and then read the sentence.

Sentences to Read	**Answer Key**
1. **cap:** This is my favorite baseball cap.	*boy with baseball cap*
2. **bat:** I hit the ball with a wooden bat.	*baseball bat*
3. **cap:** Will you take the cap off this bottle?	*bottle cap*
4. **tag:** It is fun to play tag with my friends!	*two kids playing tag*
5. **bat:** My cat likes to bat at balls of yarn.	*kitten with yarn*
6. **tag:** Please cut this tag off my shirt.	*price tag on shirt*

Read the Warm-Up Sheet for "The Cat"

Turn to page 29 in the activity book.

Have your student practice reading words and phrases that will be encountered in "The Cat."

New Teaching
(continued)

Teach Vocabulary and Activate Prior Knowledge

Point out the illustration of the sun hat on the Warm-Up Sheet. "This is a *sun hat*. A sun hat is often made of straw. Sun hats have a wide, floppy brim to help keep the hot sun off your face. You might wear a sun hat while working in the garden or relaxing at the beach."

"Has anyone or anything ever bothered you while you were trying to relax or sleep? What was it? What did you do about it?" Discuss your student's experiences.

"Sometimes people or even animals can bother us, but they usually don't mean it. In the next story, you'll see how a cat bothers its owner!"

Read "The Cat"

"Turn to page 19 in your reader and read 'The Cat' aloud." Discuss your student's ideas for the questions below as you come to them.

After page 21: "How does Sam feel about the cat batting the tag? Why does he feel that way?" Have your student look at Sam's expression in the illustration to answer the question.

After page 23: "Does the cat take the hat to be mean? Why or why not?"

After page 24: "How does Sam feel at the end of the story? Do you think he has forgiven the cat? Why?"

Read-Aloud Time

Read a Story or Poem

Read aloud to your student for twenty minutes.

Read-Aloud Tip!

Increase a Short Attention Span
Since young children have short attention spans, start small with your read-alouds. Begin by choosing shorter books or books with less text. As your student's attention span increases, gradually add in a mix of longer, more complex stories.

Mark the Progress Chart

Have your student mark Lesson 5 on the Progress Chart.

Lesson 6   Letters H, K, and R

Objective

This lesson teaches words containing the letters <u>h</u>, <u>k</u>, and <u>r</u> and the Leap Word *a*.

You Will Need

☐ Phonogram Cards 13-15

☐ *Blast Off to Reading!* pages 31-37

☐ Word Cards 24-32

☐ raisins, M&Ms, coins, dried beans, or Cheerios

Before You Begin

Preview the Sounds of the Letters

h   The letter <u>h</u> says /h/ as in *hat*.

k   The letter <u>k</u> says /k/ as in *kite*.

r   The letter <u>r</u> says /r/ as in *rake*. A common mistake is to pronounce <u>r</u> as /ruh/. If the sound /r/ is difficult for your student to say in isolation, try having him make a growling noise like a dog: /grrr/. Then say the sound without the initial /g/ sound, leaving just the /rrr/ sound.

    Refer to the Letter Tiles app or Phonogram Sounds app for a demonstration of the <u>h</u>, <u>k</u>, and <u>r</u> phonogram sounds.

Review the Practice Sheets

Beginning with this lesson, every Practice Sheet has a section called "Sentences." Each sentence is divided into phrases, like this:

The sad rat
The sad rat ran.

This type of practice is called *phrased reading*, and it improves your student's phrasing. Phrasing is important for fluency; fluent readers are able to phrase, or break text into meaningful parts.

If your student does not need practice with phrasing, feel free to skip the shorter phrases and have your student read just the full sentence.

Review the Phonogram Cards that are behind the Review divider in your student's Reading Review Box. Show each card to your student and have him say the sound. If necessary, remind your student of the sound.

 Shuffle and review the Word Cards that are behind the Review divider in your student's Reading Review Box. If your student has difficulty reading a word, build the word with letter tiles and have your student sound it out using the blending procedure shown in Appendix C.

 Choose just ten Word Cards for review each day. Shuffle the cards so your student reviews a variety of patterns.

Don't Forget!

 Ask your student to point to some vowels and some consonants.

New Teaching

Teach New Letter Sounds

Teach the Phonogram Cards for the letters <u>h</u>, <u>k</u>, and <u>r</u>.

For each card:
1. Hold up the Phonogram Card and demonstrate the sound.
2. Have your student repeat the sound.
3. Shuffle the new Phonogram Cards and do a mixed review.

File the Phonogram Cards behind the Review divider of the Reading Review Box.

Now move these three letter tiles into the workspace and practice the same sounds using the tiles.

Lesson 6: Letters H, K, and R

New Teaching
(continued)

Point to each tile in random order and ask your student to tell you the sound that the letter makes. Practice until your student can say the sound of each letter accurately.

 You might like to have some fun with today's new Phonogram Cards by playing the game "Phonogram Go Fish." For instructions, look for this icon in Appendix G.

Blend Sounds with Letter Tiles

Build the word *rat* with letter tiles.

"I'll sound out this first word, and then you'll sound out the next word."

Touch under the r and say /r/.

Touch under the a and say /ă/.

Touch under the t and say /t/.

Now go back to the beginning of the word and blend the sounds together as follows.

Slide your finger under the letters r-a and say /ră/.

Start at the beginning of the word again. Slide your finger under the letters r-a-t and say *rat* slowly.

Finally, read the word *rat* at a normal pace as we do when we speak.

Using the same blending procedure, have your student sound out the word *had*.

Leave the word *had* in the workspace.

Play "Change the Word"

"I'm going to change the last letter of this word."

"What does this new word say?" Encourage your student to sound out the new word, *ham*.

Continue to change one letter at a time to form the following words. Each time, have your student sound out the new word.

ham → hat → rat → mat → mad

> You may wish to make up simple sentences for each new word to give meaning to the word and maintain your student's interest. **Tip!**

Complete Activity Sheets

"Let's play a game of bingo!"

Letter Sounds Bingo
Remove pages 31-33 from the *Blast Off* activity book.

Give your student something fun to use for markers, like raisins, M&Ms, coins, dried beans, or Cheerios.

Randomly call out the sounds of the letters. When a sound is called, your student should put a marker over the corresponding letter. When your student gets three in a row, he says "Bingo!"

For a longer game, have your student fill the card completely before calling bingo.

"Let's match some more words and pictures."

Word Match
Remove page 35 from the activity book.

If necessary, explain that a yak is a large animal with very long, thick hair and horns.

Cut out the word cards from the bottom of the page and have your student place the appropriate card under the matching picture.

Ask the following questions.

1. "Which word starts with the sound /y/?" *Yak.*
2. "Which two words end with the sound /t/?" *Rat and hat.*
3. "What is the last sound in the word *ham*?" */m/.*
4. "Which of these are animals?" *Rat and yak.*
5. "Which is something you can wear?" *Hat.*
6. "What would look really silly if you put it on your head?" *Rat, yak, or ham.*

New Teaching
(continued)

Practice Reading Words

Have your student practice reading the words on Word Cards 24-31.

AAR Level 1 — Lesson 6 – Word Card 24	AAR Level 1 — Lesson 6 – Word Card 25	AAR Level 1 — Lesson 6 – Word Card 26	AAR Level 1 — Lesson 6 – Word Card 27
rat	hat	rag	had
AAR Level 1 — Lesson 6 – Word Card 28	**AAR Level 1 — Lesson 6 – Word Card 29**	**AAR Level 1 — Lesson 6 – Word Card 30**	**AAR Level 1 — Lesson 6 – Word Card 31**
ram	ham	ran	yak

File the Word Cards behind the Review divider of the Reading Review Box.

Teach a Leap Word: *a*

Show Word Card 32 to your student.

"Most words follow the rules and say the sounds that we expect them to say. But there are a few words that do not. Here is one of those words."

"This word is *a*, as in *I have a dog*." Pronounce *a* as /ŭ/, which is the most common pronunciation of this short word.

"What is this word?" *A.*

> You may wish to explain that we usually pronounce this word as /ŭ/. Sometimes we do say /ā/, but for the purpose of flashcard review, say the more common pronunciation: /ŭ/.

Review this Leap Word several times today and then file it behind the Review divider in the Reading Review Box.

Lesson 6: Letters H, K, and R

New Teaching
(continued)

Practice Fluency

Remove page 37 from the activity book.

The sentences on this activity sheet end with a period. Remind your student that a period is a punctuation mark used to end a sentence.

Have your student read from the Practice Sheet.

How Much Time?

How much time should you spend on the Practice Sheets? Only you can be the judge of that, since the answer is different for every student. Some students may not need all the practice provided here. Other students may benefit from rereading the sheets multiple times over a period of a week.

The goal is to keep making progress, not to achieve immediate perfection.

Read-Aloud Time

Read a Story or Poem

Read aloud to your student for twenty minutes.

Mark the Progress Chart

Have your student mark Lesson 6 on the Progress Chart.

Lesson 6: Letters H, K, and R

Lesson 7   Read "Jam" and "A Hat"

Objective

In this lesson, students read two short stories and "set the table" for one of the stories.

You Will Need

☐ *Blast Off to Reading!* pages 39-44   ☐ map or globe

☐ *Run, Bug, Run!* book

Before You Begin

Preview Lessons with Two Stories

Beginning with this lesson, all story lessons contain two stories. Both stories have Warm-Up Sheets, a vocabulary component, and discussion questions. The first story has an additional component: an activity sheet that is designed to increase your student's comprehension.

Please note that it is fine to stop after the first story and continue the lesson the next day. If the first story is challenging for your student, it may be too much to read a second story. Stop before your student fatigues.

The second story is included for additional practice with the concepts taught in the previous lesson, and the extra reading practice is great for building fluency. If you are working with an advanced student who doesn't need the extra practice, you may choose to skip the second story. (But be forewarned—your student may beg to read those extra stories! There are some fun storylines coming up!)

Review Tips

Review takes only a few minutes a day, yet it is critical to your student's success. But what do you do if you have a lot of Word Cards in your review pile?

Remember that you don't need to review *all* of the Word Cards every day. Instead, rotate through a selection of ten or so cards each day. If you feel that there are too many Word Cards behind the review divider and that you shouldn't move on to the next lesson, trust your instincts. Spend more time reviewing the concepts in previous lessons using the letter tiles or activity sheets, or even have a game or activity day in place of your regular lesson. See Appendix G and Appendix H for ideas for reviewing Phonogram Cards and Word Cards.

Review the Phonogram Cards that are behind the Review divider in your student's Reading Review Box. Show each card to your student and have him say the sound. If necessary, remind your student of the sound.

 Shuffle and review the Word Cards that are behind the Review divider in your student's Reading Review Box. If your student has difficulty reading a word, build the word with letter tiles and have your student sound it out using the blending procedure shown in Appendix C.

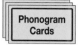 Use a favorite family board game to review Word Cards. For instructions, look for this icon in Appendix H.

New Teaching

Story 1: "Jam"

Complete Activity Sheet

"In the story you'll be reading today, a girl has a very unusual dinner guest. Before reading the story, let's help her set the table for two!"

Set the Table
Remove pages 39-41 from the *Blast Off* activity book.

Cut out the table settings cards on page 41.

Have your student arrange them as desired on the illustration of the table. Don't forget the napkins!

New Teaching
(continued)

Read the Warm-Up Sheet for "Jam"

Turn to page 43 in the activity book.

Have your student practice reading words and phrases that will be encountered in "Jam."

Teach Vocabulary and Activate Prior Knowledge

Point out the illustration of a yak on the Warm-Up Sheet. "A *yak* is a big, long-haired ox. Yaks can be found in various parts of central Asia."

Point out the illustration of a biscuit on the Warm-Up Sheet. "This is a *biscuit*. A biscuit is a type of small bread roll, often eaten as part of a meal with butter or gravy, or as a sweet treat with jam."

"In this next story, a yak enjoys yams and biscuits at dinner. Have you ever had a friend over for dinner?" Discuss what your student and his friend ate or what they did together.

"Have you ever seen a little child get really excited about a food—like ice cream—and that is all she wants to eat?"

"Let's see what happens when the girl in this story serves the yak some jam!"

Read "Jam"

Be sure to have your student read the stories aloud, not silently. Oral reading practice is much more effective in developing fluency than silent reading practice.

"Turn to page 27 in your reader and read 'Jam' aloud." Discuss your student's ideas for the questions below as you come to them.

New Teaching
(continued)

After page 31: "What do you think the yak likes most: the ham, the yam, or the jam? Why?" Point out the yak's expression in the illustration.

After page 32: "Do you think Pam is mad that the yak ate all the jam? Why? Do you think she will invite the yak to dinner again?"

Story 2: "A Hat"

Read the Warm-Up Sheet for "A Hat"

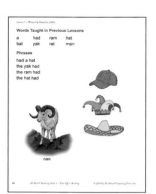

Turn to page 44 in the activity book.

Have your student practice reading words and phrases that will be encountered in "A Hat."

Teach Vocabulary and Activate Prior Knowledge

Point out the illustration of a ram on the Warm-Up Sheet. "A *ram* is an adult male sheep. Rams have big horns they use to defend themselves."

Point out the illustration of a sombrero (the hat nearest the bottom of the Warm-Up Sheet). "This is a *sombrero*. A sombrero is a type of hat made of straw. It has a high crown and a very wide brim to protect you from the sun. Sombreros are often worn in Mexico and the southern United States." Point out Mexico on a map or globe.

Point out the illustration of the middle hat on the Warm-Up Sheet. "There are many types of hats. This is a *jester hat*. Jester hats were worn by court jesters, the people that kings and queens used to hire to tell jokes and perform silly acts. What other types of hats can you think of?"

"Have you ever had a really strange dream? What was it about?"

"The girl in the next story has an odd dream about hats. Let's see how it ends."

New Teaching
(continued)

Read "A Hat"

"Turn to page 37 in your reader and read 'A Hat' aloud." Discuss your student's ideas for the questions below as you come to them.

After page 43: "How do you think this dream will end? Who or what will have a hat next?"

After reading: "Are you surprised at how the story ends? Why?"

Read-Aloud Time

Read a Story or Poem

Read aloud to your student for twenty minutes.

Track Your Progress

Mark the Progress Chart

Have your student mark Lesson 7 on the Progress Chart.

Lesson 8   Letters I, V, F, and Z

Objective   This lesson teaches words containing the letters i̱, v̱, f̱, and ẕ.

You Will Need   ☐ Phonogram Cards 16-19   ☐ Word Cards 33-42
☐ *Blast Off to Reading!* pages 45-54

Before You Begin   ## Preview the Sounds of the Letters

i The letter i̱ can say three sounds:
- /ĭ/ as in *itchy*, known as the short sound (taught in this lesson)
- /ī/ as in *ivy*, known as the long sound (taught in Lesson 44)
- /ē/ as in *radio* (taught in Lesson 44)

To help your student remember the sound of short i̱ (/ĭ/), **Tip!** we will use the following hand motion.

Scratch your forearm with your fingertips as if you are itchy. "When we say /ĭ/, let's pretend that we are itchy. Say the sound of i̱ like this: /ĭ/–/ĭ/–itchy." *Student pretends to have an itch and says /ĭ/–/ĭ/–itchy.*

v The letter v̱ says /v/ as in *vase*. Be sure that you and your student don't add /uh/ to the end of the sound, as in /vuh/.

f The letter f̱ says /f/ as in *fish*.

z The letter ẕ says /z/ as in *zipper*.

 Refer to the Letter Tiles app or Phonogram Sounds app for a demonstration of the i̱, v̱, f̱, and ẕ phonogram sounds.

Preview Word Flippers

Word Flippers are used in seven lessons and are a fun way to practice fluency. This particular activity requires several minutes of assembly, so you may want to do this before the lesson begins. Refer to Appendix E for instructions.

It's time to review the cards behind the Mastered dividers to ensure they stay fresh in your student's mind.

Shuffle the cards behind both Mastered dividers and choose a selection for review.

New Teaching

Teach New Letter Sounds

Hold up the Phonogram Card for the letter i̲.

"This letter says /ĭ/."

Scratch your forearm with your fingertips as if you are itchy. "When we say /ĭ/, let's pretend that we are itchy. Say the sound of i̲ like this: /ĭ/–/ĭ/–itchy." *Student pretends to have an itch and says /ĭ/–/ĭ/–itchy.*

Teach the Phonogram Cards for the letters v̲, f̲, and z̲.

For each card:
1. Hold up the Phonogram Card and demonstrate the sound.
2. Have your student repeat the sound.
3. Shuffle the new Phonogram Cards and do a mixed review.

File the Phonogram Cards behind the Review divider of the Reading Review Box.

Now move these four letter tiles into the workspace and practice the same sounds using the tiles.

Point to each tile in random order and ask your student to tell you the sound that the letter makes. Practice until your student can say the sound of each letter accurately.

New Teaching
(continued)

 Let your student get creative with the new phonograms with the activity "Color It." For instructions, look for this icon in Appendix G.

Blend Sounds with Letter Tiles

Build the word *dip* with letter tiles.

"I'll sound out this first word, and then you'll sound out the next word."

Touch under the <u>d</u> and say /d/.

Touch under the <u>i</u> and say /ĭ/.

Touch under the <u>p</u> and say /p/.

Now go back to the beginning of the word and blend the sounds together as follows.

Slide your finger under the letters <u>d</u>-<u>i</u> and say /dĭ/.

Start at the beginning of the word again. Slide your finger under the letters <u>d</u>-<u>i</u>-<u>p</u> and say *dip* slowly.

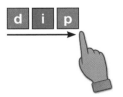

New Teaching
(continued)

Finally, read the word *dip* at a normal pace as we do when we speak.

Using the same blending procedure, have your student sound out the word *fan*.

Starting over at the beginning of the word is optional. Some students need the extra support provided by this step, while others do not.

Whenever you feel that your student is ready, blend all three letters without this additional step.

Play "Change the Word"

Build the word *him* with letter tiles.

"What is this word?" *Him*.

"I'm going to change the last letter of this word."

"What does this new word say?" Encourage your student to sound out the new word, *hit*.

Continue to change one letter at a time to form the following words. Each time, have your student sound out the new word.

hit → sit → pit → bit → fit → fig →
big → bid → hid → rid → rip

Lesson 8: Letters I, V, F, and Z

New Teaching
(continued)

Complete Activity Sheet

"Now it's time to flip some vowels!"

<u>Word Flippers for Short Vowel Sounds</u>
Remove pages 45-51 from the *Blast Off* activity book.

There are four Word Flippers in this lesson. Each page will create one flipper.

Refer to Appendix E for assembly instructions.

Have your student turn the pages and read the words that are formed.

Tip!

If the vowels cause difficulty, have your student point to the vowel and say the sound of the vowel before starting to sound out the word. For example, with the word *bit*, your student would point to the vowel and say /ĭ/, and then sound out the word from the beginning.

Use this tip whenever your student has difficulty with vowels.

Practice Reading Words

Have your student practice reading the words on Word Cards 33-42.

File the Word Cards behind the Review divider of the Reading Review Box.

New Teaching
(continued)

> Question marks are used in the stories your student will read in the next lesson.

Practice Fluency

Turn to pages 53-54 in the activity book.

Point to a sentence that ends in a question mark. "This is a question mark. It is used to show that the sentence is a question, like *How are you?*"

Model for your student the difference between reading a sentence with a period and reading a sentence with a question mark.

Have your student read from the Practice Sheets.

Don't Forget!

Today's Practice Sheet is two pages long, and you'll need to be the judge of whether your student needs all of this practice.

For older learners needing remedial work, this extra practice is critical to their success. For younger learners whose eye muscles are still developing, you should choose a reasonable number of lines to practice. Every situation is different, and you need to do what is best for your student.

Read-Aloud Time

Read a Story or Poem

Read aloud to your student for twenty minutes.

Mark the Progress Chart

Have your student mark Lesson 8 on the Progress Chart.

Lesson 9   Read "Hit the Gas" and "The Bad Rat"

Objective

In this lesson, students read two short stories and practice punctuation marks.

You Will Need

☐ *Blast Off to Reading!* pages 55-58

☐ *Run, Bug, Run!* book

Before You Begin

Review Punctuation Marks with Your Student

The story "Hit the Gas" uses the question mark, which was introduced in Lesson 8. Before beginning the "On Your Mark" activity sheet, review the terms *period*, *exclamation point*, and *question mark* with your student.

You may wish to use these simple definitions:
- **period:** A period is used to show the end of a sentence.
- **exclamation point:** An exclamation point is used to show emotion or excitement.
- **question mark:** A question mark is used to show that the sentence is a question, as in *How are you?*

Review

Review the Phonogram Cards that are behind the Review divider in your student's Reading Review Box. Show each card to your student and have him say the sound. If necessary, remind your student of the sound.

Shuffle and review the Word Cards that are behind the Review divider in your student's Reading Review Box. If your student has difficulty reading a word, build the word with letter tiles and have your student sound it out using the blending procedure shown in Appendix C.

Have some fun with today's Word Card review by playing the game "Word Card Slapjack." For instructions, look for this icon in Appendix H.

Story 1: "Hit the Gas"

Complete Activity Sheet

"Let's practice using punctuation marks."

On Your Mark

Remove page 55 from the *Blast Off* activity book.

Cut out the punctuation mark cards on the bottom of the page and lay them face up on the table.

Have your student read each sentence and then decide which punctuation mark should be used at the end. Once he's decided, he should place the punctuation card in the space provided. You may help your student choose the correct punctuation mark by discussing the sentences.

Read the Warm-Up Sheet for "Hit the Gas"

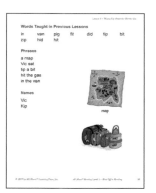

Turn to page 57 in the activity book.

Have your student practice reading words and phrases that will be encountered in "Hit the Gas."

Point out the name *Vic* in the Names section. "In the next story, the girl is named Vic. Vic is short for Victoria. When we shorten a person's name or call her by a different name, we call it a *nickname*. Do you or does someone you know have a nickname?"

New Teaching
(continued)

Teach Vocabulary and Activate Prior Knowledge

Point out the illustration of luggage on the Warm-Up Sheet. "This is *luggage.* Luggage is all the bags, suitcases, and other items that you take with you when you go on a trip."

"Have you ever gone on a trip in a car? Where did you put the luggage?" Discuss where your student went or what he saw on the trip.

"If you could take a trip anywhere, where would you go?"

Turn to page 47 in the reader and point out the title of the story. "If I tell the driver of a car to 'hit the gas,' do I mean to go or to stop? What if I say 'hit the brakes'?"

"In this story, a girl goes on a trip with a lot of unusual friends. Let's see what happens."

Read "Hit the Gas"

"Turn to page 47 in your reader and read 'Hit the Gas' aloud." Discuss your student's ideas for the questions below as you come to them.

After page 49: "Look at the illustration. What items is Vic bringing with her?" *Plant, doghouse, food bowl, suitcase, pig feed, apples, cheese.*

"Based on those items, what kind of friends do you think will go on the trip with Vic?"

After page 54: "Where do you think Vic and the animals are going?"

Point to the comma. "This is a comma. Commas are used to indicate a short pause." If necessary, model for your student how to read the sentence.

Story 2: "The Bad Rat"

The remaining story lessons contain two stories to read. If you see that your student is fatigued after reading the first story, you may wish to split the lesson in two and read the second story the next day.

Read the Warm-Up Sheet for "The Bad Rat"

Turn to page 58 in the activity book.

Have your student practice reading words and phrases that will be encountered in "The Bad Rat."

Teach Vocabulary and Activate Prior Knowledge

Point out the illustration of the toppling dominoes on the Warm-Up Sheet. "These are dominoes. If you set up dominoes like this and knock over the first one, that domino will knock over the second domino, the second domino will knock over the third domino, and so on until all the dominoes fall down. This is called a *chain reaction*. A chain reaction is when one event leads to another event, and so on and so on."

"In this next story, a rat sets off a chain reaction."

Read "The Bad Rat"

"Turn to page 57 in your reader and read 'The Bad Rat' aloud." Discuss your student's ideas for the questions below as you come to them.

After page 60: "Why do you think the pig bites the cat?"

After page 64: "Do you think the rat will bite anyone anymore? Why?"

Read a Story or Poem

Read aloud to your student for twenty minutes.

Read-Aloud Tip!

Model Good Reading Habits

During your read-aloud times, model how you sometimes stop and think about what you are reading. You want your student to understand that good readers think about what they are reading and that they should expect the text to make sense. Reading is like a conversation between the author and the reader.

Mark the Progress Chart

Have your student mark Lesson 9 on the Progress Chart.

M, A, B, J, Y,
O, C, K, Z, F ...

Whew!
All those letters warped my woofer
for a while, but now I have them all straight.
And you're doing great, too!

Keep it up, fellow space dog!

Lesson 10   Letters O, L, and W

Objective

This lesson teaches words containing the letters <u>o</u>, <u>l</u>, and <u>w</u> and the Leap Word *of.*

You Will Need

☐ Phonogram Cards 20-22   ☐ Word Cards 43-52

☐ *Blast Off to Reading!* pages 59-62

Before You Begin

Preview the Sounds of the Letters

o   The letter <u>o</u> can say four sounds:
- /ŏ/ as in *otter,* known as the short sound (taught in this lesson)
- /ō/ as in *open,* known as the long sound (taught in Lesson 46)
- /o͞o/ as in *to* (taught in Lesson 46)
- /ŭ/ as in *oven* (taught in lesson 46)

> To help your student remember the sound of short <u>o</u> (/ŏ/), **Tip!** we will use the following hand motion.
>
> Form an "o" shape with one hand and hold it to your nose. "When we say /ŏ/, let's pretend that we have a nose like an otter. Say the sound of <u>o</u> like this: /ŏ/–/ŏ/–otter." *Student makes an otter nose and says /ŏ/–/ŏ/–otter.*

l   The letter <u>l</u> says /l/ as in *leaf.* Be sure that you and your student don't add /uh/ to the end of the sound, as in /luh/.

w   The letter <u>w</u> says /w/ as in *wave.* It is impossible to say /w/ in isolation without any trace of /uh/ at the end, but clip the /uh/ as short as possible.

   Refer to the Letter Tiles app or Phonogram Sounds app for a demonstration of the <u>o</u>, <u>l</u>, and <u>w</u> phonogram sounds.

Allow for Regional Variations

Regional variations may affect how your student pronounces some words, and that is okay! Just keep in mind that you may need to make a few accommodations as you teach. The letter <u>o</u> is a great example.

Before You Begin
(continued)

In some regions, all short o̱'s are pronounced the same. The vowel sound in words such as *got* and *dog* are identical.

But in other regions, all short o̱'s are not equal. The vowel sounds in *got* and *dog* are different. *Got* is pronounced with a pure short o̱ sound, while *dog* is pronounced with an /aw/ sound, as in /dawg/.

If your student sounds out a word such as *hot* and the pronunciation seems awkward, acknowledge that sounding out the word gets us really close to the correct pronunciations, and it's okay to adjust the word so it matches your own dialect.

Review

Review the Phonogram Cards that are behind the Review divider in your student's Reading Review Box. Show each card to your student and have him say the sound. If necessary, remind your student of the sound.

Shuffle and review the Word Cards that are behind the Review divider in your student's Reading Review Box. If your student has difficulty reading a word, build the word with letter tiles and have your student sound it out using the blending procedure shown in Appendix C.

New Teaching

Teach New Letter Sounds

Hold up the Phonogram Card for the letter o̱.

"This letter says /ŏ/."

Form an "o" shape with one hand and hold it to your nose. "When we say /ŏ/, let's pretend that we have a nose like an otter. Say the sound of o̱ like this: /ŏ/–/ŏ/–otter." *Student makes an otter nose and says /ŏ/–/ŏ/–otter.*

New Teaching
(continued)

Teach the Phonogram Cards for the letters l and w.

For each card:
1. Hold up the Phonogram Card and demonstrate the sound.
2. Have your student repeat the sound.
3. Shuffle the new Phonogram Cards and do a mixed review.

File the Phonogram Cards behind the Review divider of the Reading Review Box.

Now move these three letter tiles into the workspace and practice the same sounds using the tiles.

Point to each tile in random order and ask your student to tell you the sound that the letter makes. Practice until your student can say the sound of each letter accurately.

 You may wish to have your student practice the new phonograms by writing them in a salt tray. For instructions, look for this icon in Appendix G.

Blend Sounds with Letter Tiles

Build the word *lid* with letter tiles.

"I'll sound out this first word, and then you'll sound out the next word."

Touch under the l and say /l/.

Touch under the i and say /ĭ/.

New Teaching
(continued)

Touch under the <u>d</u> and say /d/.

Now go back to the beginning of the word and blend the sounds together as follows.

Slide your finger under the letters <u>l</u>-<u>i</u> and say /lĭ/.

Start at the beginning of the word again. Slide your finger under the letters <u>l</u>-<u>i</u>-<u>d</u> and say *lid* slowly.

Finally, read the word *lid* at a normal pace as we do when we speak.

Using the same blending procedure, have your student sound out the word *wig*.

Start at the beginning of the word again. Slide your finger under the letters <u>l</u>-<u>i</u>-<u>d</u> and say *lid* slowly.

This is the last lesson in which we start at the beginning of the word for a second time. If you feel that your student still needs this step, feel free to add it in.

New Teaching
(continued)

Play "Change the Word"

Build the word *sob* with letter tiles.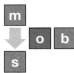

"What is this word?" *Sob.*

"I'm going to change the first letter of this word."

"What does this new word say?" Encourage your student to sound out the new word, *mob.*

Continue to change one letter at a time to form the following words. Each time, have your student sound out the new word.

mob → mop → top → hop → hot →
rot → pot → got

Complete Activity Sheet

"Let's match some more words and pictures."

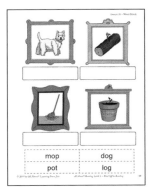

Word Match

Remove page 59 from the *Blast Off* activity book.

Cut out the word cards from the bottom of the page and have your student place the appropriate card under the matching picture.

Ask the following questions.

1. "Which word starts with the sound /m/?" *Mop.*
2. "Which two words end with the sound /g/?" *Dog and log.*

Practice Reading Words

Have your student practice reading the words on Word Cards 43-51.

File the Word Cards behind the Review divider of the Reading Review Box.

 Don't Forget! Remember: if the vowels cause difficulty, have your student point to the vowel and say its sound before beginning to sound out the word. For example, with the word *job*, your student would point to the vowel and say /ŏ/, and then sound out the word from the beginning.

Teach a Leap Word: *of*

Show Word Card 52 to your student.

AAR Level 1   Lesson 10 – Word Card 52

of

"Most words follow the rules and say the sounds that we expect them to say. But there are a few words that do not. Here is one of those words."

"This word is *of*, as in *Let's get more of those fish.*"

"The <u>o</u> and the <u>f</u> don't say the sounds we expect them to say, so this is a Leap Word."

The word *of* is the only word in which the letter <u>f</u> says /v/.

Review this Leap Word several times today and then file it behind the Review divider in the Reading Review Box.

New Teaching

(continued)

Practice Fluency

Turn to pages 61-62 in the activity book.

Have your student read from the Practice Sheets.

To engage your student in the fluency exercises, try the activity "Buddy Reading." For instructions, look for this icon in Appendix F.

Read-Aloud Time

Read a Story or Poem

Read aloud to your student for twenty minutes.

Track Your Progress

Mark the Progress Chart

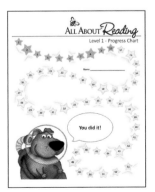

Have your student mark Lesson 10 on the Progress Chart.

Lesson 10: Letters O, L, and W

Lesson 11   Read "Jan Did It" and "The Job"

Objective

In this lesson, students read two short stories and create a chore chart.

You Will Need

☐ *Blast Off to Reading!* pages 63-68   ☐ optional: video of an Irish jig

☐ *Run, Bug, Run!* book

Before You Begin

Help Your Student Read for Meaning

As your student reads today's story, monitor yourself to see if you interrupt him too often. Instead of immediately correcting your student's misread words, let him finish the sentence so he has a chance to self-correct.

For example, if the student reads *The dot ran fast*, he will probably self-correct because the sentence obviously doesn't make sense. He will look back to see where his error is and reread the sentence as *The dog ran fast*.

If he does continue reading without correcting himself, prompt him to notice the error after he has completed the sentence: "Try reading that sentence again" or "You've almost got that—try it one more time." If the error resulted in a sentence that didn't make sense, prompt your student to try again to achieve the correct meaning.

Review

Review the Phonogram Cards that are behind the Review divider in your student's Reading Review Box. Show each card to your student and have him say the sound. If necessary, remind your student of the sound.

Shuffle and review the Word Cards that are behind the Review divider in your student's Reading Review Box. If your student has difficulty reading a word, build the word with letter tiles and have your student sound it out using the blending procedure shown in Appendix C.

Try spicing up today's Word Card review by playing the game "Swat the Words." For instructions, look for this icon in Appendix H.

Story 1: "Jan Did It"

Complete Activity Sheet

"Do you have any small jobs to do around the house? What are they?"

"In this activity, you'll make your own chore chart."

Chore Chart

Remove pages 63-65 from the *Blast Off* activity book.

Cut out the chore cards on page 65.

Have your student create her own visual chore chart by attaching the chore cards to the "Jobs" list on page 63. If your student has special chores not represented in the illustrations, she may draw them on the blank chore cards provided and add them to the jobs list.

Read the Warm-Up Sheet for "Jan Did It"

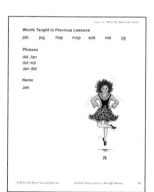

Turn to page 67 in the activity book.

Have your student practice reading words and phrases that will be encountered in "Jan Did It."

Teach Vocabulary and Activate Prior Knowledge

Point out the illustration of a jig on the Warm-Up Sheet. "A *jig* is an energetic dance. If someone dances a jig, you will see them hopping or skipping to the music. A common type of jig is an Irish jig." Locate a YouTube video of an Irish jig and show it to your student.

Make Harry Potter movies

singer

Lesson 11: Read "Jan Did It" and "The Job"

New Teaching
(continued)

"The girl in this story is very busy. Let's see what she has on her list of things to do."

Read "Jan Did It"

"Turn to page 67 in your reader and read 'Jan Did It' aloud." Discuss your student's ideas for the questions below as you come to them.

After page 68: "What jobs are on Jan's list of things to do?"

You may need to explain these words to your student: *jog* (slow run) and *sob* (cry).

After page 74: "Why do you think Jan did not sob?"

Story 2: "The Job"

Read the Warm-Up Sheet for "The Job"

Turn to page 68 in the activity book.

Have your student practice reading words and phrases that will be encountered in "The Job."

Teach Vocabulary and Activate Prior Knowledge

Point out the illustration of a drive-in restaurant on the Warm-Up Sheet. "This is a *drive-in restaurant*. At this type of restaurant, you stay in your car. A waiter comes out to take your order and then delivers your meal to your car. Sometimes they have special trays you can attach to your car door."

"Our next story takes place at a drive-in restaurant. The place where a story happens is called the *setting*."

New Teaching
(continued)

Point out the illustration of the photographer on the Warm-Up Sheet. "This is a *photographer*. Photographers take pictures for a living. They work for magazines, newspapers, advertising agencies, and many other types of companies."

"Have you ever had your picture taken with a camera?" Discuss when and where your student had his picture taken.

"In this story, someone takes a picture of a dog and makes him famous! Let's see how that happens."

Read "The Job"

"Turn to page 77 in your reader and read 'The Job' aloud." Discuss your student's ideas for the questions below as you come to them.

After page 79: "What kind of job do you think Lad has?"

After page 80: Point to the quotation marks. "These are quotation marks. They are used to show that someone is speaking. Point to the person who is speaking." *Student points to the boy.*

After page 86: "Look at the illustration. What is Lad's ad for?"

Read-Aloud Time

Read a Story or Poem

Read aloud to your student for twenty minutes.

Mark the Progress Chart

Have your student mark Lesson 11 on the Progress Chart.

Did you do all
your chores today? My to-do list
is long, but I'm chomping my way through
it bit by bit. So far I've ...

• cleaned the kibbles from the cockpit floor (oops)
• put down fresh newspapers (ahem)
• wiped space-bugs off the windshield (ew)
• spit-shined the rocket inside and out
(it really glows now!)

I'm taking an ear-scratching break
and then ... back to work!

Lesson 12   Letter U and the Second Sound of S

Objective

This lesson teaches words containing the letter <u>u</u> and the second sound of <u>s</u>.

You Will Need

☐ Phonogram Cards 2 and 23

☐ *Blast Off to Reading!* pages 69-74

☐ Word Cards 53-62

☐ raisins, M&Ms, coins, dried beans, or Cheerios

Before You Begin

Preview the Sounds of the Letters

u   The letter <u>u</u> can say three sounds:
- /ŭ/ as in *udder*, known as the short sound (taught in this lesson)
- /ū/ as in *unit*, known as the long sound (taught in Lesson 48)
- /o͝o/ as in *put* (taught in Lesson 48)

> To help your student remember the sound of short <u>u</u> (/ŭ/), we will use the following hand motion. **Tip!**
>
> Using both hands, do a hand motion like you are milking a cow. "When we say /ŭ/, let's pretend that we are farmers and we are milking a cow. Say the sound of <u>u</u> like this: /ŭ/–/ŭ/–udder." *Student pretends to milk a cow and says /ŭ/–/ŭ/–udder.*

s   Your student has already learned that <u>s</u> says /s/. In this lesson we will add the second sound of <u>s</u>: /z/ as in *has*.

 Refer to the Letter Tiles app or Phonogram Sounds app for a demonstration of the <u>u</u> and <u>s</u> phonogram sounds.

Preview More Information on S

When it occurs at the beginning of a word, <u>s</u> says /s/ as in *sun*. When it occurs at the end of the word, sometimes it says /s/ and sometimes it says /z/. In this lesson, students will learn that they should try the first sound, /s/, and if that doesn't sound like a real word, try the second sound.

Before You Begin
(continued)

There are some guidelines to figure out whether final s will say /s/ or /z/, but it involves much more mental work than simply trying the /s/ sound first. We won't be teaching these guidelines to your student, but for your information, here is the pattern:

- If the preceding sound is /f/, /k/, /p/, /t/, or /th/, final s usually says /s/.

  cliffs   sticks   lips   acts   paths

- If the preceding sound is /b/, /d/, /g/, /l/, /m/, /n/, /ng/, /r/, or /v/, final s usually says /z/.

  tabs   lids   logs   hills   moms
  hens   wings   cars   lives

- If the preceding sound is a vowel sound, final s may say /s/ or /z/.

  gas   has

It's much simpler and more effective to have the student try the first sound of s, and if that doesn't produce a real word, then try the second sound.

Review

Review the Phonogram Cards that are behind the Review divider in your student's Reading Review Box. Show each card to your student and have him say the sound. If necessary, remind your student of the sound.

Shuffle and review the Word Cards that are behind the Review divider in your student's Reading Review Box. If your student has difficulty reading a word, build the word with letter tiles and have your student sound it out using the blending procedure shown in Appendix C.

Don't Forget!

Choose just ten Word Cards for review each day. Shuffle the cards so your student reviews a variety of patterns.

Teach New Letter Sounds

Hold up the Phonogram Card for the letter <u>u</u>.

"This letter says /ŭ/."

Using both hands, do a hand motion like you are milking a cow. "When we say /ŭ/, let's pretend that we are farmers and we are milking a cow. Say the sound of <u>u</u> like this: /ŭ/–/ŭ/–udder." *Student pretends to milk a cow and says /ŭ/–/ŭ/–udder.*

Show Phonogram Card 2 to your student.

"You already know that the letter <u>s</u> says /s/. But it also makes another sound: /z/. So the letter <u>s</u> makes two sounds: /s/ and /z/. Repeat after me: /s/–/z/." *Student repeats the sounds.*

Mix in several other Phonogram Cards for mixed review and practice until your student can say the sounds accurately.

 Remember: Whenever you introduce a new Phonogram Card, file it behind the appropriate **Review** divider in your student's Reading Review Box.

Even if your student appears to remember the new phonogram during his first introduction to it, it often takes multiple sessions to master a new phonogram. You want to be sure the Phonogram Card has really been mastered before moving it behind the **Mastered** divider, so revisit it in the next lesson.

Build the words *us* and *is* with letter tiles.

"When the letter <u>s</u> is at the end of a word, sometimes it says its first sound and sometimes it says its second sound. Try the first sound, and if that doesn't sound like a real word, try the second sound."

Have your student read the words *us* and *is* to practice this concept. Mix in several other letter tiles for mixed review and practice until your student can say the sounds accurately.

Blend Sounds with Letter Tiles

Build the word *hut* with letter tiles.

"I'll sound out this first word, and then you'll sound out the next word."

Touch under the <u>h</u> and say /*h*/.

Touch under the <u>u</u> and say /*ŭ*/.

Touch under the <u>t</u> and say /*t*/.

Now go back to the beginning of the word. Slide your finger under the letters <u>h</u>-<u>u</u>-<u>t</u> and say *hut* slowly.

Finally, read the word *hut* at a normal pace as we do when we speak.

Using the same blending procedure, have your student sound out the word *rub*.

New Teaching
(continued)

Play "Change the Word"

Build the word *hum* with letter tiles.

"What is this word?" *Hum.*

"I'm going to change the first letter of this word."

"What does this new word say?" Encourage your student to sound out the new word, *gum.*

Continue to change one letter at a time to form the following words. Each time, have your student sound out the new word.

> **gum → gun → bun → sun → run → rub → rug →**
> **dug → tug → bug**

This next sequence contains the second sound of s. Change one letter at a time to form the following words.

> **is → his → has → as**

Complete Activity Sheet

"Let's play some bingo!"

Letter Sounds Bingo
Remove pages 69-71 from the *Blast Off* activity book.

Give your student something fun to use for markers, like raisins, M&Ms, coins, dried beans, or Cheerios.

Randomly call out the sounds of the letters. When a sound is called, your student should put a marker over the corresponding letter. When your student gets three in a row, he says "Bingo!"

For a longer game, have your student fill the card completely before calling bingo.

New Teaching
(continued)

Practice Reading Words

Have your student practice reading the words on Word Cards 53-62.

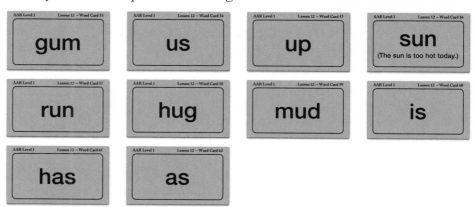

AAR Level 1	Lesson 12 – Word Card 53

gum

| AAR Level 1 | Lesson 12 – Word Card 54 |

us

| AAR Level 1 | Lesson 12 – Word Card 55 |

up

| AAR Level 1 | Lesson 12 – Word Card 56 |

sun
(The sun is too hot today.)

| AAR Level 1 | Lesson 12 – Word Card 57 |

run

| AAR Level 1 | Lesson 12 – Word Card 58 |

hug

| AAR Level 1 | Lesson 12 – Word Card 59 |

mud

| AAR Level 1 | Lesson 12 – Word Card 60 |

is

| AAR Level 1 | Lesson 12 – Word Card 61 |

has

| AAR Level 1 | Lesson 12 – Word Card 62 |

as

File the Word Cards behind the Review divider of the Reading Review Box.

Practice Fluency

Turn to pages 73-74 in the activity book.

Have your student read from the Practice Sheets.

Try using sticker dots to break up the Practice Sheet. For instructions, look for this icon in Appendix F.

Lesson 12: Letter U and the Second Sound of S

New Teaching
(continued)

> ### Freeing Up Mental Space for Comprehension
>
> Reading requires two main tasks:
> 1. Fluently decoding the printed word
> 2. Comprehending the printed word
>
> For beginning readers, decoding is very difficult because they have to work so hard to sound out words to pronounce them. This takes up so much of a beginning reader's attention that your student's mind actually switches between decoding and comprehending a few words at a time. That's why a student's reading can be somewhat choppy when he is initially learning to read. It's all a part of the process!
>
> By consistently working through the fluency exercises, though, your student will learn to decode the printed word more quickly and easily, which will free up the mental space and attention needed for reading comprehension.

Read-Aloud Time

Read a Story or Poem

Read aloud to your student for twenty minutes.

Track Your Progress

Mark the Progress Chart

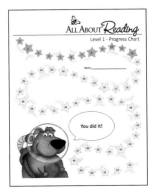

Have your student mark Lesson 12 on the Progress Chart.

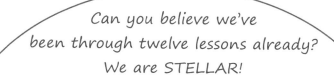

Can you believe we've
been through twelve lessons already?
We are STELLAR!

And we've read a whole galaxy of stories, too.
Did you see that dog in "The Job"?
Sure, he has cute spots and all, but I think
I would have been amazing
in that hot dog ad!

Who wouldn't like
gravity-defying hot dogs?

Lesson 13   Read "Run, Bug, Run!" and "Kip the Pup"

Objective   In this lesson, students read two short stories and imagine life from the viewpoint of a character.

You Will Need

☐ *Blast Off to Reading!* pages 75-78

☐ *Run, Bug, Run!* book

Before You Begin   ## Preview the Purpose of the Activity Sheet

Today's first short story is told from the point of view of a small bug. To help your student understand the concept of point of view, the activity sheet asks him to imagine various scenarios as if he were the character.

Review

Review the Phonogram Cards that are behind the Review divider in your student's Reading Review Box. Show each card to your student and have him say the sound(s). If necessary, remind your student of the sound(s).

Shuffle and review the Word Cards that are behind the Review divider in your student's Reading Review Box. If your student has difficulty reading a word, build the word with letter tiles and have your student sound it out using the blending procedure shown in Appendix C.

Your student may enjoy practicing Word Cards by typing a selection of them on a computer. This activity is especially good for kids who struggle with handwriting.

Shuffle the cards behind the Mastered dividers and choose a random selection of ten to twenty cards for review.

Story 1: "Run, Bug, Run!"

Complete Activity Sheet

"Imagine how scary the world would be if you were as small as a bug. Let's help this bug stay out of danger."

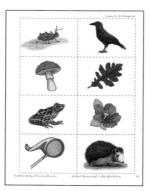

Is It Dangerous?
Remove page 75 from the *Blast Off* activity book.

Cut out the cards and set aside the bug card. Mix up the remaining seven cards and place them face down in a pile. Have your student select the cards one by one and decide whether the object pictured would be dangerous to the bug or if it's safe. If desired, your student may make separate piles for dangerous and safe objects.

Answer Key
Dangerous: bird, frog, net, hedgehog
Safe: mushroom, leaf, flower

Read the Warm-Up Sheet for "Run, Bug, Run!"

Turn to page 77 in the activity book.

Have your student practice reading words and phrases that will be encountered in "Run, Bug, Run!"

New Teaching
(continued)

Teach Vocabulary and Activate Prior Knowledge

Point out the illustration of a bud on the Warm-Up Sheet. "A *bud* is a new leaf or flower that is still closed and that is getting ready to open. There is a rosebud in today's story. That means a new rose that is just beginning to open its petals."

Point out the illustration of a mob on the Warm-Up Sheet. "A *mob* is a large group. A group of cows is called a *herd*. A group of dogs is called a *pack*. And a group of kangaroos is called a *mob*."

"The word *mob* can actually refer to any large group. For example, if there was a mob of mosquitoes outside last night, that means there were lots and lots of mosquitoes. In this next story, the main character is an insect. At first he is alone, but then he finds a mob."

"What is the opposite of a mob?" Possible answers: *one or two, a small number.*

"If you were as small as a bug, where would you hide to stay safe?" Discuss various places a small bug could hide.

"Let's see what the little bug in this story does to stay out of danger."

Read "Run, Bug, Run!"

"Turn to page 89 in your reader and read 'Run, Bug, Run!' aloud." Discuss your student's ideas for the questions below as you come to them.

After page 96: "Why isn't the bug afraid of the big mob?"

After reading: "Go back to the beginning of the story and look at the illustrations. What danger is the bug in on each page?"

Story 2: "Kip the Pup"

Read the Warm-Up Sheet for "Kip the Pup"

Turn to page 78 in the activity book.

Have your student practice reading words and phrases that will be encountered in "Kip the Pup."

Teach Vocabulary and Activate Prior Knowledge

Point out the illustration of a hut on the Warm-Up Sheet. "A *hut* is a type of shelter. It is usually small and can be made from a variety of different things. The one in this illustration is made of stone and straw. Huts can also be made of sticks, mud, or wood. An igloo is a type of hut that is made of snow and ice."

"Have you ever seen a puppy playing outside? What kinds of things do puppies like to do?" Discuss ways that puppies have fun.

"In this next story, a pup has all sorts of fun. And he even has a hut!"

Read "Kip the Pup"

"Turn to page 99 in your reader and read 'Kip the Pup' aloud." Discuss your student's ideas for the questions below as you come to them.

After reading: "Kip does two things that are a bit naughty. What are these two things?" *Biting the hose/sprinkler and digging up the flowers.*

"Why do you think Kip doesn't get in trouble for being naughty?"

Read a Story or Poem

Read aloud to your student for twenty minutes.

Stay Awake During Read-Aloud Time!

Does read-aloud time find you fighting fatigue? Here are some parent-tested ways to keep you from drifting into dreamland in the middle of a story.

- Vary your location, especially if your sofa is too comfy. Try outside or at the kitchen table.
- Read early in the day after breakfast or lunch when you are still fresh and wide awake.
- Distract yourself by sipping tea or nibbling popcorn or, even better, by creating funny voices for the characters.
- Read where there is bright, natural light.
- Have an older student read aloud to younger siblings—while you sneak off for a well-deserved doze!

Track Your Progress

Mark the Progress Chart

Have your student mark Lesson 13 on the Progress Chart.

128

Lesson 14   Letter E

Objective
This lesson teaches words containing the letter <u>e</u>.

You Will Need
☐ Phonogram Card 24   ☐ Word Cards 63-72
☐ *Blast Off to Reading!* pages 79-84

Before You Begin

Preview the Sounds of the Letter

e The letter <u>e</u> can say two sounds:
- /ĕ/ as in *echo*, known as the short sound (taught in this lesson)
- /ē/ as in *even*, known as the long sound (taught in Lesson 48)

To help your student remember the sound of short <u>e</u> (/ĕ/), we will use the following hand motion. **Tip!**

Cup your hand to your ear as if you are listening to an echo. "When we say /ĕ/, let's pretend that we are listening to an echo. Say the sound of <u>e</u> like this: /ĕ/–/ĕ/–echo." *Student pretends to listen for an echo and says /ĕ/–/ ĕ/–echo.*

Refer to the Letter Tiles app or Phonogram Sounds app for a demonstration of the <u>e</u> phonogram sounds.

Preview Function Words

Function words are short words like *the, at, an, can, am, a, if, of,* and *is.* These words can't be described (What does *if* mean?) and are normally unstressed (*I'kn ride'uh bike* instead of *I can ride a bike*)—yet they are the glue that holds our sentences together.

Function words make up a high percentage of our reading material, but some beginning readers need extra time to learn them. To give your student extra practice with function words, they have been sprinkled throughout the Practice Sheets.

A Tip Regarding Vowels I and E

Some students have difficulty with words containing short i and short e, which sound similar to untrained ears. If your student says the wrong sound, ask him to first touch the vowel and say the vowel sound with its related mnemonic (/ĕ/–/ĕ/–echo or /ĭ/–/ĭ/–itchy). Then he should go back and sound out the word from the beginning.

Review

Review the Phonogram Cards that are behind the Review divider in your student's Reading Review Box. Show each card to your student and have him say the sound(s). If necessary, remind your student of the sound(s).

Shuffle and review the Word Cards that are behind the Review divider in your student's Reading Review Box. If your student has difficulty reading a word, build the word with letter tiles and have your student sound it out using the blending procedure shown in Appendix C.

New Teaching

Teach New Letter Sound

Hold up the Phonogram Card for the letter e.

"This letter says /ĕ/."

Cup your hand to your ear as if you are listening to an echo. "When we say /ĕ/, let's pretend that we are listening to an echo. Say the sound of e like this: /ĕ/–/ĕ/–echo." *Student pretends to listen for an echo and says /ĕ/–/ĕ/–echo.*

Mix in several other Phonogram Cards for mixed review and practice until your student can say the sounds accurately. File the new Phonogram Card behind the Review divider in the Reading Review Box.

Move the new letter tile into the workspace.

Mix in several other letter tiles for mixed review and practice with the new letter until your student can say the sound accurately.

New Teaching
(continued)

For extra practice with the new phonogram, try the activity "Jump On It." For instructions, look for this icon in Appendix G.

Blend Sounds with Letter Tiles

Build the word *bed* with letter tiles.

"I'll sound out this first word, and then you'll sound out the next word."

Touch under the b and say /b/.

Touch under the e and say /ĕ/.

Touch under the d and say /d/.

Now go back to the beginning of the word. Slide your finger under the letters b-e-d and say *bed* slowly.

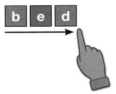

Finally, read the word *bed* at a normal pace as we do when we speak.

Using the same blending procedure, have your student sound out the word *set*.

New Teaching
(continued)

Play "Change the Word"

Build the word *jet* with letter tiles.

"What is this word?" *Jet.*

"I'm going to change the first letter of this word."

"What does this new word say?" Encourage your student to sound out the new word, *met.*

Continue to change one letter at a time to form the following words. Each time, have your student sound out the new word.

met → men → hen → pen → pet → bet → yet → yes

Complete Activity Sheet

"Let's feed bananas to some monkeys!"

Monkeys and Bananas
Remove pages 79-82 from the *Blast Off* activity book.

Cut out the monkey strips and lay them out on the table. Cut out the banana cards and place them in a pile with the words facing down.

Have your student read each monkey's name. Then have him pick one banana card at a time, read the word, and place the banana next to the monkey whose name rhymes with the word.

Continue until all the words have been read and matched with the rhyming monkey.

Answer Key
Ned: wed, bed, red, Ted, led, fed
Peg: beg, leg, Meg
Dot: hot, cot, rot, pot, tot, lot

Practice Reading Words

Have your student practice reading the words on Word Cards 63-72.

AAR Level 1 — Lesson 14 – Word Card 63	AAR Level 1 — Lesson 14 – Word Card 64	AAR Level 1 — Lesson 14 – Word Card 65	AAR Level 1 — Lesson 14 – Word Card 66
yes	**men**	**ten**	**pet**

AAR Level 1 — Lesson 14 – Word Card 67	AAR Level 1 — Lesson 14 – Word Card 68	AAR Level 1 — Lesson 14 – Word Card 69	AAR Level 1 — Lesson 14 – Word Card 70
get	**leg**	**bed**	**red** (The rose is red.)

AAR Level 1 — Lesson 14 – Word Card 71	AAR Level 1 — Lesson 14 – Word Card 72
set	**wet** (The dog is wet.)

File the Word Cards behind the Review divider of the Reading Review Box.

Practice Fluency

Turn to pages 83-84 in the activity book.

Have your student read from the Practice Sheets.

 To engage your student in the fluency exercises, make a word search puzzle. For instructions, look for this icon in Appendix F.

Read-Aloud Time

Read a Story or Poem

Read aloud to your student for twenty minutes.

Mark the Progress Chart

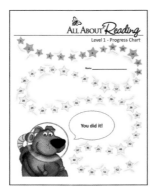

Have your student mark Lesson 14 on the Progress Chart.

Lesson 15 Read "The Gum" and "The Sad Hog"

Objective

In this lesson, students read two short stories and complete a story sequencing activity.

You Will Need

☐ *Blast Off to Reading!* pages 85-89

☐ *Run, Bug, Run!* book

Before You Begin

Preview Story Sequencing

After reading the first story, your student will complete a sequencing activity. Sequencing refers to the ability to identify, order, and retell events from a story, and it's a key strategy for reading comprehension.

Review

Review the Phonogram Cards that are behind the Review divider in your student's Reading Review Box. Show each card to your student and have him say the sound(s). If necessary, remind your student of the sound(s).

Get your student on her feet for the Phonogram Card review with the game "Phonogram Hopscotch." For instructions, look for this icon in Appendix G.

Shuffle and review the Word Cards that are behind the Review divider in your student's Reading Review Box. If your student has difficulty reading a word, build the word with letter tiles and have your student sound it out using the blending procedure shown in Appendix C.

Story 1: "The Gum"

Read the Warm-Up Sheet for "The Gum"

Turn to page 85 in the activity book.

Have your student practice reading words and phrases that will be encountered in "The Gum."

Teach Vocabulary and Activate Prior Knowledge

Point out the illustration of a headstand on the Warm-Up Sheet. "This is a *headstand*. A headstand is when someone actually stands on his head! Have you ever tried to do a headstand?"

"Have you ever made a big mess? How did you clean it up?" Discuss ways to clean up a mess.

"A girl in this next story does a headstand and makes a mess. Let's see how the whole family tries to clean it up."

Read "The Gum"

"Turn to page 109 in your reader and read 'The Gum' aloud." Discuss your student's ideas for the questions below as you come to them.

After page 110: "Look at the illustration. How do you think Peg's gum ends up on the rug?"

After page 115: "The characters have tried many ways to get the gum off the rug, but it won't budge. Do you think they will get it off at the end of the story?"

After reading: "Who do you think has the best idea for getting the gum off the rug? How would *you* do it?"

Complete Activity Sheet

"Let's see if you can remember all the ways the family tried to get the gum off the rug."

<u>**Get the Gum!**</u>
Remove page 87 from the activity book.

Cut out the story sequencing cards.

Mix up the cards and place them face up on the table. Explain that the cards show the different tools the family in the story uses to get the gum out of the rug. Have your student place the cards in the correct order as they appeared in the story. The student may refer to the story to complete this activity.

Story 2: "The Sad Hog"

Read the Warm-Up Sheet for "The Sad Hog"

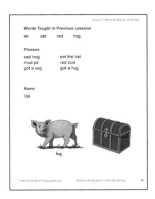

Turn to page 89 in the activity book.

Have your student practice reading words and phrases that will be encountered in "The Sad Hog."

Point out the name *Val* in the Name section. "Val is a nickname for Valerie."

Teach Vocabulary and Activate Prior Knowledge

Point out the illustration of a chest on the Warm-Up Sheet. "This is a *chest*. A chest is a big box where you can store things. People often keep chests in the attic or basement to hold old items they want to keep. Other words for chest are *trunk*, *toy chest*, or *toy box*. What kinds of things do you think can be stored in a chest?"

New Teaching
(continued)

Point out the illustration of a hog on the Warm-Up Sheet. "This is a *hog*. Hog is another name for a pig."

"If your best friend were sad, what would you do to cheer him or her up?" Discuss ways to cheer up a friend.

"In this story, a little girl finds things in an old chest to cheer up her sad pet. Let's see what happens."

Read "The Sad Hog"

"Turn to page 119 in your reader and read 'The Sad Hog' aloud." Discuss your student's ideas for the questions below as you come to them.

After page 121: "Why do you think the hog is sad?"

After reading: "Why is the hog happy now?"

Read-Aloud Time

Read a Story or Poem

Read aloud to your student for twenty minutes.

Track Your Progress

Mark the Progress Chart

Have your student mark Lesson 15 on the Progress Chart.

Lesson 16   Letters QU and X

Objective   This lesson teaches words containing the phonograms <u>qu</u> and <u>x</u>.

You Will Need   ☐ Phonogram Cards 25-26   ☐ Word Cards 73-80
                       ☐ *Blast Off to Reading!* pages 91-94

Before You Begin   ## Preview the Sounds of the Letters

qu The letters <u>q</u> and <u>u</u> work together to make the /kw/ sound as in *queen*. In English words, the letter <u>q</u> is always followed by the letter <u>u</u>, which is why we treat them as one phonogram. In this phonogram, the <u>u</u> doesn't act like a vowel.

x The letter <u>x</u> says /ks/ as in *ax*.

 Refer to the Letter Tiles app or Phonogram Sounds app for a demonstration of the <u>qu</u> and <u>x</u> phonogram sounds.

Review

 Review the Phonogram Cards that are behind the Review divider in your student's Reading Review Box. Show each card to your student and have him say the sound(s). If necessary, remind your student of the sound(s).

 Shuffle and review the Word Cards that are behind the Review divider in your student's Reading Review Box. If your student has difficulty reading a word, build the word with letter tiles and have your student sound it out using the blending procedure shown in Appendix C.

Your student may enjoy reviewing Word Cards with the activity "Tell a Story." For instructions, look for this icon in Appendix H.

Teach New Letter Sounds

Hold up the Phonogram Card for <u>qu</u>.

"See how there are two letters on one card? In English words, the letter <u>q</u> is always followed by the letter <u>u</u>. Together, these letters say /kw/. Repeat after me: /kw/." *Student repeats the sound.*

Hold up the Phonogram Card for the letter <u>x</u>.

"The letter <u>x</u> says /ks/. Repeat after me: /ks/." *Student repeats the sound.*

> Some students are helped by knowing that the sound of <u>x</u> is made by two sounds spoken in rapid succession: /k/ and /s/. **Tip!**

Mix in several other Phonogram Cards for mixed review and practice until your student can say the sounds accurately. File the new Phonogram Cards behind the Review divider in the Reading Review Box.

Move the new letter tiles into the workspace.

Mix in several other letter tiles for mixed review and practice with the new letters until your student can say the sounds accurately.

> Have some fun reviewing these phonograms by playing the game "Phonogram Go Fish." For instructions, look for this icon in Appendix G.

Blend Sounds with Letter Tiles

Build the word *fix* with letter tiles.

"I'll sound out this first word, and then you'll sound out the next word."

New Teaching
(continued)

Touch under the f and say /f/.

Touch under the i and say /ĭ/.

Touch under the x and say /ks/.

Now go back to the beginning of the word. Slide your finger under the letters f-i-x and say *fix* slowly.

Finally, read the word *fix* at a normal pace as we do when we speak.

Using the same blending procedure, have your student sound out the word *quit*.

Leave the word *quit* in the workspace.

Play "Change the Word"

"I'm going to change the first tile of this word."

"What does this new word say?" Encourage your student to sound out the new word, *fit*.

New Teaching
(continued)

Continue to change one letter at a time to form the following words. Each time, have your student sound out the new word.

fit → fat → fax → tax → wax → ax → as → is → it

> Note that this is the first time you will be changing the vowel during this activity: *fit–fat* and *as–is*. You may wish to point this out to your student.
>
> Also, your student has already learned that the letter s̲ says two sounds. In the words *as* and *is*, s̲ says its second sound, /z/.

Complete Activity Sheet

"Are you ready to open some presents?"

What's in the Box?
Remove pages 91-92 from the *Blast Off* activity book.

Cut out each gift box, mix them up, and place them on the table with the words facing down.

To play, have your student select a gift box and turn it over to read the two-word phrase. If your student reads the phrase correctly, he can keep the gift box. If he reads the phrase incorrectly, return the box to the pile for another try.

Practice Reading Words

Have your student practice reading the words on Word Cards 73-80.

File the Word Cards behind the Review divider of the Reading Review Box.

New Teaching
(continued)

Practice Fluency

Turn to pages 93-94 in the activity book.

Have your student read from the Practice Sheets.

 To engage your student in the fluency exercises, let him illustrate a selection of words. For instructions, look for this icon in Appendix F.

Read-Aloud Time

Read a Story or Poem

Read aloud to your student for twenty minutes.

Track Your Progress

Mark the Progress Chart

Have your student mark Lesson 16 on the Progress Chart.

Hey, there, friend!
Sorry I disappeared for a while, but
I've been on a reconnaissance mission to
the future ... of this book!

And you know what? You've successfully finished
your orbit of the letters A to Z!

I won't give away all the goodies coming up, but
I will say you are going to be learning some
METEORIC stuff and reading some
ASTEROID-SMASHING stories!

All systems GO!

Lesson 17   Read "Pet Ox" and "Fox in a Box"

Objective

In this lesson, students read two short stories and create silly sentences based on a story.

You Will Need

☐ *Blast Off to Reading!* pages 95-98

☐ *Run, Bug, Run!* book

Before You Begin

Choppy Reading

It is normal for beginning students to read choppily, one word at a time. They are working very hard at decoding each individual word, so don't expect smooth reading at this stage.

However, you can help your student advance to the next level of fluency in the following two ways.

1. Have your student do a "cold reading" and then a "hot reading" of the sentences on the Practice Sheet. The first time he reads through the sentences, it is a cold reading. Have him read the same sentences several more times to warm up and improve his fluency. When he thinks he is able to read the sentences smoothly, he can announce that he is ready to do a final "hot reading." Celebrate the difference between the cold reading and the hot reading.

2. Model fluency for your student. Read a sentence aloud with expression, and then have your student read the same sentence after you. This exercise accustoms your student to the feeling of reading at a faster, smoother pace.

At this beginning level, don't be concerned about choppy reading. Just work toward the goal of fluency little by little, and recognize the hard work that your student is accomplishing.

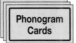

Review the Phonogram Cards that are behind the Review divider in your student's Reading Review Box. Show each card to your student and have him say the sound(s). If necessary, remind your student of the sound(s).

Shuffle and review the Word Cards that are behind the Review divider in your student's Reading Review Box. If your student has difficulty reading a word, build the word with letter tiles and have your student sound it out using the blending procedure shown in Appendix C.

Get silly with today's Word Card review with the activity "Yucky Snacks." For instructions, look for this icon in Appendix H.

New Teaching

Story 1: "Pet Ox"

Complete Activity Sheet

"Imagine if you kept a snake in your refrigerator or an elephant under your couch! In this activity, you'll make silly sentences about animals in strange places."

Silly Sentences
Remove pages 95-96 from the *Blast Off* activity book.

Cut out the animal and place cards. Note that animal cards are marked with a paw print on the back and place cards are marked with a compass rose.

Shuffle and place the cards face down in two piles, one for animals and one for places. Have your student draw one card from the animal pile and one card from the place pile and read the resulting silly sentence.

Continue until your student has read all the silly sentences.

Lesson 17: Read "Pet Ox" and "Fox in a Box"

New Teaching
(continued)

Read the Warm-Up Sheet for "Pet Ox"

Turn to page 97 in the activity book.

Have your student practice reading words and phrases that will be encountered in "Pet Ox."

Point out the name *Jax* in the Names section. "Jax is a nickname for Jackson."

Teach Vocabulary and Activate Prior Knowledge

Point out the illustration of a pen on the Warm-Up Sheet. "A *pen* is a kind of enclosure for animals. Farmers keep their pigs in a pen, for example."

Point out the illustration of an ox on the Warm-Up Sheet. "An *ox* is a large, very strong animal that is often used to pull or carry heavy loads. Where do you think a farmer would keep his ox?"

"If you could have any animal in the world as a pet, no matter how big or small, what would it be? Why?"

"Would you let that pet in the house or keep it outside? Why?"

"In this next story, a boy lets an unusual pet inside the house. Let's see what happens."

Read "Pet Ox"

"Turn to page 129 in your reader and read 'Pet Ox' aloud." Discuss your student's ideas for the questions below as you come to them.

After page 133: "Do you think Jax is supposed to have the ox in the house? Why or why not?"

After page 134: Point to the dash in the last sentence. "This line is called a dash. The dash shows that there is a pause here." If necessary, model for your student how to read the sentence.

New Teaching
(continued)

After page 135: "Why does Mom want the ox back in his pen?"

After reading: "Go back and look at the illustrations on pages 131-134. What do Jax and the ox do on each page that might make Mom mad?"

Story 2: "Fox in a Box"

Read the Warm-Up Sheet for "Fox in a Box"

Turn to page 98 in the activity book.

Have your student practice reading words and phrases that will be encountered in "Fox in a Box."

Activate Prior Knowledge

"Have you ever played with an empty box? What kinds of things can you do with a big box?" Discuss creative ways to play with a box.

"In the story you are about to read, a fox has lots of fun with a box."

Read "Fox in a Box"

"Turn to page 139 in your reader and read 'Fox in a Box' aloud." Discuss your student's ideas for the questions below as you come to them.

After page 141: "Where do you think this box comes from? How does it end up in the woods?"

After page 146: "Why does Fox spit out the piece of box?"

Lesson 17: Read "Pet Ox" and "Fox in a Box"

Read a Story or Poem

Read aloud to your student for twenty minutes.

Read-Aloud Tip!

When Your Student Reads Too Fast

Reading too fast may not seem like a problem to worry about, but there are definite drawbacks to it. Your fast reader may skip or add words, ignore punctuation, mumble, or have a hard time remembering details of the story. Here are some strategies to slow your reader down.

- Model the same passage reading fast with no expression and then again slowly with expression. Can your student hear the difference?
- See if having a physical reminder, like using a piece of paper as a guide, helps your student slow down.
- Invent a code phrase, like "speedy bunny," to remind your student to slow down.
- If your student ignores punctuation, have her pinch her fingers together when she gets to the punctuation at the end of sentences. This is a good physical reminder for her to slow down.

Mark the Progress Chart

Have your student mark Lesson 17 on the Progress Chart.

Lesson 17: Read "Pet Ox" and "Fox in a Box"

Lesson 18   Consonant Team TH

Objective

This lesson teaches the concept of consonant teams and words containing both sounds of consonant team <u>th</u>.

You Will Need

☐ Phonogram Card 27

☐ letter tile <u>th</u>

☐ Consonant Teams label

☐ *Blast Off to Reading!* pages 99-104

☐ Word Cards 81-88

☐ spatula

Before You Begin

Preview Consonant Teams

When two consonants work together to make one sound, we call them a *consonant team*. Another common term for this is *consonant digraph*.

Six consonant teams will be taught in Level 1: <u>th</u> as in *three* and *then*; <u>sh</u> as in *ship*; <u>ch</u> as in *child, school,* and *chef*; <u>ck</u> as in *duck*; <u>ng</u> as in *king*; and <u>nk</u> as in *thank*.

Preview the *Consonant Teams* Category

If you are using the Letter Tiles app, the consonant teams are organized under the Consonant Teams category.

If you are using a magnetic white board, place the Consonant Teams label and the <u>th</u> tile below the alphabet row.

To see what the magnetic white board will look like after all the Level 1 consonant teams have been placed on the board, refer to Appendix L.

Preview Consonant Team TH

Today you will be teaching the consonant team <u>th</u>.

Depending on the word, <u>th</u> says /th/ as in *three* or /t̶h̶/ as in *then*. You will notice that there is a strikethrough on the <u>th</u> in the second sound: /t̶h̶/. This strikethrough is used to differentiate between the two sounds of <u>th</u>.

Before You Begin
(continued)

The /th/ is considered an *unvoiced* sound, while the /t̶h̶/ is considered a *voiced* sound because we use our vocal cords to say it.

Your student will learn both sounds of <u>th</u> in this lesson. Examples include:

/th/: bath   moth   thin

/t̶h̶/: than   this   them

 The <u>th</u> tile is stored under the Consonant Teams category.

 Refer to the Letter Tiles app or Phonogram Sounds app for a demonstration of the <u>th</u> phonogram sounds.

Review

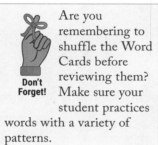

Are you remembering to shuffle the Word Cards before reviewing them? **Don't Forget!** Make sure your student practices words with a variety of patterns.

Review the Phonogram Cards that are behind the Review divider in your student's Reading Review Box. Show each card to your student and have him say the sound(s). If necessary, remind your student of the sound(s).

Shuffle and review the Word Cards that are behind the Review divider in your student's Reading Review Box. If your student has difficulty reading a word, build the word with letter tiles and have your student sound it out using the blending procedure shown in Appendix C.

New Teaching

Teach New Letter Sounds

AAR Level 1   Lesson 18 – Phonogram Card 27

th

Hold up the Phonogram Card for the consonant team <u>th</u>.

"See how there are two letters on one card? The two letters work together to make one sound."

"These letters can say /th/, or they can say /t̶h̶/."

"Repeat after me: /th/–/t̶h̶/." *Student repeats the sounds.*

Lesson 18: Consonant Team TH

New Teaching
(continued)

Mix in several other Phonogram Cards for mixed review and practice until your student can say the sounds accurately. File the new Phonogram Card behind the Review divider in the Reading Review Box.

Move the new letter tile into the workspace.

Mix in several other letter tiles for mixed review and practice with the new phonogram until your student can say the sounds accurately.

 For extra practice with the new phonogram, try the activity "Stamp It." For instructions, look for this icon in Appendix G.

Blend Sounds with Letter Tiles

"When we read words with th, we try the first sound first. If that doesn't make a word you recognize, then try the second sound of th."

Build the word *them* with letter tiles.

"I'll sound out this first word, and then you'll sound out the next word."

"First I try the first sound of th." Touch the th and say /th/.

"Then I sound out the rest of the word."

Touch the e and say /ĕ/, and then touch the m and say /m/.

Now go back to the beginning of the word and blend the sounds together, using the first sound of th. Slide your finger under the letters th-e-m and say /thĕm/.

"With the first sound of th, this word doesn't sound like a word I recognize. So now I try the second sound of th, /th̶/."

New Teaching
(continued)

Repeat the previous steps, using the second sound of <u>th</u>. Then go back and blend the sounds together. Slide your finger under the letters <u>th</u>-<u>e</u>-<u>m</u> and say /<s>th</s>ĕm/.

"So this word says *them*. It uses /<s>th</s>/, the second sound of <u>th</u>."

"Now it's your turn. Remember to always try the first sound of <u>th</u> first."

Using the same procedure for blending, have your student sound out the words *this* and *bath*. Be sure your student tries the first sound of <u>th</u> first, and then the second sound.

Leave the word *bath* in the workspace.

Play "Change the Word"

"I'm going to change the first letter of this word."

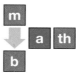

"What does this new word say?" Encourage your student to sound out the new word, *math*.

Continue to change one letter at a time to form the following words. Each time, have your student sound out the new word.

math → path → pat → pan → an → in → thin

This next sequence contains the second sound of <u>th</u>. Change one letter at a time to form the following words.

that → than → then → them

New Teaching
(continued)

Complete Activity Sheet

"It's time to fry some eggs!"

Over Easy
Remove pages 99-102 from the *Blast Off* activity book.

Cut out the eggs.

Place several eggs sunny side up in a pan. Have your student use a spatula to flip over the eggs, one at a time, and read the word.

If your student reads the word correctly, he can keep the fried egg. If he reads the word incorrectly, he should put the egg back in the pan and try again.

Practice Reading Words

Have your student practice reading the words on Word Cards 81-88.

File the Word Cards behind the Review divider in the Reading Review Box.

New Teaching
(continued)

Practice Fluency

Turn to pages 103-104 in the activity book.

Have your student read from the Practice Sheets.

 To encourage your student in fluency practice, set up a points system. For instructions, look for this icon in Appendix F.

Read-Aloud Time

Read a Story or Poem

Read aloud to your student for twenty minutes.

Track Your Progress

Mark the Progress Chart

Have your student mark Lesson 18 on the Progress Chart.

Lesson 18: Consonant Team TH

Lesson 19 Read "Get Them!" and "The Red Pen"

Objective	In this lesson, students read two short stories and complete a character motivation activity.
You Will Need	☐ *Blast Off to Reading!* pages 105-108 ☐ *Run, Bug, Run!* book
Before You Begin	**Avoid Making Corrections Too Soon**

When your student misreads a word in a sentence, resist the temptation to correct him immediately. Let him reach the end of the sentence before you interrupt, giving him the chance to realize on his own that he made a mistake.

For example, if your student reads *The hot sat with a thud*, he will probably self-correct because the sentence obviously doesn't make sense. He will look back to see where his error is and reread the sentence correctly as *The hog sat with a thud*. If he does continue reading without correcting himself, ask him if the sentence he just read makes sense.

When you interrupt your student immediately after he makes an error, he is deprived of the opportunity to monitor what he is reading for meaning. In the example above, the phrase *The hot...* does make sense in itself, as it could be *The hot day* or *The hot lunch*. If you give your student time to reach the end of the sentence, though, it will most likely be clear to him that he has misread a word.

Review

Review the Phonogram Cards that are behind the Review divider in your student's Reading Review Box. Show each card to your student and have him say the sound(s). If necessary, remind your student of the sound(s).

Shuffle and review the Word Cards that are behind the Review divider in your student's Reading Review Box. If your student has difficulty reading a word, build the word with letter tiles and have your student sound it out using the blending procedure shown in Appendix C.

Story 1: "Get Them!"

Complete Activity Sheet

"You probably have a reason for doing everything you do. This is called your *motivation*. In this activity, you'll discover the reasons various animals do what they do."

Why Did They Do That?

Remove page 105 from the *Blast Off* activity book.

Cut out the cards and place them face down on the table. Have your student draw one card at a time and then answer one of the character motivation questions below.

Q: Why is the cat licking her paw?
Possible answers: She wants to be clean; it hurts.

Q: Why is the seal balancing the ball?
Possible answers: He's been trained; to make people laugh.

Q: Why is the meerkat standing guard?
Possible answers: He wants to protect his family; to make sure enemies stay away.

Q: Why does the bird have a twig in her mouth?
Possible answer: She wants to build a nest.

Q: Why is the lion roaring?
Possible answers: He wants to show who is boss; he wants to scare others away.

Q: Why does the monkey want the banana?
Possible answer: He's hungry.

Discuss your student's answers.

New Teaching
(continued)

Read the Warm-Up Sheet for "Get Them!"

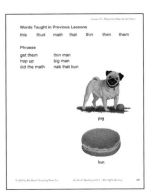

Turn to page 107 in the activity book.

Have your student practice reading words and phrases that will be encountered in "Get Them!"

Teach Vocabulary and Activate Prior Knowledge

Point out the illustration of a pug on the Warm-Up Sheet. "A *pug* is a small dog with a flat nose and a very wrinkled face. There is a pug in today's story."

Point out the illustration of a bun on the Warm-Up Sheet. "A *bun* is a small cake or bread. Have you ever had a cinnamon bun or a dinner bun with butter? The pug in the next story is very fond of buns!"

"Have you ever been on a team or in a group to play a game or do a project? How did it go?" Discuss any experience your student has had as part of a team.

"Do you prefer to do things by yourself or with a team or group? Why?"

"In this next story, a pug gets help from a group of people. Let's see what happens."

Read "Get Them!"

"Turn to page 151 in your reader and read 'Get Them!' aloud." Discuss your student's ideas for the questions below as you come to them.

After page 154: "Hopping doesn't work. What else could the pug do to get the bun?"

After pages 157-158: Point to the ellipses (three dots) on page 157. "When you see three dots like this, it means there is a big pause in the sentence." If necessary, model for your student how to read the sentence on pages 157-158.

New Teaching
(continued)

After page 158: "What is the pug going to do with all these people?"

> You may need to explain the word *nab* on page 159 to your student. *Nab* means *to grab* or *to catch*.

After page 161: "Do you think the pug is going to get away with the bun? Why or why not?"

Story 2: "The Red Pen"

Read the Warm-Up Sheet for "The Red Pen"

Turn to page 108 in the activity book.

Have your student practice reading words and phrases that will be encountered in "The Red Pen."

Point out the name *Tex* in the Name section. "Tex is a nickname for Texas."

Teach Vocabulary and Activate Prior Knowledge

Point out the illustration of a jet on the Warm-Up Sheet. "A *jet* is a large, very fast airplane."

Point out the illustration of a bog on the Warm-Up Sheet. "A *bog* is an area where the ground is wet, muddy, and spongy. It is hard to walk in a bog!"

"If you could be anything for a day, like a bird or a tree or a cloud, what would you be?" Discuss what your student would do during his day as his chosen object.

"The boy in the story you are about to read has a big imagination. Let's see what he would like to be."

New Teaching
(continued)

Read "The Red Pen"

"Turn to page 165 in your reader and read 'The Red Pen' aloud." Discuss your student's ideas for the questions below as you come to them.

After reading: "Tex imagines that he is many things. Why do you think he would like to be a pen? A log? A box?"

"Look at the illustrations on pages 167 and 176. Based on the items in Tex's bedroom, what are some things that Tex likes to do?" *Possible answers: Play basketball, play guitar, listen to music, draw, read, play with his dog.*

Read-Aloud Time

Read a Story or Poem

Read aloud to your student for twenty minutes.

Read-Aloud Tip!

Reading to Kids Who Can't Sit Still
If you have a wriggler, you know how hard it is to keep his attention during read-aloud time. Here are some strategies for making sure your active student is getting the most out of reading time.

- Read after physical activity so your student gets all his energy out.
- Look for interactive books with flaps, sounds, tabs, or things to count.
- Listen to audio books in the car.
- Find books that appeal to your student's unique interests.
- Eliminate distractions like phones, television, and computer games.
- Keep your student's hands busy with quiet toys and activities like playdough, building blocks, lacing cards, or coloring books.

Mark the Progress Chart

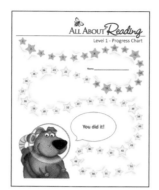

Have your student mark Lesson 19 on the Progress Chart.

HARF HARF HARF HARF!
Hoo-boy, how about that story about the pug and the bun? If that one didn't make your ears flap in the wind, I don't know what will. That little guy has a lot of spunk.

In fact, he'd make a great astro-pup, don't you think?

Lesson 20   Consonant Team SH

Objective   This lesson teaches words containing the consonant team <u>sh</u>.

You Will Need

☐ Phonogram Card 28   ☐ *Blast Off to Reading!* pages 109–116

☐ letter tile <u>sh</u>   ☐ Word Cards 89–96

Before You Begin

Preview Consonant Team SH

The consonant team <u>sh</u> says /sh/ as in *ship*.

You may wish to help your student remember the sound of /sh/ by showing him how to hold his finger to his lips and say "shhh."

sh   The <u>sh</u> tile is stored under the Consonant Teams category.

Refer to the Letter Tiles app or Phonogram Sounds app for a demonstration of the <u>sh</u> phonogram sound.

Develop Automatic Word Recognition

Automatic word recognition means that words are recognized at a glance. When a student has automatic word recognition, he doesn't have to decode the word; he just knows what the word is with a single look. Another name for this skill is *automaticity.*

The Practice Sheets give your student the practice he needs to develop automaticity. After encountering the same words multiple times, your student will move from sounding out the words to automatic word recognition, allowing him to read smoothly and with more comprehension.

When you get to the "Practice Fluency" section today, check to make sure that you are spending enough time with the Practice Sheets. If working on Practice Sheets feels like a chore to your student, check out the tips in Appendix F.

Review the Phonogram Cards that are behind the Review divider in your student's Reading Review Box. Show each card to your student and have him say the sound(s). If necessary, remind your student of the sound(s).

Shuffle and review the Word Cards that are behind the Review divider in your student's Reading Review Box. If your student has difficulty reading a word, build the word with letter tiles and have your student sound it out using the blending procedure shown in Appendix C.

New Teaching

Teach New Letter Sound

Hold up the Phonogram Card for the consonant team <u>sh</u>.

"The <u>s</u> and <u>h</u> work together to make one sound. These letters say /sh/."

"Repeat after me: /sh/." *Student repeats the sound.*

Mix in several other Phonogram Cards for mixed review and practice until your student can say the sounds accurately. File the new Phonogram Card behind the Review divider in the Reading Review Box.

Move the new letter tile into the workspace.

Mix in several other letter tiles for mixed review and practice with the new phonogram until your student can say the sounds accurately.

For extra practice with the new phonogram, play some file folder games. For download information, look for this icon in Appendix G.

New Teaching

(continued)

Blend Sounds with Letter Tiles

Build the word *shut* with letter tiles.

"I'll sound out this first word, and then you'll sound out the next word."

Touch the <u>sh</u> and say /sh/.

Touch the <u>u</u> and say /ŭ/.

Touch the <u>t</u> and say /t/.

Now go back to the beginning of the word. Slide your finger under the letters <u>sh</u>-<u>u</u>-<u>t</u> and say *shut* slowly.

Finally, read the word *shut* at a normal pace as we do when we speak.

Using the same procedure for blending, have your student sound out the word *cash*.

New Teaching
(continued)

Play "Change the Word"

Build the word *wish* with letter tiles.

"What is this word?" *Wish.*

"I'm going to change the first letter of this word."

"What does this new word say?" Encourage your student to sound out the new word, *fish.*

Continue to change one letter at a time to form the following words. Each time, have your student sound out the new word.

fish → dish → dip → ship → shop

Complete Activity Sheet

"Let's flip some more words!"

Word Flippers for SH

Remove pages 109-113 from the *Blast Off* activity book.

There are three Word Flippers in this lesson. Each page will create one flipper.

Refer to Appendix E for assembly instructions.

Have your student flip through the book randomly, reading the words that are formed.

Practice Reading Words

Have your student practice reading the words on Word Cards 89-96.

File the Word Cards behind the Review divider in the Reading Review Box.

Practice Fluency

Turn to pages 115-116 in the activity book.

Have your student read from the Practice Sheets.

Point to the last word in the New Words section. "Has anyone ever said *Sh!* to you? What does it mean?" *Be quiet.*

 To engage your student in the fluency exercises, try the activity "Word Hide and Seek." For instructions, look for this icon in Appendix F.

Read-Aloud Time

Read a Story or Poem

Read aloud to your student for twenty minutes.

Mark the Progress Chart

Have your student mark Lesson 20 on the Progress Chart.

Hey! We didn't do too
SHabby with that SH lesson,
did we? In fact, we did so great that
I want to
SHout,
SHimmy,
and SHake
with joy!

Oh, but SH!
I forgot that SH makes us whisper ...
so I'm going to tiptoe back to my spaceSHip,
SHut the door, and have a nice
diSH of kibbles.

I wiSH you could
join me!

Lesson 21 Read "Run!" and "Six Fish"

Objective

In this lesson, students read two short stories and learn about story settings.

You Will Need

- [ ] *Blast Off to Reading!* pages 117-122
- [ ] *Run, Bug, Run!* book
- [ ] map or globe

Before You Begin

Avoid Excessive Feedback

In Lesson 19, we talked about why it is important to let your student finish a sentence even after he has misread a word. This practice encourages your student to monitor for meaning, asking himself, "Does this sentence make sense?"

On the flip side of the coin is the teacher who offers immediate feedback, constantly interrupting the student for every misread word. Too often, such a stream of feedback causes the student to become dependent on the teacher to confirm that the word or phrase he just read is correct. The reader waits for the teacher to nod or say "good" or "uh-huh," which then becomes a cycle: the student reads a word or two, waits for affirmation, and then reads a few more words. This stop-and-go cycle works against the development of fluency.

If you feel yourself falling into this negative routine with your student, let him know that from now on, you will give feedback after the sentence has been completed instead of during his reading.

Review

Review the Phonogram Cards that are behind the Review divider in your student's Reading Review Box. Show each card to your student and have him say the sound(s). If necessary, remind your student of the sound(s).

Shuffle and review the Word Cards that are behind the Review divider in your student's Reading Review Box. If your student has difficulty reading a word, build the word with letter tiles and have your student sound it out using the blending procedure shown in Appendix C.

Review
(continued)

 Give your student extra incentive for today's Word Card review with the activity "Snack Stack." For instructions, look for this icon in Appendix H.

New Teaching

Story 1: "Run!"

Complete Activity Sheet

"You know that the place where a story happens is called the setting. In this activity, you'll put various objects in their correct setting."

In the Right Place
Remove pages 117-119 from the *Blast Off* activity book.

Cut out the cards on page 119.

Mix up the cards and place them face down on the table. Have your student draw one card at a time and then decide which setting that card belongs in, either the indoor setting or the outdoor setting.

Continue until all the cards have been placed in the appropriate setting.

Read the Warm-Up Sheet for "Run!"

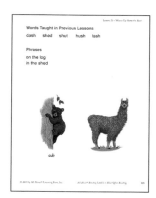

Turn to page 121 in the activity book.

Have your student practice reading words and phrases that will be encountered in "Run!"

Lesson 21: Read "Run!" and "Six Fish"

Teach Vocabulary and Activate Prior Knowledge

Point out the illustration of a cub on the Warm-Up Sheet. "A *cub* is a young bear. The word is also used for other baby animals like tigers, but in today's story, it refers to a baby bear."

Point out the illustration of a llama on the Warm-Up Sheet. "This is a *llama*. A llama is a domesticated animal in the camel family. Llamas are often raised for their soft, woolly fleece."

"Have you ever been scared by a shadow or an object that turned out to not be scary? Tell me about it."

"If you were in the woods and thought you saw a bear cub or other large animal, what would you do?"

"The boy in this story thinks he sees something in the field. Let's see what happens."

Read "Run!"

"Turn to page 179 in your reader and read 'Run!' aloud." Discuss your student's ideas for the questions below as you come to them.

After page 180: "Do you think they really see a cub outside? What else could it be?"

After reading: "Look at the illustrations on pages 183, 184, and 188. Do you think the setting of this story is in the United States or a different country?"

Find Bolivia on a map or globe. "This story is set in Bolivia, a country in South America. Bolivians harvest quinoa in fields like this, bent over the crops. Quinoa is a type of grain used for food or to make flour."

Story 2: "Six Fish"

Read the Warm-Up Sheet for "Six Fish"

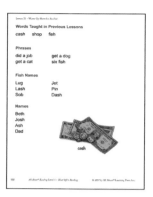

Turn to page 122 in the activity book.

Have your student practice reading words and phrases that will be encountered in "Six Fish."

Point out the name *Ash* in the Names section. "Ash is a nickname for Ashton."

Teach Vocabulary and Activate Prior Knowledge

Point out the illustration of cash on the Warm-Up Sheet. "*Cash* is another word for money. It includes both coins and paper money."

"Have you ever received cash for a job you did? What was the job?"

"Did you save the cash or did you buy something with it?"

"What kind of animal do you think makes the best pet?" Discuss your student's chosen animal and why it makes a good pet.

"Let's see what kind of pet the girl in this story chooses."

Read "Six Fish"

"Turn to page 191 in your reader and read 'Six Fish' aloud." Discuss your student's ideas for the questions below as you come to them.

After page 199: "Which pet do you think Beth will choose? Why?"

After reading: "Beth does three jobs to get cash. Look at the illustrations on pages 192-195. What are the jobs? What goes wrong with each one?"

"Look at the illustration on page 199. Based on the drawings and the names of the fish, what kind of personality do you think each fish has?"

New Teaching
(continued)

Consider recording your student as she reads the story again. It can be really helpful for kids to hear themselves reading—and having a recording session can be lots of fun! Just be sure to record a "hot" reading, not a cold reading.

After recording, let your student assess her own work. How did it sound? Was it natural or choppy? Too fast, too slow, or just right? Did she pay attention to punctuation? Encourage her to notice one thing she did well and one thing that needs improvement. Then she can practice and re-record to see if she improved.

Read-Aloud Time

Read a Story or Poem

Read aloud to your student for twenty minutes.

Track Your Progress

Mark the Progress Chart

Have your student mark Lesson 21 on the Progress Chart.

KATE STUMP

Lesson 21: Read "Run!" and "Six Fish"

Lesson 22   Consonant Team CH

Objective

This lesson teaches words containing the consonant team <u>ch</u>.

You Will Need

☐ Phonogram Card 29   ☐ *Blast Off to Reading!* pages 123-131

☐ letter tile <u>ch</u>   ☐ Word Cards 97-102

Before You Begin

Preview Consonant Team CH

The consonant team <u>ch</u> has three sounds: /ch/–/k/–/sh/. In this lesson, your student will learn the first and most common sound, /ch/ as in *child*. The other two sounds will be taught in Lesson 48.

 The <u>ch</u> tile is stored under the Consonant Teams category.

 Refer to the Letter Tiles app or Phonogram Sounds app for a demonstration of the <u>ch</u> phonogram sound.

Review

 Review the Phonogram Cards that are behind the Review divider in your student's Reading Review Box. Show each card to your student and have him say the sound(s). If necessary, remind your student of the sound(s).

Shuffle and review the Word Cards that are behind the Review divider in your student's Reading Review Box. If your student has difficulty reading a word, build the word with letter tiles and have your student sound it out using the blending procedure shown in Appendix C.

Test your student's Word Card memory with the game "Word Card Concentration." For instructions, look for this icon in Appendix H.

Teach New Letter Sound

Hold up the Phonogram Card for the consonant team <u>ch</u>.

"The <u>c</u> and <u>h</u> work together to make one sound. These letters can say /ch/."

"Repeat after me: /ch/." *Student repeats the sound.*

Mix in several other Phonogram Cards for mixed review and practice until your student can say the sounds accurately. File the new Phonogram Card behind the Review divider in the Reading Review Box.

Move the new letter tile into the workspace.

Mix in several other letter tiles for mixed review and practice with the new phonogram until your student can say the sound accurately.

Practice the new phonogram with the activity "Phonogram Card City." For instructions, look for this icon in Appendix G.

Blend Sounds with Letter Tiles

Build the word *chop* with letter tiles.

"I'll sound out this first word, and then you'll sound out the next word."

Touch the <u>ch</u> and say */ch/.*

Touch the <u>o</u> and say */ŏ/.*

New Teaching
(continued)

Touch the p and say /p/.

Now go back to the beginning of the word. Slide your finger under the letters ch-o-p and say *chop* slowly.

Finally, read the word *chop* at a normal pace as we do when we speak.

Using the same procedure for blending, have your student sound out the word *rich*.

Play "Change the Word"

Build the word *chin* with letter tiles.

"What is this word?" *Chin*.

"I'm going to change the last letter of this word."

"What does this new word say?" Encourage your student to sound out the new word, *chip*.

Continue to change one letter at a time to form the following words. Each time, have your student sound out the new word.

chip → chop → chap → chat

Complete Activity Sheets

"Let's pretend to be a mouse earning cheese by reading words with <u>ch</u>."

Little Mouse

Remove pages 123-125 from the *Blast Off* activity book.

Cut out the mouse and the cheese cards as indicated. Set out the twelve pieces of cheese with the words facing down.

You and your student take turns being the mouse. The mouse sneaks up to the pile of cheese and takes one piece. The mouse reads the word on the piece of cheese that was selected. If the word is read correctly, the mouse keeps the cheese. If the word is read incorrectly, it goes back into the cheese pile.

Continue until all the words have been read and the mouse has all the cheese.

"Now let's mail some letters!"

The "Mail a Letter" activity sheet provides mixed review of words containing <u>th</u>, <u>sh</u>, and <u>ch</u>. You may choose to do this second activity sheet during a different lesson if your student is tiring.

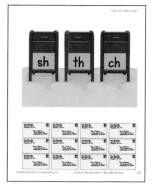

Mail a Letter

Remove pages 127-128 from the activity book.

Make a small slot in each mailbox by cutting along the dotted line on the back.

Cut out the "letters" on the bottom of the page and place them in a pile with the words facing down.

Have your student choose one "letter" at a time, turn it over, read the word, and decide which mailbox he needs to deliver it to. He may then slip the letter into the correct mailbox.

Continue until your student has delivered all the letters.

Lesson 22: Consonant Team CH

New Teaching
(continued)

Practice Reading Words

Have your student practice reading the words on Word Cards 97-102.

AAR Level 1 Lesson 22 – Word Card 97	AAR Level 1 Lesson 22 – Word Card 98
chip	**chin**

File the Word Cards behind the Review divider in the Reading Review Box.

Practice Fluency

Turn to pages 129-131 in the activity book.

Have your student read from the Practice Sheets.

To engage your student in the fluency exercises, try the activity "Roll the Dice." For instructions, look for this icon in Appendix F.

Read-Aloud Time

Read a Story or Poem

Read aloud to your student for twenty minutes.

Mark the Progress Chart

Have your student mark Lesson 22 on the Progress Chart.

A-roooooooooooo!
I can hardly hear youuuuuuuuuuuu!
Every astro-dog in orbit is reviewing
flashcards and they are really woofing it up!
I can barely hear myself howl.

Have you been reviewing yours?

(See you soooooooooon!)

Lesson 23   Read "The Tub" and "Get the Moth, Meg!"

Objective

In this lesson, students read two short stories and use illustrations to retell a story.

You Will Need

- [ ] *Blast Off to Reading!* pages 133-137
- [ ] *Run, Bug, Run!* book
- [ ] map or globe

Before You Begin

Preview the Purpose of the Activity Sheet

With the help of the illustrations in the first activity, your student will retell a story, which is an important skill for beginning readers to learn. Besides being a great way for you to evaluate comprehension, retelling has other benefits too:

- It fosters visualization, encouraging students to imagine the story line and characters.
- It helps develop expressive vocabulary.
- It develops sequencing skills.

Review

Review the Phonogram Cards that are behind the Review divider in your student's Reading Review Box. Show each card to your student and have him say the sound(s). If necessary, remind your student of the sound(s).

Your student may enjoy reviewing Phonogram Cards with the "Feed the Monster" activity. For instructions, look for this icon in Appendix G.

Shuffle and review the Word Cards that are behind the Review divider in your student's Reading Review Box. If your student has difficulty reading a word, build the word with letter tiles and have your student sound it out using the blending procedure shown in Appendix C.

Story 1: "The Tub"

Read the Warm-Up Sheet for "The Tub"

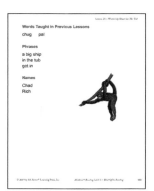

Turn to page 133 in the *Blast Off* activity book.

Have your student practice reading words and phrases that will be encountered in "The Tub."

Teach Vocabulary and Activate Prior Knowledge

Point out the illustration of a spider monkey on the Warm-Up Sheet. "This is a *spider monkey*. Spider monkeys are small monkeys that live in the rain forests of Costa Rica."

Find Costa Rica on a map or globe. "This story is set in Costa Rica, a country in Central America. The story features a couple of spider monkeys having a great time with their water toys."

"What are your favorite toys to play with in the bathtub or at the beach?"

"Let's see what these monkeys do for fun."

Read "The Tub"

"Turn to page 203 in your reader and read 'The Tub' aloud." Discuss your student's ideas for the question below when you come to it.

After page 207: "What do you think they'll put in the tub next? What would you put in it?"

New Teaching
(continued)

Complete Activity Sheet

"Now it's your turn to tell the story of the tub."

Tell Me a Story

Remove page 135 from the activity book.

Cut out the cards on the top of the page.

Have your student retell the story "The Tub," using the illustrated cards as props. As each item appears in your student's story, he may add it to the illustration of the tub.

Continue until your student has finished his story.

Story 2: "Get the Moth, Meg!"

Read the Warm-Up Sheet for "Get the Moth, Meg!"

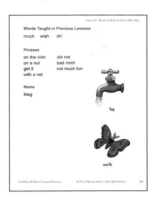

Turn to page 137 in the activity book.

Have your student practice reading words and phrases that will be encountered in "Get the Moth, Meg!"

Point out the exclamation "Sh!" on the Warm-Up Sheet and review it with your student. The exclamation is used in the story.

Teach Vocabulary and Activate Prior Knowledge

Point out the illustration of a water tap on the Warm-Up Sheet. "This is a *water tap*. *Tap* is another word for *faucet*."

Point out the illustration of a moth on the Warm-Up Sheet. "A *moth* is an insect with two pairs of wings. Unlike butterflies, moths don't have antennae and their colors are not as bright. Moths are mostly nocturnal. Do you ever see moths fluttering around your porch light at night?"

New Teaching
(continued)

"Did you ever have a mosquito or fly that just wouldn't leave you alone? Maybe it kept buzzing around your head! What could you have done to try to catch it?" Discuss your student's experience and how he could have caught the insect.

"Let's see what happens when the girl in this story tries to catch a moth."

Read "Get the Moth, Meg!"

"Turn to page 211 in your reader and read 'Get the Moth, Meg!' aloud." Discuss your student's ideas for the questions below as you come to them.

After page 214: "Is the moth really doing something bad? Why does Meg think it is bad?"

After page 218: "Why is Meg mad?"

Read-Aloud Time

Read a Story or Poem

Read aloud to your student for twenty minutes.

Read-Aloud Tip!

A Picture Is Worth...
Before, during, or after reading, be sure to take the time to talk about the book's illustrations. Not only do the illustrations in picture books tell half the story, there are often secondary "silent" stories going on as well.

Have your student point out favorite characters, objects, colors, and recurring elements, or ask him why the artist may have drawn something a certain way.

Mark the Progress Chart

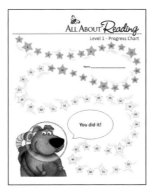

Have your student mark Lesson 23 on the Progress Chart.

Lesson 23: Read "The Tub" and "Get the Moth, Meg!"

Lesson 24   Words with Final Blends

Objective

This lesson teaches words containing consonant blends at the end and the Leap Word *was*.

You Will Need

☐ *Blast Off to Reading!* pages 139-152

☐ Word Cards 103-112

Before You Begin

Preview Consonant Blends

In this lesson, your student will learn to read words with consonant blends.

A consonant blend consists of two sounds that are said together quickly. For example, the word *lamp* has a consonant blend at the end. The /m/ and /p/ sounds are said in rapid succession, but each consonant keeps its own sound.

> A consonant blend is different from a consonant team. In a consonant blend, each letter retains its own sound. In consonant teams, such as <u>th</u>, <u>sh</u>, and <u>ch</u>, two letters combine to make a completely new sound.

A blend at the end of a word is called a **final blend**. Final blends are easier to read than blends at the beginning of the word, so we will introduce final blends first. Read the following examples and listen for the blends.

dust   help   risk   felt   bump

Words with consonant blends will be decoded using the same blending procedure that your student has already been using.

Some phonics programs teach blends as a unit; for example, they may teach blends <u>sp</u> and <u>nd</u> as their own sounds on flashcards. But that method requires much more memory work for students because they have to memorize dozens of blends. It is much simpler to learn the basic phonograms and blend them to sound out words.

Reminder about the Practice Sheets

The goal of the Practice Sheets is to help your student achieve *automaticity*. Automaticity—or automatic word recognition—means that words are recognized at a glance. Automaticity enables your student to read more fluently. When he doesn't have to laboriously decode each and every word, he can read smoothly and with greater comprehension.

Because there are so many words in this "final blends" category, this lesson contains several additional Practice Sheets. Please remember that the Practice Sheets aren't meant to be completed in a single sitting! It is critical to stop before your student fatigues. You may take several days or weeks to cover all of the activities in this lesson, depending on your circumstances. See Appendix F for ideas on using the Practice Sheets.

Review

Review the Phonogram Cards that are behind the Review divider in your student's Reading Review Box. Show each card to your student and have him say the sound(s). If necessary, remind your student of the sound(s).

Shuffle and review the Word Cards that are behind the Review divider in your student's Reading Review Box. If your student has difficulty reading a word, build the word with letter tiles and have your student sound it out using the blending procedure shown in Appendix C.

New Teaching

Blend Sounds with Letter Tiles

Build the word *land* with letter tiles.

"Sometimes there are two consonants at the end of a word, as in the word *land*. Listen and watch as I blend the letters in this word."

Touch the l and say /l/.

New Teaching
(continued)

Touch the <u>a</u> and say /ă/.

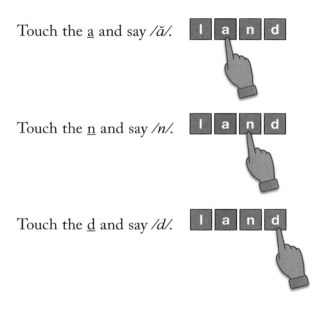

Touch the <u>n</u> and say /n/.

Touch the <u>d</u> and say /d/.

Now go back to the beginning of the word. Slide your finger under the letters <u>l</u>-<u>a</u>-<u>n</u>-<u>d</u> and say *land* slowly.

Finally, read the word *land* at a normal pace as we do when we speak.

Using the same procedure for blending, have your student sound out the word *best*.

Decode Words Containing Two-Letter Phonograms

Build the word *lunch* with letter tiles.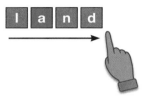

Point to the <u>ch</u> tile. "Listen and watch as I sound out a word that has <u>ch</u> at the end."

Touch the <u>l</u> and say /l/.

New Teaching
(continued)

Touch the u and say /ŭ/.

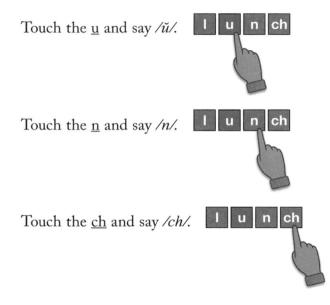

Touch the n and say /n/.

Touch the ch and say /ch/.

Now go back to the beginning of the word. Slide your finger under the letters l-u-n-ch and say *lunch* slowly.

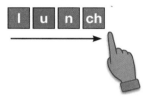

Finally, read the word *lunch* at a normal pace as we do when we speak.

Using the same procedure for blending, have your student sound out the word *tenth*.

Complete Activity Sheets

"Let's flip some words with final blends."

Word Flippers for Final Blends
Remove pages 139-145 from the *Blast Off* activity book.

There are four Word Flippers in this lesson. Each page will create one flipper.

Refer to Appendix E for assembly instructions.

Have your student turn the pages and read the words that are formed.

Lesson 24: Words with Final Blends

New Teaching
(continued)

"Now let's see if we can match these socks."

Matching Socks

Remove pages 147-148 from the activity book.

Cut out the individual socks and put them in random order on the table, with the words facing down.

Have your student find two socks that match and then read the words on the back of the socks.

Practice Reading Words

Have your student practice reading the words on Word Cards 103-111.

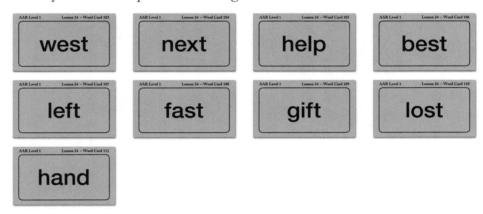

File the Word Cards behind the Review divider in the Reading Review Box.

Teach a Leap Word: *was*

Show Word Card 112 to your student.

"Most words follow the rules and say the sounds that we expect them to say. But there are a few words that do not. Here is one of those words."

"This word is *was*, as in *She was a lion tamer.*"

Point to the <u>a</u>. "The <u>a</u> doesn't say the sound we expect it to."

New Teaching
(continued)

Review this Leap Word several times today and then file it behind the Review divider in the Reading Review Box.

Practice Fluency

Turn to pages 149-152 in the activity book.

Have your student read from the Practice Sheets.

Read-Aloud Time

Read a Story or Poem

Read aloud to your student for twenty minutes.

Track Your Progress

Mark the Progress Chart

Have your student mark Lesson 24 on the Progress Chart.

Lesson 25 Read "Tin Raft" and "Lost in the Bog"

Objective

In this lesson, students read two short stories and practice matching text and illustrations.

You Will Need

☐ *Blast Off to Reading!* pages 153-159

☐ *The Runt Pig* book

Before You Begin

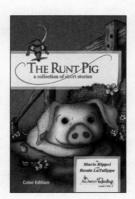

Today your student will read the first story in the second reader, *The Runt Pig*.

The stories in *The Runt Pig* will increase your student's fluency and comprehension skills even further. The wide variety of content will help keep your student interested and motivated.

Remember to check out the tips in Appendix J if your student runs into difficulties while reading the stories.

Review

It's time to review the cards behind the Mastered dividers to ensure they stay fresh in your student's mind.

Shuffle the cards behind both Mastered dividers and choose a selection for review.

Story 1: "Tin Raft"

Read the Warm-Up Sheet for "Tin Raft"

Turn to page 153 in the *Blast Off* activity book.

Have your student practice reading words and phrases that will be encountered in "Tin Raft."

Point out the name *Tish* in the Names section. "Tish is a nickname for Patricia."

Teach Vocabulary and Activate Prior Knowledge

Point out the illustration of a raft on the Warm-Up Sheet. "A *raft* is a flat structure that floats and is used as a boat. Rafts are often made of wood lashed together with cord."

Point out the illustration of a workbench on the Warm-Up Sheet. "This is a *workbench*. A workbench is a table where you can keep your tools, do small carpentry or electrical work, or repair small items."

"Have you ever had a favorite toy that was damaged or broken? What did you do to fix it?"

"The boy in this story has a damaged toy raft. Let's see if someone can fix it."

Read "Tin Raft"

"Turn to page 9 in your reader and read 'Tin Raft' aloud." Discuss your student's ideas for the questions below as you come to them.

After page 14: "Look at the raft in the illustration. Do you think it will be able to float now? Why or why not?"

After reading: "Why does Kent think this is the best gift?"

New Teaching
(continued)

Complete Activity Sheet

"Now let's read some of the words from the story and see if you can match them to the illustrations."

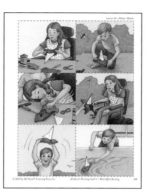

Make a Match

Remove pages 155-157 from the activity book.

Cut out the text and illustration cards.

Set the text cards in a pile face down. Spread the illustration cards face up on the table. Have your student draw one text card at a time, read it, and match it to the most appropriate illustration. If your student does not find the right match, return the card to the bottom of the stack to try again later.

Continue until your student has read all the text cards and matched them to the illustrations.

Story 2: "Lost in the Bog"

Read the Warm-Up Sheet for "Lost in the Bog"

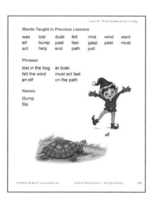

Turn to page 159 in the activity book.

Have your student practice reading words and phrases that will be encountered in "Lost in the Bog."

Point out the name *Sis* in the Names section. "Sis is a nickname for Sister."

Teach Vocabulary and Activate Prior Knowledge

Point out the illustration of an elf on the Warm-Up Sheet. "An *elf* is a small, imaginary human, often shown with pointy ears."

New Teaching
(continued)

Point out the illustration of a box turtle on the Warm-Up Sheet. "This is a *box turtle*. A box turtle is a land turtle with a low shell that can be completely closed around the animal inside. This type of turtle lives in North America and Mexico and is often kept as a pet."

"Have you ever seen a turtle? What do turtles do when they get scared? What do *you* do when you get scared?" Discuss how turtles hide in their shells and what your student does when he is afraid of something.

"Let's see what happens when the turtle in this story gets scared."

Read "Lost in the Bog"

"Turn to page 19 in your reader and read 'Lost in the Bog' aloud." Discuss your student's ideas for the questions below as you come to them.

After page 22: "What do you think bumps Gump?"

After page 28: "Who or what do you think is on the path?"

Read-Aloud Time

Read a Story or Poem

Read aloud to your student for twenty minutes.

Track Your Progress

Mark the Progress Chart

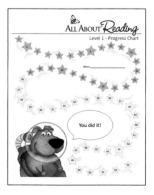

Have your student mark Lesson 25 on the Progress Chart.

Lesson 25: Read "Tin Raft" and "Lost in the Bog"

Lesson 26   Words with Initial Blends

Objective

This lesson teaches words containing consonant blends at the beginning and the Leap Word *to*.

You Will Need

☐ *Blast Off to Reading!* pages 161-174

☐ Word Cards 113-122

Before You Begin

Preview Initial Blends

In this lesson, your student will learn to read words with consonant blends at the beginning. For most students, initial blends are slightly more difficult than final blends. Read the following examples and listen for the blends.

step   plan   swim   frog   glad

Don't Forget! Remember that a consonant blend is different from a consonant team. In consonant blends such as <u>st</u>, <u>pl</u>, and <u>fr</u>, each letter retains its own sound. In consonant teams, such as <u>th</u>, <u>sh</u>, and <u>ch</u>, two letters combine to make a completely new sound.

Review

Phonogram Cards

Review the Phonogram Cards that are behind the Review divider in your student's Reading Review Box. Show each card to your student and have him say the sound(s). If necessary, remind your student of the sound(s).

Make phonogram review more energetic with the "Jump On It" activity. For instructions, look for this icon in Appendix G.

Word Cards

Shuffle and review the Word Cards that are behind the Review divider in your student's Reading Review Box. If your student has difficulty reading a word, build the word with letter tiles and have your student sound it out using the blending procedure shown in Appendix C.

Blend Sounds with Letter Tiles

Build the word *spot* with letter tiles.

"Sometimes there are two consonants at the beginning of a word, as in the word *spot*. Listen and watch as I blend the letters in this word."

Touch the s̲ and say /s/.

Touch the p̲ and say /p/.

Touch the o̲ and say /ŏ/.

Touch the t̲ and say /t/.

Now go back to the beginning of the word. Slide your finger under the letters s̲-p̲-o̲-t̲ and say *spot* slowly.

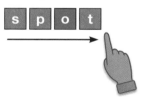

Finally, read the word *spot* at a normal pace as we do when we speak.

Using the same procedure for blending, have your student sound out the word *flag*.

Lesson 26: Words with Initial Blends

New Teaching
(continued)

Decode Words Containing Two-Letter Phonograms

Build the word *throb* with letter tiles.

Point to the <u>th</u> tile. "Listen and watch as I sound out a word that has <u>th</u> at the beginning."

Touch the <u>th</u> and say /*th*/.

Touch the <u>r</u> and say /*r*/.

Touch the <u>o</u> and say /*ŏ*/.

Touch the <u>b</u> and say /*b*/.

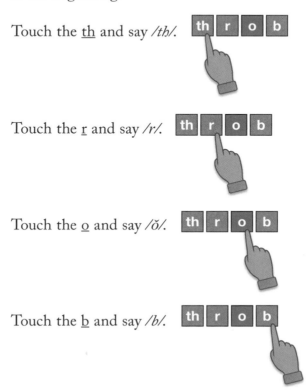

Now go back to the beginning of the word. Slide your finger under the letters <u>th</u>-<u>r</u>-<u>o</u>-<u>b</u> and say *throb* slowly.

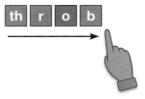

Finally, read the word *throb* at a normal pace as we do when we speak.

Using the same procedure for blending, have your student sound out the word *shred*.

Complete Activity Sheets

"Let's flip some words with blends at the beginning."

Word Flippers for Initial Blends

Remove pages 161-167 from the *Blast Off* activity book.

There are four Word Flippers in this lesson. Each page will create one flipper.

Refer to Appendix E for assembly instructions.

Have your student turn the pages and read the words that are formed.

"Now let's make these animals move!"

How Animals Move

Remove page 169 from the activity book.

Cut out the movement cards and the animal cards. Have your student match the picture of each animal with the movement it makes.

- *hop* (frog, grasshopper)
- *trot* (horse, zebra)
- *swim* (fish, duck)

Practice Reading Words

Have your student practice reading the words on Word Cards 113-121.

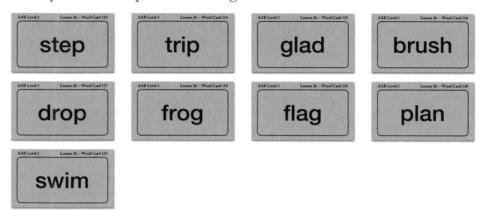

Lesson 26: Words with Initial Blends

New Teaching
(continued)

In some regions, *flag* is pronounced with a long <u>a</u> instead of a short <u>a</u>. If your student has difficulty reading the word *flag* due to pronunciation, make it a Leap Word, following the general format for the word *to* in the next section.

File the Word Cards behind the Review divider in the Reading Review Box.

Teach a Leap Word: *to*

We are treating the word *to* as a Leap Word because it contains the third sound of <u>o</u>, which has not been taught yet.

Show Word Card 122 to your student.

"This word is *to*, as in *Did you go to the lake?*"

Point to the <u>o</u>. "The <u>o</u> doesn't say the sound we expect it to."

Review this Leap Word several times today and then file it behind the Review divider in the Reading Review Box.

Practice Fluency

If you adapted the teaching of the word *flag* when you taught the Word Cards in this lesson, it is likely that you will need to adapt the words *drag*, *snag*, *stag*, and *brag* on this Practice Sheet as well.

 This lesson contains extra Practice Sheets. You may wish to take a few days to cover all of them and to make them more engaging by using games and activities from Appendix F.

New Teaching
(continued)

Turn to pages 171-174 in the activity book.

Have your student read from the Practice Sheets.

Read-Aloud Time

Read a Story or Poem

Read aloud to your student for twenty minutes.

Track Your Progress

Mark the Progress Chart

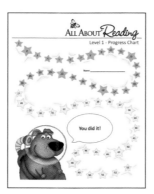

Have your student mark Lesson 26 on the Progress Chart.

Lesson 27 Read "Lunch" and "The Big Top"

Objective

In this lesson, students read two short stories and learn about onomatopoeia.

You Will Need

☐ *Blast Off to Reading!* pages 175-178 ☐ map or globe
☐ *The Runt Pig* book

Before You Begin

Preview Onomatopoeia

Onomatopoeia is when a word imitates the natural sound of a particular thing. For example, the words *plop, plip, splash, drizzle, drip, sprinkle,* and *gush* are all onomatopoeic words that can describe water.

Onomatopoeia is pronounced /ŏn–ō–mah–tō–pē–uh/.

Here are some other common examples of onomatopoeia.

buzz	**honk**	**quack**
choo-choo	**jingle**	**snarl**
crash	**oink**	**swish**
ding-dong	**pitter-patter**	**zoom**

Review

Review the Phonogram Cards that are behind the Review divider in your student's Reading Review Box. Show each card to your student and have him say the sound(s). If necessary, remind your student of the sound(s).

Shuffle and review the Word Cards that are behind the Review divider in your student's Reading Review Box. If your student has difficulty reading a word, build the word with letter tiles and have your student sound it out using the blending procedure shown in Appendix C.

Let your student get creative with the Word Card review by illustrating a selection of words. For instructions, look for this icon in Appendix H.

Teach Onomatopoeia

"Some words imitate sound." Knock on a solid surface and say *knock knock.*

"You already know a lot of words that imitate sounds. What do cows say?" *Moo.*

"What do cats say?" *Meow* or *purr.*

"What do birds say?" *Tweet* or *chirp.*

"What does it sound like when a balloon breaks?" *Pop.*

Story 1: "Lunch"

Complete Activity Sheet

"Now let's swish and flip like a fish!"

Swish and Flip!
Remove page 175 from the *Blast Off* activity book.

Cut out the word cards at the bottom of the page and spread them out on the table with the words facing up.

Have your student match each word with the drawing that makes that sound. For example, "chomp, chomp" should be matched with the drawing of the dog chomping on a bone.

Continue until all word cards have been matched to their illustrations.

Answer Key

twig	*snap*
dog	*chomp, chomp*
rabbit	*thump*
fish	*swish, swish, swish*
pancakes	*flip*
faucet	*drip*

New Teaching
(continued)

Read the Warm-Up Sheet for "Lunch"

Turn to page 177 in the activity book.

Have your student practice reading words and phrases that will be encountered in "Lunch."

Teach Vocabulary and Activate Prior Knowledge

Point out the illustration of a bunch of bananas on the Warm-Up Sheet. "A *bunch* is a number of things that are grouped or fastened together, like this bunch of bananas."

Point out the illustration of the fruit vendor on the Warm-Up Sheet. "This is a *fruit vendor*. A vendor is someone who sells something. This woman sells bananas and other fruits."

Find India on a map or globe. "This next story is set in India, a country in the southern part of Asia. Many vendors in India are experts at loading up their bicycles with their goods. This is how they transport their goods to the market. Do you think you could ride a bike loaded with bananas?"

"What is your favorite food? Pretend you live on a desert island and your favorite food is dangling from a palm tree out of your reach. What are some ways you could try to get it?"

"In this next story, a chimp takes some chances to get his favorite food. Let's see what happens."

Read "Lunch"

"Turn to page 33 in your reader and read 'Lunch' aloud." Discuss your student's ideas for the questions below as you come to them.

After page 35: "How do you think the chimp will get the bananas from the bicycle?"

After page 41: "How do you think this story will end? Will the chimp be happy or sad? Why?"

New Teaching
(continued)

After reading: "This story uses a lot of onomatopoeia. Flip through the pages to find some examples." *Possible answers: swish, snap, thump, flop, chomp, gulp, munch.*

Story 2: "The Big Top"

Read the Warm-Up Sheet for "The Big Top"

Turn to page 178 in the activity book.

Have your student practice reading words and phrases that will be encountered in "The Big Top."

Teach Vocabulary and Activate Prior Knowledge

> The story "The Big Top" is inspired by Cavalia, an entertainment company that produces creative equestrian and acrobatic performances. Your student may be interested in seeing some of their beautiful performances on YouTube or on the Cavalia website.

Point out the illustration of acrobats on the Warm-Up Sheet. "These people are acrobats. Acrobats perform all sorts of physical tricks and are often included in traveling shows."

Point out the title on page 45 of the reader. "The title of the next story is 'The Big Top.' The largest tent of a traveling show is called the *big top*, and many types of performances are held inside it."

"Have you ever been to a traveling show in a tent? What kinds of things can you see at such a show?" Discuss the different people and animals at a traveling show, such as horses, clowns, and trapeze artists.

"The story you are going to read now is inspired by a real traveling show."

New Teaching
(continued)

Read "The Big Top"

"Turn to page 45 in your reader and read 'The Big Top' aloud." Discuss your student's answers for the questions below.

After reading: "Let's go back to look at some of the pictures. See if you can name some of the things found in a traveling show."

Page 46:   "What do we call this big tent?" *The big top.*
Page 49:   "Drums are a big part of this show. What do we call people who play music?" *Musicians, drummers.*
Page 52:   "Do you know what we call this circle?" *Ring, trapeze.*
Page 54:   "Do you know what we call a person who rides a horse?" *Equestrian.*
Page 55:   "What do we call a person who jumps and flips?" *Acrobat.*

Read-Aloud Time

Read a Story or Poem

Read aloud to your student for twenty minutes.

Track Your Progress

Mark the Progress Chart

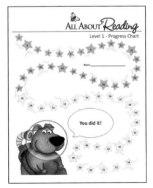

Have your student mark Lesson 27 on the Progress Chart.

Onomatopoeia!
What a concept! But what's with all the cats, cats, cats? Every time someone talks about onomatopoeia, they bring up MEOW and PURR.

Well, I can tell you that we dogs have PLENTY of onomatopoeia of our own. Try these on for size:

BARK

RUFF

ARF

WOOF

YIP

HOWL

WHINE
(I never do that, by the way.)

Take that, cats!

Lesson 28 Read "Slim Went West" and "The Hit"

Objective	In this lesson, students read two short stories that give them more practice with blends. The lesson also explores how objects can have multiple uses.
You Will Need	☐ *Blast Off to Reading!* pages 179-182 ☐ *The Runt Pig* book
Before You Begin	**Provide Additional Practice with Blends** In Lesson 26, your student learned how to decode words containing initial blends. As noted in that lesson, initial blends can be more difficult for students than final blends. For this reason, we've provided two extra stories to give your student additional practice with initial blends. Your student may breeze right through these stories, or he may need extra time for decoding. The beauty of mastery-based lessons is that you can move at your student's individual pace.

Review

Review the Phonogram Cards that are behind the Review divider in your student's Reading Review Box. Show each card to your student and have him say the sound(s). If necessary, remind your student of the sound(s).

Shuffle and review the Word Cards that are behind the Review divider in your student's Reading Review Box. If your student has difficulty reading a word, build the word with letter tiles and have your student sound it out using the blending procedure shown in Appendix C.

Have fun with today's Word Card review with the activity "Word Card Racetrack." For instructions, look for this icon in Appendix H.

Story 1: "Slim Went West"

Complete Activity Sheet

"What are some of the different things you could do with a rubber band? A bed sheet?"

"Let's look for different ways we can use a single object."

What Could It Be?
Remove page 179 from the *Blast Off* activity book.

One at a time, have your student look at the four items. Your student should brainstorm as many ways as possible that the object could be used. For example, the hat could be used to keep cool on a hot day or to carry small objects. If you wish, write down your student's ideas.

Read the Warm-Up Sheet for "Slim Went West"

Turn to page 181 in the activity book.

Have your student practice reading words and phrases that will be encountered in "Slim Went West."

Point out the name *Slim* in the Name section. "Slim is a nickname for someone who is tall and skinny."

Teach Vocabulary and Activate Prior Knowledge

Point out the illustration of an ax on the Warm-Up Sheet. "An *ax* is a tool for cutting wood. It has a heavy, sharp blade on the end of a wooden handle."

New Teaching
(continued)

"The man in today's story uses an ax when he goes on an adventure to the vast Wild West. If something is *vast*, it is *very big*. Say the word with me: *vast*."

"The *ocean* is vast. If you are in the middle of an ocean, it feels like it will go on and on forever. You can look in all directions and all you can see is water. The *desert* is another vast place. You can look in all directions and all you can see is sand."

"What is the opposite of *vast*?" *Possible answers: small, tiny, not large.*

"If you could go on a trip, where would you go?" Discuss where your student would go and mention whether the destination is east, west, north, or south.

"Let's see what happens on this man's big adventure in the West."

Read "Slim Went West"

"Turn to page 59 in your reader and read 'Slim Went West' aloud." Discuss your student's ideas for the questions below as you come to them.

After page 62: "How do you think Slim will get rich in the West?"

After page 72: "Why do you think the items on this page make Slim rich?"

After reading: "What do you think Slim and his dog will do now? What would you do?"

"What different ways does Slim use the red rag?" Encourage your student to skim the story to find out.

Story 2: "The Hit"

Read the Warm-Up Sheet for "The Hit"

Turn to page 182 in the activity book.

Have your student practice reading words and phrases that will be encountered in "The Hit."

Teach Vocabulary and Activate Prior Knowledge

Point out the illustration of mulch on the Warm-Up Sheet. "A material made of decaying leaves, bark, or compost is called *mulch*. Mulch is spread around plants to enrich the soil and protect the plants."

Point out the illustration of a baseball diamond on the Warm-Up Sheet. "This is a *baseball diamond*. A baseball diamond is the field where you play baseball. The four bases on the field are placed in the shape of a diamond, with the pitcher's mound in the middle."

"Have you ever lost something you really liked? Where did you look for it? Did you ever find it?" Discuss your student's lost item and if and how he found it.

"Let's see what happens when the boys in this story lose their baseball."

Read "The Hit"

"Turn to page 75 in your reader and read 'The Hit' aloud." Discuss your student's ideas for the questions below as you come to them.

After page 80: "Do you think the boys will find the ball?"

After pages 85: "The boys have looked everywhere. Where do you think the ball could be?"

Read a Story or Poem

Read aloud to your student for twenty minutes.

Read-Aloud Tip!

Choose a Wide Range of Books

If you've ever picked up a book outside of your expertise (such as a book on musical theory if you aren't a musician), then you've encountered unfamiliar vocabulary words that you don't understand. It would be difficult for you to read these books fluently because you wouldn't know what many of the words mean or how to pronounce them.

In the same way, it is difficult for your student to read fluently if he doesn't understand what the words mean. You can help your student develop a large listening vocabulary by reading aloud from a wide selection of books and discussing unfamiliar words.

Track Your Progress

Mark the Progress Chart

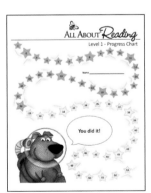

Have your student mark Lesson 28 on the Progress Chart.

Lesson 28: Read "Slim Went West" and "The Hit"

Lesson 29   FF, LL, and SS

Objective

This lesson teaches words ending in <u>ff</u>, <u>ll</u>, and <u>ss</u> and the Leap Words *said* and *I*.

You Will Need

☐ *Blast Off to Reading!* pages 183-195   ☐ Word Cards 123-132

☐ extra <u>f</u>, <u>l</u>, and <u>s</u> letter tiles

Before You Begin

Preview Words Ending in FF, LL, and SS

The letters <u>f</u>, <u>l</u>, and <u>s</u> are doubled at the end of approximately one hundred common one-syllable words, as in the examples below.

ff:	cliff	fluff	staff
ll:	well	still	smell
ss:	miss	dress	glass

Occasionally other consonants are doubled at the end of one-syllable words, too, such as <u>z</u> (*buzz, fizz*), <u>n</u> (*inn, Ann*), <u>d</u> (*add, odd*) and <u>g</u> (*egg*), although not as regularly.

In this lesson, your student will learn that when a doubled consonant appears at the end of a word, he only has to pronounce one of them.

> In the *All About Spelling* series, we call this pattern the Floss Rule because the word *floss* follows the rule and contains the letters <u>f</u>, <u>l</u>, and <u>s</u>. In spelling, your student will learn that these letters are often doubled after a single vowel at the end of a one-syllable word, and he will learn the exceptions to this pattern. This information isn't needed for reading purposes, however.

Organize the Extra Letter Tiles

If you are using letter tiles on a white board instead of the Letter Tiles app, you will need extra <u>f</u>, <u>l</u>, and <u>s</u> tiles for this lesson. Place them on the board as follows.

Preview Direct Quotations

The word *said* is used quite often in books in which there is a lot of dialogue. Consider these examples:

- My brother said, "The turtle bit me!"
- "I told you to keep your fingers out of his cage!" said Mom.

When we talk, we normally use the noun-verb pattern, as in *Frank said, "Let's eat."* But in books, it tends to be the opposite. Authors usually use the verb-noun pattern, as in *"Let's eat," said Frank.*

Because you have been reading aloud to your student every day, he should be used to hearing this verb-noun pattern. Today's Practice Sheets will give your student practice with reading direct quotations.

Review

Review the Phonogram Cards that are behind the Review divider in your student's Reading Review Box. Show each card to your student and have him say the sound(s). If necessary, remind your student of the sound(s).

For today's phonogram review, try the activity "Stamp It." For instructions, look for this icon in Appendix G.

Shuffle and review the Word Cards that are behind the Review divider in your student's Reading Review Box. If your student has difficulty reading a word, build the word with letter tiles and have your student sound it out using the blending procedure shown in Appendix C.

Blend Sounds with Letter Tiles

Build the word *stiff* with letter tiles.

"I'll sound out this first word, and then you'll sound out the next word."

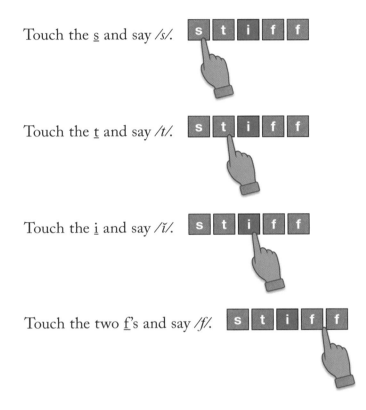

Touch the s̲ and say /s/.

Touch the t̲ and say /t/.

Touch the i̲ and say /ĭ/.

Touch the two f̲'s and say /f/.

"Notice that there are two f̲'s here. I only have to pronounce one of them."

Now go back to the beginning of the word. Slide your finger under the letters s̲-t̲-i̲-f̲-f̲ and say *stiff* slowly.

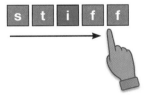

Finally, read the word *stiff* at a normal pace as we do when we speak.

"When we see two of the same letter at the end of a word, we only pronounce it once. We wouldn't say *stiff-ff* because that would sound funny."

New Teaching
(continued)

Using the same procedure for blending, have your student sound out the words *glass* and *bill*.

Complete Activity Sheets

"Let's flip some words with double letters."

Word Flippers for FF, LL, and SS

Remove pages 183-187 from the *Blast Off* activity book.

There are three Word Flippers in this lesson. Each page will create one flipper.

Refer to Appendix E for assembly instructions.

Have your student turn the pages and read the words that are formed.

"Now let's see what Frisky Fox is up to."

On the Trail

Remove pages 189-192 from the activity book.

Cut out the sixteen game cards on page 191 and place one on each square of the game board with the words facing down.

"Frisky Fox is chasing a dragonfly. Follow Frisky to see what she sees."

Have your student follow the path of the cards to reach the dragonfly by turning the cards over one by one and reading the words aloud.

New Teaching
(continued)

Practice Reading Words

Have your student practice reading the words on Word Cards 123-130.

File the Word Cards behind the Review divider in the Reading Review Box.

Teach Two Leap Words: *said* and *I*

Show Word Card 131 to your student.

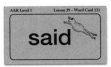

"Most words follow the rules and say the sounds that we expect them to say. But there are a few words that do not. Here is one of those words."

"This word is *said*, as in *She said hello*."

Show Word Card 132 to your student.

We are treating the word *I* as a Leap Word because it contains the long sound of i̲, which has not been taught yet.

"This word is *I*, as in *I am a student*. The word *I* is always spelled with a capital i̲."

Review these Leap Words several times today and then file them behind the Review divider in the Reading Review Box.

New Teaching
(continued)

Practice Fluency

Turn to pages 193-195 in the activity book.

Have your student read from the Practice Sheets.

 To engage your student in the fluency exercises, try the activity "Letter Search." For instructions, look for this icon in Appendix F.

Read-Aloud Time

Read a Story or Poem

Read aloud to your student for twenty minutes.

Track Your Progress

Mark the Progress Chart

Have your student mark Lesson 29 on the Progress Chart.

Lesson 29: FF, LL, and SS

8-22-22

Lesson 30 Read "Mud Milk" and "The Ant Hill"

Objective	In this lesson, students read two short stories and follow recipe instructions.
You Will Need	☐ *Blast Off to Reading!* pages 197-202 ☐ *The Runt Pig* book
Before You Begin	**Preview the Purpose of the Activity Sheet** Today's first short story follows the steps a girl takes to make "mud milk." Before reading, your student will complete a recipe activity that requires him to follow specific steps. Following recipes helps develop your student's reading, listening, and sequencing skills.

Review

Review the Phonogram Cards that are behind the Review divider in your student's Reading Review Box. Show each card to your student and have him say the sound(s). If necessary, remind your student of the sound(s).

Shuffle and review the Word Cards that are behind the Review divider in your student's Reading Review Box. If your student has difficulty reading a word, build the word with letter tiles and have your student sound it out using the blending procedure shown in Appendix C.

Shuffle the cards behind the Mastered dividers and choose a selection for review.

Story 1: "Mud Milk"

Complete Activity Sheet

"Have you ever used a recipe? In this activity, you'll follow a recipe to make a pie for a pig."

Pie for a Pig
Remove pages 197-200 from the *Blast Off* activity book.

Cut out the pie tin on page 197. Cut out the ingredient cards and spoon along the dotted lines shown on page 200.

Place the pie tin in front of your student and spread the ingredient cards above it. Tell your student that she is going to make a pie for a pig by listening to your recipe directions. With each direction, your student will put the proper ingredient in the pie tin.

Continue until your student has finished her pie for a pig.

Recipe directions
1. Put the potato peelings in the pie dish.
2. Put the cheese under the potato peelings.
3. Put the carrot tops over the potato peelings.
4. Sprinkle the bread crumbs over the whole pie.
5. Use the wooden spoon to pat down all the ingredients.
6. Carefully fold the top pie crust over all the ingredients.
7. Feed the pie to your pig!

New Teaching
(continued)

Read the Warm-Up Sheet for "Mud Milk"

Turn to page 201 in the activity book.

Have your student practice reading words and phrases that will be encountered in "Mud Milk."

Teach Vocabulary and Activate Prior Knowledge

Point out the illustration of mint on the Warm-Up Sheet. "*Mint* is a plant with leaves that have a strong, fresh taste. You have probably tasted mint in candies or even toothpaste."

Point out the illustration of a milkshake on the Warm-Up Sheet. "And there are even mint *milkshakes*! What is your favorite drink when you are thirsty?"

"Sometimes when people like the taste of something, they say it *really hits the spot*. Let's see what hits the spot for the girl in this story."

Read "Mud Milk"

 As always, if your student has any difficulty reading the stories, review the Practice Sheets of the previous lessons. Refer to Appendix J for more tips.

"Turn to page 89 in your reader and read 'Mud Milk' aloud." Discuss your student's ideas for the questions below as you come to them.

After reading: "Did you notice that this story rhymes? Let's look at it again to see if we can find the rhyming words." *Possible answers: glass/ grass, grit/fit, bud/mud, zest/best, plop/top, sand/land, lot/spot.*

"Do you think the girl is really going to drink her mud milk? Would you?"

New Teaching
(continued)

Read the Warm-Up Sheet for "The Ant Hill"

Turn to page 202 in the activity book.

Have your student practice reading words and phrases that will be encountered in "The Ant Hill."

Teach Vocabulary and Activate Prior Knowledge

Point out the illustration of an ant hill on the Warm-Up Sheet. "An *ant hill* is the mound of dirt or sand that ants throw to the surface as they dig their tunnels underground."

Point out the word *ants* under the illustration of the ants. Cover up the s with your finger. "What is this word?" *Ant.*

Uncover the s to reveal the full word, *ants.* "When we add an s to the word, we get *ants.*"

"Have you ever observed ants working on an ant hill? They are very busy, aren't they? What do you see ants do as they work?" Discuss how ants climb and carry bits of dirt and grass.

"The ants in the next story work very hard. Let's see what they are building."

Read "The Ant Hill"

"Turn to page 97 in your reader and read 'The Ant Hill' aloud." Discuss your student's ideas for the questions below as you come to them.

After page 100: "What do you think the ants are building?"

Lesson 30: Read "Mud Milk" and "The Ant Hill"

New Teaching
(continued)

After page 101: "What keeps the ants from getting lost?" *Possible answers: Their antennae, sticking together as they work, the scent trail of other ants.*

After page 105: "The ants work hard for a long time. Why do you think they need such a big hill?"

After page 106: "Sometimes authors like to surprise their readers. Are you surprised by what the ants built?"

Read-Aloud Time

Read a Story or Poem

Read aloud to your student for twenty minutes.

Track Your Progress

Mark the Progress Chart

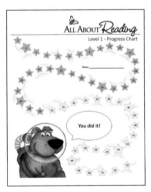

Have your student mark Lesson 30 on the Progress Chart.

You know, that pie
didn't sound half bad.
Did you try some?
Was it paw-licking good?

Can you guess what <u>my</u> favorite pie is?
MOON PIE, of course!

Graham crackers, chocolate, marshmallow ... mmm.
If you'll excuse me, I have to run to the space store
to stock up before our next blastoff!

YUM!

Lesson 31　Three Leap Words

Objective　　This lesson teaches the Leap Words *or*, *for*, and *no*.

You Will Need　☐ *Blast Off to Reading!* pages 203-206
　　　　　　　　☐ Word Cards 133-135

Before You Begin　## Preview Leap Words

Today's lesson is a relatively short one. Your student will learn three Leap Words: *or*, *for*, and *no*. If your student learns these words quickly, you may wish to continue on to the stories in Lesson 32 or expand your read-aloud time.

The first two Leap Words include phonogram <u>or</u>. The words *or* and *for* are common words that should be introduced at this stage, although phonogram <u>or</u> won't be taught until Level 2, Lesson 35.

Review

Review the Phonogram Cards that are behind the Review divider in your student's Reading Review Box. Show each card to your student and have him say the sound(s). If necessary, remind your student of the sound(s).

Shuffle and review the Word Cards that are behind the Review divider in your student's Reading Review Box. If your student has difficulty reading a word, build the word with letter tiles and have your student sound it out using the blending procedure shown in Appendix C.

Use a favorite family board game to review Word Cards. For instructions, look for this icon in Appendix H.

Teach Three Leap Words: *or*, *for*, and *no*

> We are treating *or* and *for* as Leap Words because they contain the phonogram <u>or</u>, which has not been taught yet.
>
> The word *no* is also treated as a Leap Word at this stage because long vowels have not been taught yet.

Show Word Card 133 to your student.

"This word is *or*, as in *Do you want cake or pie?*"

Show Word Card 134 to your student.

"This word is *for*, as in *I have a surprise for you.*"

Show Word Card 135 to your student.

"This word is *no*, as in *There are no more cookies.*"

Review these Leap Words several times today and then file them behind the Review divider in the Reading Review Box.

New Teaching
(continued)

Complete Activity Sheet

"Let's give some gifts to these kids."

Who Is It For?
Remove page 203 from the *Blast Off* activity book.

Cut out the three child cards at the top of the page and the three gift cards at the bottom of the page.

Have your student match each gift card to the appropriate child by reading and verbally answering the three questions. Your student should refer to the gift cards for answers.

Practice Fluency

Turn to pages 205-206 in the activity book.

Have your student read from the Practice Sheets.

To engage your student in the fluency exercises, try making her progress more concrete. For ideas on how to do that, look for this icon in Appendix F.

Read-Aloud Time

Read a Story or Poem

Read aloud to your student for twenty minutes.

Mark the Progress Chart

Have your student mark Lesson 31 on the Progress Chart.

Lesson 32 Read "The Plan" and "The Big Mess"

Objective

In this lesson, students read two short stories that give them more practice with previously taught concepts.

You Will Need

☐ *Blast Off to Reading!* pages 207-210

☐ *The Runt Pig* book

Before You Begin

Give Your Student an Audience

If your student enjoys a particular story in his readers, encourage him to read the story aloud to someone else, like a sibling, a visiting neighbor, Grandma, or a parent. Having an audience can be motivating and can give your student an opportunity to practice meaningful expression.

Review

Review the Phonogram Cards that are behind the Review divider in your student's Reading Review Box. Show each card to your student and have him say the sound(s). If necessary, remind your student of the sound(s).

Review phonograms with the game "Phonogram Bingo." For instructions, look for this icon in Appendix G.

Shuffle and review the Word Cards that are behind the Review divider in your student's Reading Review Box. If your student has difficulty reading a word, build the word with letter tiles and have your student sound it out using the blending procedure shown in Appendix C.

Story 1: "The Plan"

Complete Activity Sheet

"Lots of people like to use old clothes and blankets to create new items. Let's create something new out of something old."

Make a Quilt

Remove pages 207-208 from the *Blast Off* activity book.

Cut out the quilt squares on page 207.

Mix up the cards and place them in a pile with the illustrations of the shorts, shirts, sundresses, and pants facing up. Have your student turn the cards over one by one to reveal a close-up of the pattern on the item. Your student should arrange the cards in a pattern to create a quilt.

Read the Warm-Up Sheet for "The Plan"

Turn to page 209 in the activity book.

Have your student practice reading words and phrases that will be encountered in "The Plan."

New Teaching
(continued)

Teach Vocabulary and Activate Prior Knowledge

Point out the illustration of silk on the Warm-Up Sheet. "*Silk* is a strong, soft fiber used to make thread and fabric. It is produced by silkworms when they make their cocoons."

"Do you have a favorite blanket or pillow? Why do you like it so much?" Discuss where your student got the favorite item and why it's so special.

"What do you call your grandmother? Some families use different names, like Grandma or Nana. In this story, the girl calls her grandmother *Gram*. She receives a wonderful gift from Gram, too. Let's see what it is!"

Read "The Plan"

"Turn to page 109 in your reader and read 'The Plan' aloud." Discuss your student's ideas for the questions below as you come to them.

After page 114: "What do you think Gram is making?"

After reading: "Which items does Gram cut up to make the quilt? Skim the story to find out."

Story 2: "The Big Mess"

Read the Warm-Up Sheet for "The Big Mess"

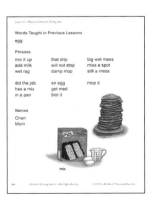

Turn to page 210 in the activity book.

Have your student practice reading words and phrases that will be encountered in "The Big Mess."

Teach Vocabulary and Activate Prior Knowledge

Point out the illustration of a mix on the Warm-Up Sheet. "A box of prepared ingredients is called a *mix*. You can use a mix to make brownies, cakes, pancakes, and other goodies."

Point out the illustration of pancakes on the Warm-Up Sheet. "A *pancake* is a thin, flat cake made of batter that is fried on both sides in a pan. Another name for pancakes is *flapjacks*. Many people eat pancakes with maple syrup, butter, or jam."

"Do you like to cook and bake? What kinds of things do you like to make?" Discuss your student's experiences in the kitchen.

"The boy in this story likes to make pancakes. Let's see what happens."

Read "The Big Mess"

"Turn to page 119 in your reader and read 'The Big Mess' aloud." Discuss your student's ideas for the question below when you come to it.

After reading: "What ingredients does Chen use to make the pancakes? Skim the story to find out."

Read a Story or Poem

Read aloud to your student for twenty minutes.

Read-Aloud Tip!

Motivate a Reluctant Reader

If you have a reluctant reader on your hands, use read-aloud time to help motivate him. Here are some tips:

- Avoid making reading feel like a chore by scheduling a leisurely read-aloud time that isn't squished between other activities.
- Try books of different genres until you hit upon some that interest your student. Possibilities include horse books, how-to books related to hobbies or current interests, nature topics, mysteries, fairy tales, and many more.
- Let your student peruse the aisles at the library or bookstore and choose the next read-alouds. Check out the magazines, comic books, and joke books as well as chapter books.

Mark the Progress Chart

Have your student mark Lesson 32 on the Progress Chart.

Lesson 32: Read "The Plan" and "The Big Mess"

Lesson 33 Read "The Runt Pig" and "Fish Class"

Objective

In this lesson, students learn about main conflicts in stories and read two short stories that give them more practice with previously taught concepts.

You Will Need

☐ *Blast Off to Reading!* pages 211-214

☐ *The Runt Pig* book

Before You Begin

Preview the Purpose of the Activity Sheet

In most stories—including today's first story—the main character has a problem, or conflict, that he must solve on his own. Before reading, your student will complete an activity that requires her to solve various problems. The ability to identify the primary conflict of a story will help your student's comprehension of the meaning of the story.

Review

Review the Phonogram Cards that are behind the Review divider in your student's Reading Review Box. Show each card to your student and have him say the sound(s). If necessary, remind your student of the sound(s).

Shuffle and review the Word Cards that are behind the Review divider in your student's Reading Review Box. If your student has difficulty reading a word, build the word with letter tiles and have your student sound it out using the blending procedure shown in Appendix C.

Let your student get creative with the Word Card review with the activity "Color It." For instructions, look for this icon in Appendix H.

Story 1: "The Runt Pig"

Complete Activity Sheet

"Are you ready to solve some problems?"

Can You Solve It?

Remove pages 211-212 from the *Blast Off* activity book.

Cut out the cards on the left side of the page (the "problems," which have a P on the back) and place them face down in a stack. Cut out the cards on the right side of the page (the "solutions," which have an S on the back) and arrange them on the table with the solutions facing up.

Have your student select a "problem" card and read it aloud. Then have him select an appropriate "solution" card to solve the problem. Discuss your student's choices.

Continue until all the problems have been solved.

Answer Key

Problem: I fell in the mud.
Solution: I will get in the tub.

Problem: A fish is lost.
Solution: Get him in the pond.

Problem: The grass is up, up, up!
Solution: The ox can munch it.

Problem: A yak is on the path!
Solution: Run fast!

Problem: The sled is wet.
Solution: Dab it with a rag.

Read the Warm-Up Sheet for "The Runt Pig"

Turn to page 213 in the activity book.

Have your student practice reading words and phrases that will be encountered in "The Runt Pig."

Lesson 33: Read "The Runt Pig" and "Fish Class"

New Teaching
(continued)

Teach Vocabulary and Activate Prior Knowledge

This discussion introduces the idiomatic expression *to lend a hand*. An idiomatic expression, or idiom, is a phrase whose meaning is different from that of the literal words that make it up.

You may wish to point out idiomatic expressions as your student comes across them in other stories or in everyday conversation.

Point out the illustration of a ramp on the Warm-Up Sheet. "A *ramp* is a sloping platform that connects two different levels. Ramps are often used instead of stairs to make it easier to push heavy objects from one level to another, or to help people in wheelchairs."

Point out the illustration of a runt on the Warm-Up Sheet. "This kitten is a *runt*. That means she is the smallest kitten in the litter. Other animals can be runts, too, such as puppies, pigs, or chipmunks."

"Has a friend or relative ever needed your help with something? How did you feel after you helped this person?" Discuss your student's experience.

"When you help someone, we say that you *lend them a hand*. It's just an expression. You don't really give them one of your hands!"

"In the next story, a runt pig lends a hand to his fellow animals on the farm. Let's see what happens."

Read "The Runt Pig"

"Turn to page 131 in your reader and read 'The Runt Pig' aloud." Discuss your student's ideas for the questions below as you come to them.

After page 133: "Do you think Bret likes being a runt pig? Why or why not?"

After page 143: "Do you think Bret will be able to help the hen? How?"

After page 148: "Bret is sad at the beginning of the story. How do you think he feels now? Why?"

New Teaching
(continued)

Discuss the Main Conflict

"In a story, the problem that a character faces is called the *conflict*. What do you think is the biggest conflict in this story?" Encourage your student to skim the text for clues if necessary.

"What does Bret do to solve the problem?"

"Why is Bret the only character who is able to solve the problem?"

After listening to years of read-alouds, your student is probably familiar with how you interpret dialogue. Still, it can take a lot of practice for novice readers to get the hang of adding expression to their own voices.

One fun way to encourage reading with expression is through buddy reading. You read a page first, using full expression for the dialogue and different characters, and then your student reads the same page. See if he can outdo you!

Story 2: "Fish Class"

Read the Warm-Up Sheet for "Fish Class"

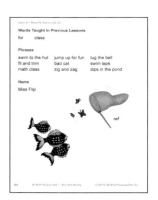

Turn to page 214 in the activity book.

Have your student practice reading words and phrases that will be encountered in "Fish Class."

Teach Vocabulary and Activate Prior Knowledge

Point out the illustration of a net on the Warm-Up Sheet. "A *net* is a type of open bag made of strong cord. It is used for catching fish or butterflies."

Lesson 33: Read "The Runt Pig" and "Fish Class"

New Teaching
(continued)

Point to the illustration of a school of fish. "Many fish travel in large groups like this. The group is called a *school of fish*. The fish stay together for protection from bigger fish and other animals that might eat them."

"This next story is about a school of fish, but not this type of school! Let's find out what kind of school it is."

Read "Fish Class"

"Turn to page 151 in your reader and read 'Fish Class' aloud." Discuss your student's ideas for the questions below as you come to them.

After page 155: "Why is class #2 important for the fish?"

After reading: "Look at all the classes again. Which class do you think is the most important for these fish? Which one is the least important? Why?"

Read-Aloud Time

Read a Story or Poem

Read aloud to your student for twenty minutes.

Track Your Progress

Mark the Progress Chart

Have your student mark Lesson 33 on the Progress Chart.

Wow, four stories in a row!
Now I need a new book for nap time
in the rocket. Any suggestions?

You probably didn't know that dogs are big readers,
but we are! I like stories about simple things like
tail-chasing, as well as big tales of space adventure.

The best thing about reading is all the people I meet
and places I go in the stories. The other day a
spaceship full of rookie pilots almost crashed into a
satellite. Lucky for them that Rocket the Dog was
there to save their hides!

What have you been reading during
Read-Aloud Time?

Lesson 34   Consonant Team CK

Objective

This lesson teaches words containing the consonant team <u>ck</u>.

You Will Need

☐ Phonogram Card 30   ☐ *Blast Off to Reading!* pages 215-229

☐ letter tile <u>ck</u>   ☐ Word Cards 136-145

Before You Begin

Preview Consonant Team CK

The consonant team <u>ck</u> says /k/ as in *duck*. It is typically found immediately after a short vowel.

 When we practice the Phonogram Card for <u>ck</u>, we say "/k/, two-letter /k/." This phrase distinguishes <u>ck</u> from the other ways of spelling /k/, such as <u>c</u> and <u>k</u>. By learning the full wording for phonogram <u>ck</u> now, your student won't have to relearn the flashcard for spelling purposes later.

The <u>ck</u> tile is stored under the Consonant Teams category.

 Refer to the Letter Tiles app or Phonogram Sounds app for a demonstration of the <u>ck</u> phonogram sound. When we use the <u>ck</u> letter tile, we only say the sound /k/. To facilitate blending, we don't say the second part, "two-letter /k/."

Review

Review the Phonogram Cards that are behind the Review divider in your student's Reading Review Box. Show each card to your student and have him say the sound(s). If necessary, remind your student of the sound(s).

Shuffle and review the Word Cards that are behind the Review divider in your student's Reading Review Box. If your student has difficulty reading a word, build the word with letter tiles and have your student sound it out using the blending procedure shown in Appendix C.

 Test your student's Word Card memory with the game "Guess the Word." For instructions, look for this icon in Appendix H.

Teach New Letter Sound

"Point to the letter tiles that can say /k/." *Student points to the <u>c</u> and <u>k</u> tiles.*

"Today you will learn another letter tile that can say /k/."

Move the <u>ck</u> tile into the workspace.

"The <u>c</u> and <u>k</u> work together to make one sound: /k/."

Hold up the Phonogram Card for the consonant team <u>ck</u>.

 "When we practice this card, we say */k/, two-letter /k/.* Repeat after me: /k/, two-letter /k/." *Student repeats the sound.*

Mix in several other Phonogram Cards for mixed review and practice until your student can say the sounds accurately. File the new Phonogram Card behind the Review divider in the Reading Review Box.

Point to the <u>ck</u> tile. "When you see this tile, say its sound, /k/. You don't have to say *two-letter /k/* when we are building with tiles, just when we are using the flashcards."

Mix in several other letter tiles for mixed review and practice with the new phonogram until your student can say the sound accurately.

> For extra practice with the new phonogram, play the game "Phonogram Cup Hunt." For instructions, look for this icon in Appendix G.

Blend Sounds with Letter Tiles

Build the word *pick* with letter tiles.

"I'll sound out this first word, and then you'll sound out the next word."

New Teaching
(continued)

Touch the p and say /p/.

Touch the i and say /ĭ/.

Touch the ck and say /k/.

Now go back to the beginning of the word. Slide your finger under the letters p-i-ck and say *pick* slowly.

Finally, read the word *pick* at a normal pace as we do when we speak.

Using the same procedure for blending, have your student sound out the word *neck*.

Play "Change the Word"

Build the word *snack* with letter tiles.

"What is this word?" *Snack.*

"I'm going to change the second letter of this word."

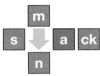

"What does this new word say?" Encourage your student to sound out the new word, *smack*.

Continue to change one letter at a time to form the following words. Each time, have your student sound out the new word.

smack → sack → sick → pick → lick → luck → pluck

New Teaching
(continued)

Complete Activity Sheets

"Let's flip some <u>ck</u> words."

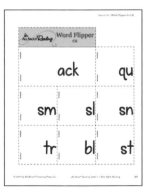

<u>Word Flippers for CK</u>
Remove pages 215-221 from the *Blast Off* activity book.

There are four Word Flippers in this lesson. Each page will create one flipper.

Refer to Appendix E for assembly instructions.

Have your student turn the pages and read the words that are formed.

"Now let's reunite some baby ducks with their parents!"

<u>A Flock of Ducks</u>
Remove pages 223-225 from the activity book.

Cut out the ducks.

Place the adult duck cards in a pile and arrange the baby duck cards in the pond. Have your student select an adult duck card and read the word aloud. Then choose a baby duck card and read the word aloud. If he reads the word correctly, reunite the baby duck with its parent. If he reads the word incorrectly, return the baby duck to the pond for another try.

Optional: Match up the rhyming pairs of adult and baby duck cards.

Continue until all the ducks have been reunited with their babies.

Lesson 34: Consonant Team CK

Practice Reading Words

Have your student practice reading the words on Word Cards 136-145.

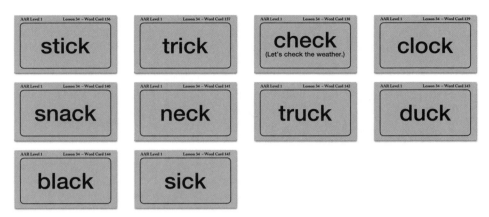

| AAR Level 1 | Lesson 34 – Word Card 136 |
| **stick** |

| AAR Level 1 | Lesson 34 – Word Card 137 |
| **trick** |

| AAR Level 1 | Lesson 34 – Word Card 138 |
| **check**
 (Let's check the weather.) |

| AAR Level 1 | Lesson 34 – Word Card 139 |
| **clock** |

| AAR Level 1 | Lesson 34 – Word Card 140 |
| **snack** |

| AAR Level 1 | Lesson 34 – Word Card 141 |
| **neck** |

| AAR Level 1 | Lesson 34 – Word Card 142 |
| **truck** |

| AAR Level 1 | Lesson 34 – Word Card 143 |
| **duck** |

| AAR Level 1 | Lesson 34 – Word Card 144 |
| **black** |

| AAR Level 1 | Lesson 34 – Word Card 145 |
| **sick** |

File the Word Cards behind the Review divider in the Reading Review Box.

Practice Fluency

Turn to pages 227-229 in the activity book.

Have your student read from the Practice Sheets.

 To engage your student in the fluency exercises, try the activity "Fun with Emotions." For instructions, look for this icon in Appendix F.

Read a Story or Poem

Read aloud to your student for twenty minutes.

Mark the Progress Chart

Have your student mark Lesson 34 on the Progress Chart.

Lesson 35　Read "The Pet Duck" and "Fun at the Pond"

Objective	In this lesson, students learn about character traits and read two short stories that give them practice with words containing <u>ck</u>.
You Will Need	☐ *Blast Off to Reading!* pages 231-237 ☐ *The Runt Pig* book
Before You Begin	**Preview the Purpose of the Activity Sheet** In today's activity, your student will discuss the character traits of the duck in the first story. Character traits are aspects of a person or animal's behavior, such as friendly, selfish, or naughty. A person can have many traits. Identifying character traits aids your student's comprehension of the story and the characters.

Review

Review the Phonogram Cards that are behind the Review divider in your student's Reading Review Box. Show each card to your student and have him say the sound(s). If necessary, remind your student of the sound(s).

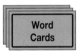

Shuffle and review the Word Cards that are behind the Review divider in your student's Reading Review Box. If your student has difficulty reading a word, build the word with letter tiles and have your student sound it out using the blending procedure shown in Appendix C.

Have fun with today's Word Card review with the activity "Word Card Racetrack." For instructions, look for this icon in Appendix H.

Story 1: "The Pet Duck"

Read the Warm-Up Sheet for "The Pet Duck"

Turn to page 231 in the activity book.

Have your student practice reading words and phrases that will be encountered in "The Pet Duck."

Teach Vocabulary and Activate Prior Knowledge

Point out the illustration of a bill on the Warm-Up Sheet. "*Bill* is another word for the beak of a bird. The bird in this illustration is a woodpecker. It uses its long bill as a chisel to remove tree bark and find insects."

Point out the illustration of a top hat on the Warm-Up Sheet. "This is a *top hat*. Top hats are usually black and have a high cylindrical crown. Abraham Lincoln was famous for wearing a top hat. Nowadays top hats are worn only when gentlemen dress up for formal occasions."

"The little girl in the next story has a pet duck that wears a top hat. Let's see what this duck does."

Read "The Pet Duck"

"Turn to page 163 in your reader and read 'The Pet Duck' aloud." Discuss your student's ideas for the questions below as you come to them.

After page 173: "What does *six on the dot* mean?"

After reading: "Rick is quite a naughty duck. What kind of trouble does he get into? Skim the story to find out."

"Even though Rick is naughty, Quinn thinks he is the best pet. Why?"

Complete Activity Sheet

"The way that a person or even an animal is—such as friendly, selfish, or naughty—is called a *character trait*. A person can have many traits. In this activity, you'll discover the character traits of the pet duck."

What Is Rick Like?
Remove pages 233-236 from the activity book.

Cut out the word cards on page 235.

Mix up the cards and place them in a pile with the illustrations facing up. Have your student turn the cards over one by one, read the word, and decide whether that word describes Rick the duck. If it does, the student should set the card on top of the illustration of Rick. If it does not, the student should set the card aside.

If your student puts a word on Rick that does not describe the character, allow him to defend his choice. More advanced readers may understand the explanation that nothing in the text supports that idea, but younger readers may tend to put their own feelings onto the duck. Ask your student to explain his answers, and then accept them at this early stage.

Answer Key

Words that describe Rick	*Words that do not describe Rick*
fun	sad
bad	hot
fast	rich
mad	stuck
glad	lost
quick	thin

Story 2: "Fun at the Pond"

Read the Warm-Up Sheet for "Fun at the Pond"

Turn to page 237 in the activity book.

Have your student practice reading words and phrases that will be encountered in "Fun at the Pond."

Teach Vocabulary and Activate Prior Knowledge

Point out the illustration of a lily pad on the Warm-Up Sheet. "A *pad*, or lily pad, is the large, floating leaf of the water lily plant. These plants grow in the water of a pond or pool, and frogs like to sit on them to bask in the sun. The word *bask* means to relax in the warmth of the sun. That's what frogs do on lily pads!"

"Have you ever been to a pond? What things can you see at a pond?" *Possible answers: frogs, lily pads, cattails, fish, water, birds, sand, butterflies.*

Point to the illustration of a crayfish. "Sometimes you might even see a *crayfish* at a pond. In some areas, these are called *crawfish* or *crawdads*. Crayfish resemble small lobsters and live in streams and rivers."

"In the next story, three children have lots of fun at the pond. Let's see what they find there."

Read "Fun at the Pond"

"Turn to page 179 in your reader and read 'Fun at the Pond' aloud." Discuss your student's ideas for the questions below as you come to them.

After page 192: "Do you think the kids will catch a fish?"

After reading: "What kinds of animals do the children meet at the pond? Skim the story to find out."

Read a Story or Poem

Read aloud to your student for twenty minutes.

Read-Aloud Tip!

Read a Range of Nonfiction Texts

Reading nonfiction helps kids develop specialized vocabulary as well as background knowledge, which in turn gives kids a wider foundation for all other reading.

Here are a few types of informational texts to share with your student:

- Nonfiction picture books and chapter books
- Life-cycle books
- Experiment and activity books
- Special interest books
- Photographic essay books
- Biographies and autobiographies
- Newspapers and magazines
- Browsable books of facts
- How-to guides, cookbooks, field guides, and craft books

Mark the Progress Chart

Have your student mark Lesson 35 on the Progress Chart.

Lesson 35: Read "The Pet Duck" and "Fun at the Pond"

Lesson 36 Consonant Team NG

Objective

This lesson teaches words containing the consonant team ng.

You Will Need

☐ Phonogram Card 31
☐ letter tile ng
☐ *Blast Off to Reading!* pages 239-247
☐ Word Cards 146-155

Before You Begin

Preview Consonant Team NG

The consonant team ng says /ng/ as in *ring*. Listen for the /ng/ sound in the following words.

sing   rang   long   bring   thing

When phonogram ng comes after a and i, the vowels don't say their pure short vowel sound. Instead, the sound falls between the short and long vowel sounds, as in the words *sang* and *thing*.

This concept is generally easy for students to grasp, since it is difficult to say the pure short vowel sound in these word parts. It is easier to say the word parts correctly.

Less commonly, ng combines with e to form the word part *eng*, as in *English* and *strength*. There are only a few words with the *eng* word part, and since none of them appear at this reading level, words containing *eng* have not been included in this lesson.

The ng tile is stored under the Consonant Teams category.

Refer to the Letter Tiles app or Phonogram Sounds app for a demonstration of the ng phonogram sound.

Review the Phonogram Cards that are behind the Review divider in your student's Reading Review Box. Show each card to your student and have him say the sound(s). If necessary, remind your student of the sound(s).

Shuffle and review the Word Cards that are behind the Review divider in your student's Reading Review Box. If your student has difficulty reading a word, build the word with letter tiles and have your student sound it out using the blending procedure shown in Appendix C.

New Teaching

Teach New Letter Sound

Hold up the Phonogram Card for the consonant team <u>ng</u>.

"The <u>n</u> and g work together to make one sound. These letters say /ng/."

"Repeat after me: /ng/." *Student repeats the sound.*

Mix in several other Phonogram Cards for mixed review and practice until your student can say the sounds accurately. File the new Phonogram Card behind the Review divider in the Reading Review Box.

Move the <u>ng</u> tile into the workspace.

Mix in several other letter tiles for mixed review and practice with the new phonogram until your student can say the sound accurately.

 For some tasty extra practice with the new phonogram, try the "Snack Track" activity. For instructions, look for this icon in Appendix G.

New Teaching
(continued)

Build Words with NG

Build the word part *ang* with letter tiles.

"This word part says /ang/. Let's make some words with /ang/."

One at a time, build the words *bang, fang, hang,* and *rang* and read them with your student.

Build the word part *ing*.

"This word part says /ing/."

One at a time, build the words *sing, king, ring, thing,* and *wing* and read them with your student.

Build the word part *ong*.

"Ng can be combined with o, too. The o says /ŏ/ just like we expect it to say."

One at a time, build the words *song, long,* and *gong* and read them with your student.

Build the word part *ung*.

"And ng can be combined with u. The u says /ŭ/ just like we expect it to say."

One at a time, build the words *hung, sung, flung,* and *lung* and read them with your student.

New Teaching
(continued)

Arrange the letter tiles as follows.

Point to the *ang* word part. "Say this word part." /*ang*/.

Move the <u>ng</u> down to form the *ing* word part. "Say this word part." /*ing*/.

Repeat with the remaining vowels and then do mixed review until your student can easily read all four word parts.

Play "Change the Word"

Build the word *thing* with letter tiles.

"What is this word?" *Thing.*

"I'm going to change the first letter of this word."

"What does this new word say?" Encourage your student to sound out the new word, *ring*.

Continue to change one letter at a time to form the following words. Each time, have your student sound out the new word.

ring → rang → sang → sing → song → sung → stung → sting

Lesson 36: Consonant Team NG

New Teaching
(continued)

Complete Activity Sheets

"Let's help a kitten find some mittens."

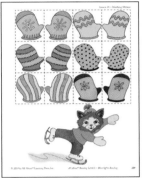

Matching Mittens
Remove pages 239-240 from the *Blast Off* activity book.

Cut out the kitten and all the mittens.

Mix up the mittens and lay them on a table with the words facing down.

Have your student choose a pair of matching mittens, flip them over to read the rhyming words, and then place the matching mittens on the kitten's paws.

Repeat until the kitten has tried on all the mittens.

"Now let's see if we can help these bunnies find their homes."

Baby Bunnies
Remove pages 241-244 from the activity book.

Cut the sheet with the mother rabbits in half horizontally. Cut out all the baby bunny cards on page 243.

Mix the baby bunny cards and place them in a pile on the table between the two mother rabbits.

Have your student select a card from the pile and read the word aloud. He should then determine whether the word belongs with the *ing* rabbit or the *ang* rabbit, and then place the baby rabbit card on the appropriate mother rabbit.

Continue until all the baby bunnies have found homes.

Practice Reading Words

Have your student practice reading the words on Word Cards 146-155.

File the Word Cards behind the Review divider in the Reading Review Box.

Practice Fluency

Turn to pages 245-247 in the activity book.

Have your student read from the Practice Sheets.

 To engage your student in the fluency exercises, try the activity "Fluency Hopscotch." For instructions, look for this icon in Appendix F.

Read a Story or Poem

Read aloud to your student for twenty minutes.

Explore the Whole Book

Read-Aloud Tip!

Before diving into a new book for the first time, explore the front and back covers, the spine, and the jacket flaps. Read and discuss the title, the author, and the illustrator, and look for interesting info about them on the flaps. If you're reading a picture book, spend some time admiring the endpapers, too!

Mark the Progress Chart

Have your student mark Lesson 36 on the Progress Chart.

Lesson 36: Consonant Team NG

Lesson 37 Read "The Bat and King Sam" and "The Long Nap"

Objective	In this lesson, students discuss the five senses and read two short stories that give them practice with words containing <u>ck</u> and <u>ng</u>.

You Will Need

☐ *Blast Off to Reading!* pages 249-252

☐ *The Runt Pig* book

☐ a small snack (e.g., apple, cracker)

Before You Begin

Preview the Purpose of the Activity Sheet

Authors often use the five senses of taste, sight, sound, touch, and smell in their imagery and description. In today's activity, your student will practice distinguishing and discussing the five senses. You will need to provide a small snack for this activity.

Review

Review the Phonogram Cards that are behind the Review divider in your student's Reading Review Box. Show each card to your student and have him say the sound(s). If necessary, remind your student of the sound(s).

Shuffle and review the Word Cards that are behind the Review divider in your student's Reading Review Box. If your student has difficulty reading a word, build the word with letter tiles and have your student sound it out using the blending procedure shown in Appendix C.

Your student may enjoy reviewing today's Word Cards with the activity "Word Cloud." For instructions, look for this icon in Appendix H.

Story 1: "The Bat and King Sam"

Complete Activity Sheet

"Today we will use our five senses to describe a food." Give your student a small snack to eat, like a slice of apple or a cracker.

That Makes Sense!
Remove page 249 from the *Blast Off* activity book.

Set the five senses pie chart in front of your student. Point to each section of the chart as you discuss the questions below, adjusting the wording according to the snack provided.

- Point to the hand (sense of touch). "How does the apple feel?" *Possible answers: smooth, damp.*
- Point to the eye (sense of sight). "How does the apple look?" *Possible answers: red, shiny.*
- Point to the ear (sense of sound). "How does the apple sound when you bite it?" *Possible answers: crunchy, crisp.*
- Point to the nose (sense of smell). "How does the apple smell?" *Possible answers: sweet, tart.*
- Point to the mouth (sense of taste). "How does the apple taste?" *Possible answers: juicy, sweet, sour.*

"Writers often use descriptive words to explain what things look, feel, smell, sound, and taste like."

New Teaching
(continued)

Read the Warm-Up Sheet for "The Bat and King Sam"

Turn to page 251 in the activity book.

Have your student practice reading words and phrases that will be encountered in "The Bat and King Sam."

Teach Vocabulary and Activate Prior Knowledge

Point out the illustration of a cliff on the Warm-Up Sheet. "A *cliff* is a steep rock face, especially at the edge of the sea."

Point out the illustration of an oil lamp on the Warm-Up Sheet. "This is an *oil lamp*. Oil lamps work by putting a type of oil in the base and then lighting a wick, as you do with a candle. These lamps were used before there was electricity and are still often used for camping."

"Do you like to sing songs? What song makes you feel happy and cheerful?" Discuss your student's favorite songs to sing.

"In this next story, a very special animal sings songs to cheer up a new friend. Let's see what happens."

Read "The Bat and King Sam"

"Turn to page 199 in your reader and read 'The Bat and King Sam' aloud." Discuss your student's ideas for the questions below as you come to them.

After page 200: "Why do you think the king's pets and animals ran off?"

After page 205: "The king is sad at the beginning of the story. How do you think he feels at the end of the story? Why?"

New Teaching
(continued)

Discuss the Five Senses

After reading the story, take out the five senses pie chart. "Listen to the following sentences and point to the sense that is being used."

- The bat ate a yummy snack. *Student points to taste.*
- The bat sang a happy song. *Student points to sound.*
- The bat gave King Sam a big hug. *Student points to touch.*

Story 2: "The Long Nap"

Read the Warm-Up Sheet for "The Long Nap"

Turn to page 252 in the activity book.

Have your student practice reading words and phrases that will be encountered in "The Long Nap."

Teach Vocabulary and Activate Prior Knowledge

Point out the illustration of a finch on the Warm-Up Sheet. "A *finch* is a colorful songbird."

Point out the illustration of a fox den on the Warm-Up Sheet. "A *den* is a wild animal's hidden home or lair. For example, foxes and bears live in dens. Dens keep animals warm and safe."

"Pretend you are a baby bear and you are very tired. What is your favorite place to take a nap?" Discuss your student's ideas.

"What would be a bad place to take a nap if you were a baby bear?"

"Let's see what happens when the bear cub in this story takes a nap."

New Teaching
(continued)

Read "The Long Nap"

"Turn to page 209 in your reader and read 'The Long Nap' aloud." Discuss your student's ideas for the questions below as you come to them.

After reading: "How many and what kind of creatures pass by the bear while he is sleeping? Skim the story to find out."

"The bear is able to take a long nap, but what could have made his nap much shorter?" *Possible answers: The bird could have landed on his nose, the spider could have bitten him, the moths could have tickled his ear, and so on.*

Read-Aloud Time

Read a Story or Poem

Read aloud to your student for twenty minutes.

Track Your Progress

Mark the Progress Chart

Have your student mark Lesson 37 on the Progress Chart.

YAWN!

I don't know about you, but a long nap
sounds pretty good to me right now. Do you
have any idea how much energy it takes to bury
a bone on a planet with no gravity?

A LOT! Dig, dig, dig. Float, float, float. Catch, catch,
catch. Dig, dig, dig. I'm too pooped to party!

So if you don't mind, I'm just going to curl up
next to Lesson 38 until you come back
to learn about this NK business. I trust you
to tell me all ...
about it ...
later ...
zzzzzzzzzzzzznk!

Lesson 38   Consonant Team NK

Objective

This lesson teaches words containing the consonant team <u>nk</u>.

You Will Need

☐ Phonogram Card 32   ☐ *Blast Off to Reading!* pages 253-259

☐ letter tile <u>nk</u>   ☐ Word Cards 156-165

Before You Begin

Preview Consonant Team NK

The consonant team <u>nk</u> says /ngk/ as in *think*. Listen for the /ngk/ sound in the following words.

trunk   bank   stink   thank   rink

Consonant team <u>nk</u> influences the vowels <u>a</u> and <u>i</u> just as <u>ng</u> does. The vowels don't say their pure short vowel sound. Instead, the sound falls between the short and long vowel sounds, as in the words *rank* and *think*.

This concept is generally easy for students to grasp, since it is difficult to say the pure short vowel sound in these word parts. It is easier to say the word parts correctly.

It is interesting to note that <u>nk</u> never combines with <u>e</u> to form words. There is no word part *enk*.

nk   The <u>nk</u> tile is stored under the Consonant Teams category.

     Refer to the Letter Tiles app or Phonogram Sounds app for a demonstration of the <u>nk</u> phonogram sound.

Review

It's time to review the cards behind the Mastered dividers to ensure they stay fresh in your student's mind.

Shuffle the cards behind both Mastered dividers and choose a selection for review.

Teach New Letter Sound

 Hold up the Phonogram Card for the consonant team <u>nk</u>.

"The <u>n</u> and <u>k</u> work together to make one sound. These letters say /ngk/."

"Repeat after me: /ngk/." *Student repeats the sound.*

Mix in several other Phonogram Cards for mixed review and practice until your student can say the sounds accurately. File the new Phonogram Card behind the Review divider in the Reading Review Box.

Move the <u>nk</u> tile into the workspace.

Mix in several other letter tiles for mixed review and practice with the new phonogram until your student can say the sound accurately.

> For extra practice with the new phonogram, play the game "Fun with Phonograms." For instructions, look for this icon in Appendix G.

Build Words with NK

Arrange the letter tiles as follows.

Point to the *ank* word part. "Say this word part." */ank/.*

Move the <u>nk</u> down to form the *ink* word part. "Say this word part." */ink/.*

Repeat with word parts *onk* and *unk* and then do mixed review until your student can easily read all four word parts.

New Teaching
(continued)

"Let's make some words with *ank*." One at a time, build the words *bank*, *sank*, and *thank* and read them with your student.

"Let's make some words with *ink*." One at a time, build the words *think*, *clink*, and *drink* and read them with your student.

"Let's make some words with *onk*." One at a time, build the words *honk* and *bonk* and read them with your student.

"Let's make some words with *unk*." One at a time, build the words *hunk*, *bunk*, and *sunk* and read them with your student.

Play "Change the Word"

Build the word *pink* with letter tiles.

"What is this word?" *Pink.*

"I'm going to change the first letter of this word."

"What does this new word say?" Encourage your student to sound out the new word, *rink.*

Continue to change one letter at a time to form the following words. Each time, have your student sound out the new word.

rink → shrink → shrunk

sunk → junk → bunk → bank → thank → think → ink

New Teaching
(continued)

Complete Activity Sheet

"Let's flip some words with <u>nk</u>."

<u>Word Flippers for NK</u>

Remove pages 253-255 from the *Blast Off* activity book.

There are two Word Flippers in this lesson. Each page will create one flipper.

Refer to Appendix E for assembly instructions.

Have your student turn the pages and read the words that are formed.

Practice Reading Words

Have your student practice reading the words on Word Cards 156-165.

File the Word Cards behind the Review divider in the Reading Review Box.

Lesson 38: Consonant Team NK

New Teaching
(continued)

Practice Fluency

Turn to pages 257-259 in the activity book.

Have your student read from the Practice Sheets.

To engage your student in the fluency exercises, try the activity "Word Road." For instructions, look for this icon in Appendix F.

Read-Aloud Time

Read a Story or Poem

Read aloud to your student for twenty minutes.

Read-Aloud Tip!

Build Comprehension with Wordless Picture Books
Yes, that's right—sometimes less is a lot more! You can practice comprehension and other reading skills by sharing wordless picture books and simply asking questions. For example, practice comprehension by asking, "What is happening here?" Questions like "What makes you think that?" strengthen inferring skills, while prediction and oral language skills can be honed with questions like "What do you think will happen next?" and "Why?"

Mark the Progress Chart

Have your student mark Lesson 38 on the Progress Chart.

Zzzzzzzzzzznk ... huh?

Oh! I'm up! I'm up!
I'm ready to learn what you found out
about NK.

I thiNK you are so smart for doing that lesson all by
yourself. But thaNK you for rousing me from my
buNK so I can learn, too.

I hope I don't stiNK!
(wiNK, wiNK)

Lesson 39 Read "Frank Shrank" and "At Camp"

Objective

In this lesson, students learn about cause and effect and read two short stories that give them practice with words containing <u>nk</u>.

You Will Need

☐ *Blast Off to Reading!* pages 261-264

☐ *The Runt Pig* book

Before You Begin

Preview the Purpose of the Activity Sheet

In today's activity, your student will practice identifying cause and effect. He will learn that a cause is an event that makes something else (the effect) happen. Being able to identify cause and effect aids your student's comprehension of what and why things happen in a story.

Review

Review the Phonogram Cards that are behind the Review divider in your student's Reading Review Box. Show each card to your student and have him say the sound(s). If necessary, remind your student of the sound(s).

Shuffle and review the Word Cards that are behind the Review divider in your student's Reading Review Box. If your student has difficulty reading a word, build the word with letter tiles and have your student sound it out using the blending procedure shown in Appendix C.

Test your student's Word Card memory with the game "Word Card Concentration." For instructions, look for this icon in Appendix H.

Story 1: "Frank Shrank"

Complete Activity Sheet

"Anything that happens has a reason for happening. This is called *cause and effect*. Cause is *why* something happens; effect is *what* happens. This activity is all about cause and effect."

Cause and Effect

Remove pages 261-262 from the *Blast Off* activity book.

Cut out the cards on page 261.

Spread out the cards on the table with the illustrations facing up. Have your student choose a card and flip it over to read aloud. Ask your student for ideas of what could happen next.

Continue to discuss several more cards of your student's choosing. Talk about the effects that could occur as a result of the "cause" listed on each card.

Read the Warm-Up Sheet for "Frank Shrank"

Turn to page 263 in the activity book.

Have your student practice reading words and phrases that will be encountered in "Frank Shrank."

New Teaching
(continued)

Teach Vocabulary and Activate Prior Knowledge

Point out the illustration of an ink pad on the Warm-Up Sheet. "A *pad of ink* is like a little sponge filled with ink. You can press stamps into it to make words and designs, or you can press your fingers in it to make fingerprints."

Point out the illustration of a can of pop on the Warm-Up Sheet. "*Pop* is another word for soda. Depending on where you live, you might call it pop or soda. What is it called where you live?"

Point out the illustration of the ruler on the Warm-Up Sheet. "This is a *ruler*. Have you used a ruler to measure things?"

"Pretend that you are only two inches tall. Where would you sleep at night? How would you travel from place to place?" Ask your student how he might use various common objects, such as a teacup, a sponge, a ruler, and a straw.

"The boy in this story starts out big, but then gets very small. Let's see what kind of adventures he has."

Read "Frank Shrank"

"Turn to page 223 in your reader and read 'Frank Shrank' aloud." Discuss your student's ideas for the questions below as you come to them.

After page 226: "Do you think Frank is afraid of shrinking? Would you be? Why or why not?"

After page 235: "What do you think will happen when Frank drinks that last drop of milk?"

After page 236: "Why is Frank happy to be big again?"

Discuss Cause and Effect in "Frank Shrank"

"There are several examples of cause and effect in the story 'Frank Shrank.' Let's look at some of them."

"Turn to page 226. What causes Frank to shrink?" *Drinking the pink milk.*

"Turn to page 233. What causes Frank to fall?" *The wind of the fan.*

"Turn to page 234. Why does Frank end up in the pad of ink?" *Because he fell off the moth.*

Story 2: "At Camp"

Read the Warm-Up Sheet for "At Camp"

Turn to page 264 in the activity book.

Have your student practice reading words and phrases that will be encountered in "At Camp."

Teach Vocabulary and Activate Prior Knowledge

Point out the illustration of a pack on the Warm-Up Sheet. "A *pack* is a small bag to carry items in. It is also called a *backpack*, *knapsack*, or *rucksack*."

"Have you ever been camping? What are some things you could do at a campsite?" *Possible answers: set up a tent, build a campfire, go fishing, collect leaves, watch the animals, roll out the sleeping bags.*

"The two boys in this story go camping on the top of a hill. Let's see what happens."

New Teaching
(continued)

Read "At Camp"

"Turn to page 239 in your reader and read 'At Camp' aloud." Discuss your student's ideas for the questions below as you come to them.

After page 244: "Why do you think the fox is not in a rush?"

After page 250: "Look at the illustration. Why do you think the fox is staying near the tent?"

Read-Aloud Time

Read a Story or Poem

Read aloud to your student for twenty minutes.

Read-Aloud Tip!

__Explain New Vocabulary__
If your student asks you what a word means during a read-aloud, by all means stop and define the word for her. But don't feel that you need to explain every unfamiliar word you come across. It would take a long time to get through a book if you did that!

Even if your student doesn't know the specific meaning of a word, more often than not she will pick up on context clues to form meaning. So as you read, choose just a few words to stop and define. You can always explain different new words the next time you read the book together.

Mark the Progress Chart

Have your student mark Lesson 39 on the Progress Chart.

Lesson 39: Read "Frank Shrank" and "At Camp"

Lesson 40 Compound Words

Objective

This lesson teaches compound words and the Leap Word *do*.

You Will Need

☐ *Blast Off to Reading!* pages 265-275   ☐ Word Cards 166-175

☐ second set of letter tiles

Before You Begin

Preview Compound Words

Compound words are special words that are made up of two smaller words, such as *sandbox*. Read the following examples and look for the two smaller words.

panfish   sunset   wetland   cannot   backpack

The small words that comprise the larger compound word have already been taught, so the compound words in this lesson are 100% decodable.

In Level 2, students will learn a syllable division rule specifically for compound words.

Add Letter Tiles to the Magnetic White Board

Building compound words will require more letters. If you are using a magnetic white board instead of the Letter Tiles app, add the remaining tiles from the second set of a-z letter tiles to complete your setup.

a b c d e f g h i j k l m n o p qu r s t u v w x y z
a b c d e f g h i j k l m n o p qu r s t u v w x y z

You may notice that there is a third s tile. Save it for Lesson 42.

Review

Review the Phonogram Cards that are behind the Review divider in your student's Reading Review Box. Show each card to your student and have him say the sound(s). If necessary, remind your student of the sound(s).

Shuffle and review the Word Cards that are behind the Review divider in your student's Reading Review Box. If your student has difficulty reading a word, build the word with letter tiles and have your student sound it out using the blending procedure shown in Appendix C.

Teach Compound Words

Build the word *bathtub* with letter tiles.

"The word *bathtub* has two smaller words in it. Can you find the two smaller words?" *Bath, tub.*

"Good! Two smaller words put together form a special type of word. We call this type of word a *compound word.*"

Complete Activity Sheets

"Let's see if these birds can help us make some compound words."

Bird Friends
Remove pages 265-267 from the *Blast Off* activity book.

Cut out the branch and the bird cards. Lay the birds on the table and mix them up. Your student should select two matching birds, set them on the branch side by side, and read the resulting compound word.

If you wish to identify the birds with your student, here is the list of species represented.

Card / Bird Species	Card / Bird Species
quicksand / cardinal	pigpen / scarlet tanager
bobcat / goldfinch	milkman / hairy woodpecker
bathtub / robin	catfish / rose-breasted grosbeak
itself / magpie	backpack / red-winged blackbird
cannot / meadowlark	lipstick / blue jay

New Teaching
(continued)

"Are you ready to chop some veggies?"

Chop-Chop
Remove pages 269-272 from the activity book.

Cut out the knife and the foods. If you wish to identify the items with your student, the foods represented are pumpkin, eggplant, grapes, cucumber, bread, pepper, pineapple, apple, and banana.

Have your student pretend to cut each compound word between its two smaller words. He should first read each smaller word, and then the entire compound word.

Answer Key
chop–stick
cod–fish
milk–man
dust–bin
drum–stick
sun–lit
egg–shell
dish–pan
flap–jack

Practice Reading Words

Have your student practice reading the words on Word Cards 166-174.

File the Word Cards behind the Review divider in the Reading Review Box.

New Teaching
(continued)

Teach a Leap Word: *do*

> We are treating the word *do* as a Leap Word because it contains the third sound of o͟, which has not been taught yet.

Show Word Card 175 to your student.

"This word is *do*, as in *What did you do today?*"

Point to the o͟. "The o͟ doesn't say the sound we expect it to."

Review this Leap Word several times today and then file it behind the Review divider in the Reading Review Box.

Practice Fluency

Turn to pages 273-275 in the activity book.

Have your student read from the Practice Sheets.

> To engage your student in the fluency exercises, try the activity "Silly Sentences." For instructions, look for this icon in Appendix F.

Read a Story or Poem

Read aloud to your student for twenty minutes.

Read-Aloud Tip!

Let Others Do the Work
Make use of audio books. Your student will have the opportunity to hear demonstrations of excellent reading as it is modeled by the narrator. You'll also give your voice a rest!

Track Your Progress

Mark the Progress Chart

Have your student mark Lesson 40 on the Progress Chart.

Oh, these compound words are too much fun! I came up with a few favorites ...

pancakes
fireworks
moonlight
spaceship
watchdog
superstar
superhero

and of course ... SPACEDOG! Can you make a list of _your_ favorites?

Lesson 41 Read "Cobweb the Cat" and "Yuck!"

Objective

In this lesson, students discuss realism vs. fantasy and read two short stories that give them practice with compound words.

You Will Need

☐ *Blast Off to Reading!* pages 277-283   ☐ map or globe

☐ *Cobweb the Cat* book

Before You Begin

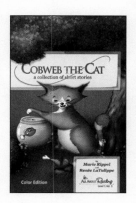

Today your student will read the first two stories in the third reader, *Cobweb the Cat*.

The subtle underlining that is found in the first two readers is no longer used in this reader because most students don't need it. If your student would still benefit from the underlining, feel free to pencil it in or continue to use the top edge of the Viewfinder Bookmark.

Many of the stories in this third collection are longer. Remember that you can stop the lesson after twenty minutes (or whatever time you have determined to be the ideal lesson length) and continue the story during your next class. Completing an entire lesson in one session is not expected.

Words and concepts introduced in earlier lessons continue to be reviewed in these stories.

Preview Realism vs. Fantasy

Part of reading comprehension is judging whether the text reflects reality or fantasy. After reading the first story, your student will discuss this concept and complete an activity in which he determines whether an action is realistic or pretend.

Review the Phonogram Cards that are behind the Review divider in your student's Reading Review Box. Show each card to your student and have him say the sound(s). If necessary, remind your student of the sound(s).

Shuffle and review the Word Cards that are behind the Review divider in your student's Reading Review Box. If your student has difficulty reading a word, build the word with letter tiles and have your student sound it out using the blending procedure shown in Appendix C.

Your student may enjoy reviewing Word Cards with the "Feed the Monster" activity. For instructions, look for this icon in Appendix H.

New Teaching

Story 1: "Cobweb the Cat"

Read the Warm-Up Sheet for "Cobweb the Cat"

Turn to page 277 in the *Blast Off* activity book.

Have your student practice reading words and phrases that will be encountered in "Cobweb the Cat."

Teach Vocabulary and Activate Prior Knowledge

Point out the illustration of a feather duster on the Warm-Up Sheet. "This is a *feather duster.* People use feather dusters to dust the furniture in their houses."

New Teaching
(continued)

Point out the illustration of a windmill on the Warm-Up Sheet. "A *windmill* is a building with big sails on it that spin like a fan in the wind."

Find the Netherlands on a map or globe. "The next story is set in the Netherlands, a country in Western Europe on the North Sea. The Netherlands is famous for its many windmills, which were once used to pump water and to help make products like paper, mustard, chalk, paint, and grain."

"The cat in this story lives in a windmill. Let's see what he does all day."

Read "Cobweb the Cat"

"Turn to page 9 in your reader and read 'Cobweb the Cat' aloud." Discuss your student's ideas for the questions below as you come to them.

After page 19: "What do you think Cobweb is hunting?"

After reading: Point out pages 13-15. "Is Cobweb actually checking the milk, fixing the tub, and dusting the desktop? What is he doing instead?"

Discuss Realism vs. Fantasy

"Do you think the cat in this story really could have done all the things he did? Why or why not?"

"Go back to the beginning of the story and look for sentences that describe something that the cat couldn't do in real life." *Possible answers: check the milk, fix the bathtub, dust the desktop, feed the fish, hang his rug.*

"Why do you think a cat couldn't do those things?"

"This story is fantasy. That means that it isn't real—it is make-believe."

"I will read a list of activities, and you will tell me if the activity could happen in real life or if it is fantasy." For each fantasy activity, ask your student why it couldn't happen.

"A friend saved up his money to buy a new toy." *It could happen.*
"A donkey invited us to a barbecue." *It's fantasy.*
"The daisies sang me a song about rain." *It's fantasy.*
"My sister did somersaults on the playground." *It could happen.*

Complete Activity Sheet

"Now let's see if you can figure out which of these things a real cat can do."

Can a Real Cat Do It?
Remove pages 279-281 from the activity book.

Cut out the cards on page 279.

Have your student look at the illustrations and read the text. If the action is something that a real cat could do, have your student place the card on the large illustration of the real cat.

If your student places a "fantasy" action on the real cat, allow him to defend his choice. Ask your student to explain his answer, and then accept it at this early stage.

Story 2: "Yuck!"

Read the Warm-Up Sheet for "Yuck!"

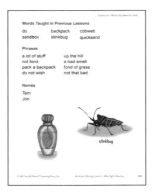

Turn to page 283 in the activity book.

Have your student practice reading words and phrases that will be encountered in "Yuck!"

Point out the name *Tam* in the Names section. "Tam is a nickname for Tamara."

Teach Vocabulary and Activate Prior Knowledge

Point out the illustration of a stinkbug on the Warm-Up Sheet. "A *stinkbug* is a small bug that gives off a bad smell. Stinkbugs might stick to your clothes, so be careful!"

New Teaching
(continued)

Point out the illustration of perfume on the Warm-Up Sheet. "This is *perfume*. Perfume comes in many different scents. People wear perfume so that they smell good. Do you know anyone who wears perfume?"

"What are some things or activities that you don't like? Why don't you like them?"

"How could a friend convince you to try something you don't like?"

"The girl in this story doesn't like a lot of things—at first. Let's see if she ends up liking anything at all."

Read "Yuck!"

"Turn to page 25 in your reader and read 'Yuck!' aloud." Discuss your student's ideas for the questions below as you come to them.

After page 32: "Why isn't Tam fond of the hill?"

After page 35: "So far Tam has ended up liking all the things she disliked at first. Do you think she will end up liking the stinkbug? Why?"

After page 38: "Why do you think Jon is hiding the stinkbug? What might he do with it?"

After reading: "Why do you think Tam is so quick to dislike things, even before she knows what they are?"

"Do you think this story could be mostly real, or is it fantasy? Why?"

Read-Aloud Time

Read a Story or Poem

Read aloud to your student for twenty minutes.

Mark the Progress Chart

Have your student mark Lesson 41 on the Progress Chart.

Lesson 42 Plural Words

Objective

This lesson teaches plural words and verbs ending in s and es.

You Will Need

☐ *Blast Off to Reading!* pages 285-289   ☐ Word Cards 176-185

☐ extra s letter tile

Before You Begin

Preview Plural Words

The s at the end of a plural word can say either /s/ or /z/. Most students will naturally say the correct sound for the letter s, since it is actually hard to say the wrong sound. But if your student has difficulty, remind him to say the singular form of the word first and then the plural form. He will naturally pronounce the word correctly.

Read the following examples of plural words and listen for the /s/ or /z/ sound.

/s/:	lips	sinks	hilltops	belts	rats
/z/:	flags	spills	stems	fishes	boxes

It is interesting to note that the letter s says /z/ after vowel sounds (as in *plays*) and after voiced consonants (as in *bugs*).

The suffix es is found after the sounds /s/, /z/, /ch/, /sh/, and /ks/. The syllable es at the end of a word is unaccented, and therefore the vowel sound is muffled. In normal speech, es often sounds like /ĭz/ instead of /ĕz/.

Add Letter Tile to the Magnetic White Board

In today's lesson your student will begin building plural words. If you are using a magnetic white board instead of the Letter Tiles app, add the third s tile to your setup.

Preview Verbs Ending in S and ES

Many present tense verbs end in s or es, such as *chomps* and *splashes*. Students will encounter these words on the Practice Sheets and in the upcoming short stories. Because of their experience with plural words, it will be easy for them to decode these verbs.

Review the Phonogram Cards that are behind the Review divider in your student's Reading Review Box. Show each card to your student and have him say the sound(s). If necessary, remind your student of the sound(s).

 Shuffle and review the Word Cards that are behind the Review divider in your student's Reading Review Box. If your student has difficulty reading a word, build the word with letter tiles and have your student sound it out using the blending procedure shown in Appendix C.

New Teaching

Teach Plural Words

Build the word *hats* with letter tiles.

Cover the s̲ with your finger.

"We say one *hat*..."

"...and we say two *hats*."

"*Hats* is **plural** because it means **more than one**."

"I'll say a word and you make it plural."

"One *map*, two _____." If necessary, prompt your student to say *maps*.

"One *ant*, two _____." *Ants.*

"One *star*, two _____." *Stars.*

"At the end of a word, the s̲ can say either /s/ or /z/. First try the /s/ sound, and if that doesn't sound right, try the /z/ sound."

Build the following words and have your student read them.

New Teaching
(continued)

Build the word *glasses* with tiles.

Cover the e-s with your finger.

"We say one *glass*..."

"...and we say two *glasses*."

"*Glasses* is **plural** because it means **more than one**."

Build the following words and have your student read them.

Complete Activity Sheet

"Let's play some ball!"

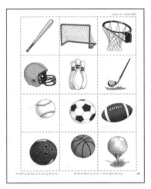

Have a Ball
Remove pages 285-286 from the *Blast Off* activity book.

Cut out the twelve sports items. Mix up the six balls and lay them out in one group with the words facing down.

Lay out the six items of sports equipment in another group with the words facing down.

Have your student match each ball with its corresponding piece of sports equipment. He should then flip the cards over and read the singular and plural versions of the words.

Answer Key
baseball / baseball bat *(windmill, windmills)*
soccer ball / goal net *(foxes, fox)*
football / helmet *(glass, glasses)*
bowling ball / bowling pins *(wish, wishes)*
basketball / basketball hoop *(rings, ring)*
golf ball / golf club *(clocks, clock)*

Practice Reading Words

Have your student practice reading the words on Word Cards 176-185.

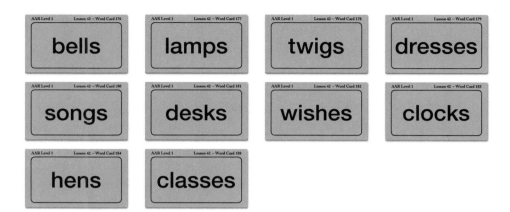

File the Word Cards behind the Review divider in the Reading Review Box.

Practice Fluency

Turn to pages 287-289 in the activity book.

Have your student read from the Practice Sheets.

On page 288, you'll find a section titled "Verbs ending in -s or -es." These present tense verbs can be decoded in a similar way to the plural nouns taught earlier in this lesson. You can still cover up the s or e-s to help your student read the base word, if necessary. But instead of saying "one desk, two desks," we use phrases such as "I fix, he fixes."

 To engage your student in the fluency exercises, try the activity "Eat Your Words." For instructions, look for this icon in Appendix F.

Read a Story or Poem

Read aloud to your student for twenty minutes.

Read-Aloud Tip!

Read Fairy Tales
If your student isn't familiar with classic fairy tales, now is a good time to read them aloud! Here are some you might consider:

- Goldilocks and the Three Bears
- The Ugly Duckling
- Rumpelstiltskin
- Beauty and the Beast
- The Gingerbread Man
- The Steadfast Tin Soldier
- Tom Thumb
- Aladdin

Track Your Progress

Mark the Progress Chart

Have your student mark Lesson 42 on the Progress Chart.

Lesson 42: Plural Words

Lesson 43   Read "Ten Wishes" and "Fast Fun"

Objective

In this lesson, students complete an activity about rhyme and read two short stories that give them practice with plural words.

You Will Need

☐ *Blast Off to Reading!* pages 291-295

☐ *Cobweb the Cat* book

☐ hyphen tile

☐ Other Tiles label

Before You Begin

Preview the Purpose of the Activity Sheet

Both of the stories in this lesson make use of rhyme. After reading the first story, your student will complete a rhyming activity. Rhyming is an important component of reading since it helps develop overall memory, language, and reading skills. It can also be a fun motivator for reluctant readers.

Preview the *Other Tiles* Category

If you are using the Letter Tiles app, you'll see that the hyphen tile has been added to the Other Tiles category.

If you are using a magnetic white board, place the Other Tiles label and the hyphen tile below the alphabet row.

| a | b | c | d | e | f | g | h | i | j | k | l | m |

Consonant Teams						Other Tiles
ch	ck	ng				-
nk	sh	th

Review

Review the Phonogram Cards that are behind the Review divider in your student's Reading Review Box. Show each card to your student and have him say the sound(s). If necessary, remind your student of the sound(s).

Liven up today's Phonogram Card review with the "Snowball Fight" activity. For instructions, look for this icon in Appendix G.

Review
(continued)

Shuffle and review the Word Cards that are behind the Review divider in your student's Reading Review Box. If your student has difficulty reading a word, build the word with letter tiles and have your student sound it out using the blending procedure shown in Appendix C.

New Teaching

Story 1: "Cobweb the Cat"

Read the Warm-Up Sheet for "Ten Wishes"

Turn to page 291 in the *Blast Off* activity book.

Have your student practice reading words and phrases that will be encountered in "Ten Wishes."

Teach Vocabulary and Activate Prior Knowledge

Point out the illustrations of the masks on the Warm-Up Sheet. "A *mask* is a disguise that covers all or part of your face. Do you recognize any of these masks?"

"Have you ever dressed up in a costume with a mask? What kind of mask was it?"

"Suppose that for one day you could have the one thing you want most in the world. What would you ask for?" Discuss your student's ideas.

"Let's see what the children in this story would ask for."

Lesson 43: Read "Ten Wishes" and "Fast Fun"

New Teaching
(continued)

Read "Ten Wishes"

> Your student may notice that the king in "Ten Wishes" is the same King Sam as in the story "The Bat and King Sam."

"Turn to page 41 in your reader and read 'Ten Wishes' aloud." Discuss your student's ideas for the question below when you come to it.

After reading: "Which of these wishes would you like the most? The least? Why?"

Complete Activity Sheet

"Did you notice that many of the wishes rhyme? In this activity, you'll match the characters with their rhyming wishes."

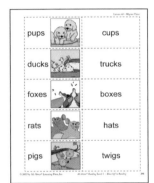

Rhyme Time
Remove page 293 from the activity book.

Cut out the character cards and rhyme cards.

Mix the character cards and place them face down in a pile. Mix the rhyme cards and spread them face up on the table. Have your student draw the character cards one at a time, read the card out loud, and then choose the matching rhyme card.

Continue until your student has matched all the cards.

New Teaching
(continued)

Story 2: "Fast Fun"

Read the Warm-Up Sheet for "Fast Fun"

Turn to page 295 in the activity book.

Have your student practice reading words and phrases that will be encountered in "Fast Fun."

Your student may notice the hyphen in the words *flip-flop* and *trip-traps*. A hyphen joins two words together to combine their meanings.

Teach Vocabulary and Activate Prior Knowledge

Point out the illustration of a dishcloth on the Warm-Up Sheet. "A *dishcloth* is a piece of fabric used to wash or dry dishes. It's also called a *dishrag*, *washcloth*, and *kitchen cloth*. What does your family call it?"

Point out the illustration of children playing leapfrog on the Warm-Up Sheet. "These kids are playing a game called *leapfrog*. In this game, one person bends down and another person vaults right over his back, like a frog."

"Do you know what a tongue twister is? It's a silly sentence that's hard to say, like *Rubber baby buggy bumpers*. Do you know any tongue twisters?"

"Let's see if you can say the tongue twisters in the next story."

Read "Fast Fun"

"Turn to page 57 in your reader and read 'Fast Fun' aloud."

Encourage your student to repeat each tongue twister several times in a row. How fast can he go?

Lesson 43: Read "Ten Wishes" and "Fast Fun"

Read a Story or Poem

Read aloud to your student for twenty minutes.

Read-Aloud Tip!

Read Poetry

Besides being a delightful and engaging form of writing, poetry benefits students in many ways.

- Rhyming poems help develop your student's memory, memorization skills, and rhythmic awareness.
- Poetry helps develop an awareness of language and phonic patterns.
- The distilled nature of poetry helps students focus on sentence-level skills such as adjectives, adverbs, powerful verbs, and specific nouns.
- Poetry helps students express their own experiences through writing.

Check out our poetry picture book reading list on our blog at blog.allaboutlearningpress.com/poetry-books-for-kids for some ideas to get you started.

Mark the Progress Chart

Have your student mark Lesson 43 on the Progress Chart.

Lesson 44 Additional Sounds for A, I, and C

Objective

This lesson teaches additional sounds for the letters <u>a</u>, <u>i</u>, and <u>c</u>.

You Will Need

☐ Phonogram Cards 4, 11, and 16

☐ *Blast Off to Reading!* page 297

☐ raisins, M&Ms, coins, dried beans, or Cheerios

Before You Begin

Look Back at Previous Progress

Your student has come a long way! He can now decode any CVC (consonant-vowel-consonant) word as well as words containing these concepts:

- words with blends
- words with consonant teams <u>th</u>, <u>sh</u>, <u>ch</u>, <u>ck</u>, <u>ng</u>, and <u>nk</u>
- compound words

The one thing that ties these words together is that they are all short vowel words.

The sequence has been very intentional. We wanted your student to become confident in reading short vowel words because it is a developmentally appropriate approach to teaching reading.

And starting with this lesson, we're ready to build on this solid base!

Look Ahead to Remaining Lessons

As you know by now, the vowels and some of the consonants have more than one sound. Your student has learned the first, most common sound for these letters, and now it is time to learn the remaining sounds.

Here's a summary of the remaining lessons in Level 1:

- The "new concept" lessons (Lessons 44, 46, 48, and 50) teach the remaining sounds of the letters. There are no new Word Cards taught during these lessons; the teaching time is devoted to the new phonogram sounds.

- The "read a story" lessons (Lessons 45, 47, 49, and 51) present eight new stories. These stories provide great practice with the words taught in Lessons 1-42 and help your student build fluency and reading stamina. No new words are introduced.

Before You Begin
(continued)

- Lesson 52 puts all the newly learned long vowel sounds to use, and seven open syllable words are taught, including *she*, *go*, and *we*.

- The final lesson, Lesson 53, includes two stories that give practice with these new open syllable words.

Preview the Sounds of the Letters

In this lesson, your student will be learning the remaining sounds of <u>a</u>, <u>i</u>, and <u>c</u>. Here's a quick reminder of the sounds of these letters.

a   The letter <u>a</u> can say three sounds:

- /ă/ as in *apple*, known as the short sound (taught in Lesson 1)
- /ā/ as in *acorn*, known as the long sound
- /ah/ as in *father*

i   The letter <u>i</u> can say three sounds:

- /ĭ/ as in *itchy*, known as the short sound (taught in Lesson 8)
- /ī/ as in *ivy*, known as the long sound
- /ē/ as in *radio*

c   The letter <u>c</u> can say two sounds:

- /k/ as in *cat*, or hard <u>c</u> (taught in Lesson 4)
- /s/ as in *city*, or soft <u>c</u>

 Refer to the Letter Tiles app or Phonogram Sounds app for a demonstration of the <u>a</u>, <u>i</u>, and <u>c</u> phonogram sounds.

Review

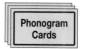
Phonogram Cards

Review the Phonogram Cards that are behind the Review divider in your student's Reading Review Box. Show each card to your student and have him say the sound(s). If necessary, remind your student of the sound(s).

Review
(continued)

Shuffle and review the Word Cards that are behind the Review divider in your student's Reading Review Box. If your student has difficulty reading a word, build the word with letter tiles and have your student sound it out using the blending procedure shown in Appendix C.

New Teaching

Teach New Letter Sounds

Show Phonogram Card 4 to your student.

"You already know that the letter a says /ă/. But it also makes two other sounds: /ā/ and /ah/. So the letter a makes three sounds: /ă/, /ā/, and /ah/. Repeat after me: /ă/–/ā/–/ah/." *Student repeats the sounds.*

Show Phonogram Card 16 to your student.

"You already know that the letter i says /ĭ/. But it also makes two other sounds: /ī/ and /ē/. So the letter i makes three sounds: /ĭ/, /ī/, and /ē/. Repeat after me: /ĭ/–/ī/–/ē/." *Student repeats the sounds.*

Show Phonogram Card 11 to your student.

"You already know that the letter c says /k/. But it also makes another sound, /s/. So the letter c makes two sounds: /k/ and /s/. Repeat after me: /k/–/s/." *Student repeats the sounds.*

Move the letter tiles into the workspace and practice until your student can say the sounds accurately.

Get your student on her feet to practice these and other phonograms with the game "Phonogram Hopscotch." For instructions, look for this icon in Appendix G.

New Teaching
(continued)

Complete Activity Sheet

"Let's load this train with freight."

Load the Train
Remove page 297 from the *Blast Off* activity book.

Give your student something fun to use for markers, like raisins, M&Ms, coins, jelly beans, or Cheerios.

Randomly call out the sounds of the letters. As you call each sound or group of sounds, your student should put a marker over the corresponding letter. For instance, for the letter i̱, ask your student to place a jelly bean over the letter that can say /ĭ/–/ī/–/ē/.

When your student has filled all eight parts of the train, he says, "Choo-choo!"

Read-Aloud Time

Read a Story or Poem

Read aloud to your student for twenty minutes.

Track Your Progress

Mark the Progress Chart

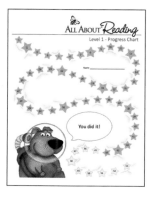

Have your student mark Lesson 44 on the Progress Chart.

Lesson 44: Additional Sounds for A, I, and C

Lesson 45   Read "The Lost List" and "No Mud for Max"

Objective

In this lesson, students read two short stories and skim the text to answer questions.

You Will Need

☐ *Blast Off to Reading!* pages 299-303   ☐ M&Ms, raisins, or nuts

☐ *Cobweb the Cat* book

Before You Begin

Preview Skimming

Part of being a fluent and flexible reader is knowing how to skim text. *Skimming* is a reading technique in which the reader moves quickly through the text to get a general idea of the material. The post-reading activity sheet gives your student practice in skimming.

Related to skimming is *scanning*, another fast-reading technique readers use to find specific facts quickly.

Review

Review the Phonogram Cards that are behind the Review divider in your student's Reading Review Box. Show each card to your student and have him say the sound(s). If necessary, remind your student of the sound(s).

Shuffle and review the Word Cards that are behind the Review divider in your student's Reading Review Box. If your student has difficulty reading a word, build the word with letter tiles and have your student sound it out using the blending procedure shown in Appendix C.

Get silly with today's Word Card review with the activity "Yucky Snacks." For instructions, look for this icon in Appendix H.

Story 1: "The Lost List"

Read the Warm-Up Sheet for "The Lost List"

Turn to page 299 in the *Blast Off* activity book.

Have your student practice reading words and phrases that will be encountered in "The Lost List."

Teach Vocabulary and Activate Prior Knowledge

Point out the illustration of hot cross buns on the Warm-Up Sheet. "A *hot cross bun* is a spiced, sweet bun made with currants or raisins and marked with a cross on the top."

Point out the illustration of a badger on the Warm-Up Sheet. "This is a *badger*. Badgers are strong, nocturnal mammals in the weasel family. They usually have a gray and black coat."

"There is a badger in the next story that likes to help with the grocery shopping. Let's see if he does a good job."

Read "The Lost List"

"Turn to page 69 in your reader and read 'The Lost List' aloud." Discuss your student's ideas for the questions below as you come to them.

After page 73: "Uh-oh, Finn lost the list! Do you remember the four items he is supposed to get?"

After page 78: "Did Finn get all the right items? How do you think his mother will react to his purchases?"

After reading: "Why do you think Mom and Dad aren't mad at Finn?"

New Teaching
(continued)

Complete Activity Sheet

"Let's use the story to answer some questions about the facts."

Check the Facts

Remove page 301 from the activity book.

Have your student read each question in the first column and then mark his answer in the appropriate *yes* or *no* column. If desired, mark each answer with an M&M, raisin, or nut.

Show your student how to skim the text to find the answers.

Story 2: "No Mud for Max"

Read the Warm-Up Sheet for "No Mud for Max"

Turn to page 303 in the activity book.

Have your student practice reading words and phrases that will be encountered in "No Mud for Max."

Teach Vocabulary and Activate Prior Knowledge

Point out the illustration of the hippopotamus on the Warm-Up Sheet. "This is a *hippopotamus*, or *hippo* for short. A hippo is a large African mammal with thick skin, huge jaws, and big tusks. Hippos live on land and in the water."

Point out the illustration of a remote control on the Warm-Up Sheet. "This is a *remote control*. You probably have a remote control for your television. Remote controls are used to operate machines or even toys from a distance."

New Teaching
(continued)

"Have you ever lost a toy in a tree or in a hole or under something? How did you get it back?"

"The hippo in this story loses his favorite toy. Let's see if he gets it back."

Read "No Mud for Max"

"Turn to page 83 in your reader and read 'No Mud for Max' aloud." Discuss your student's ideas for the questions below as you come to them.

After page 87: "If you were to help Max, how would you get the plane out of the mud?"

After page 91: "What do you think is going to happen?"

After reading: "Do you think Max has anything in common with Tam from the story 'Yuck!'?" *Possible answer: They both think they don't like something but then find out it is not so bad.*

Read-Aloud Time

Read a Story or Poem

Read aloud to your student for twenty minutes.

Track Your Progress

Mark the Progress Chart

Have your student mark Lesson 45 on the Progress Chart.

Lesson 45: Read "The Lost List" and "No Mud for Max"

Lesson 46   Additional Sounds for O and G

Objective

This lesson teaches additional sounds for the letters o and g.

You Will Need

☐ Phonogram Cards 9 and 20

☐ *Blast Off to Reading!* page 305

☐ raisins, M&Ms, coins, dried beans, or Cheerios

Before You Begin

Preview the Sounds of the Letters

In this lesson, your student will be learning the remaining three sounds of o and the remaining sound of g. Here is a quick reminder of the sounds of these letters.

o The letter o can say four sounds:

- /ŏ/ as in *otter*, known as the short sound (taught in Lesson 10)
- /ō/ as in *open*, known as the long sound
- /o͞o/ as in *to*
- /ŭ/ as in *oven*

g The letter g can say two sounds:

- /g/ as in *goat*, or hard g (taught in Lesson 4)
- /j/ as in *gem*, or soft g

 Refer to the Letter Tiles app or Phonogram Sounds app for a demonstration of the o and g phonogram sounds.

Review

Phonogram Cards

Review the Phonogram Cards that are behind the Review divider in your student's Reading Review Box. Show each card to your student and have him say the sound(s). If necessary, remind your student of the sound(s).

Word Cards

Shuffle and review the Word Cards that are behind the Review divider in your student's Reading Review Box. If your student has difficulty reading a word, build the word with letter tiles and have your student sound it out using the blending procedure shown in Appendix C.

Teach New Letter Sounds

 Show Phonogram Card 20 to your student.

"You already know that the letter o says /ŏ/. But it also makes three other sounds: /ō/, /ōō/, and /ŭ/. So the letter o makes four sounds: /ŏ/, /ō/, /ōō/, and /ŭ/. Repeat after me: /ŏ/–/ō/–/ōō/–/ŭ/." *Student repeats the sounds.*

 Show Phonogram Card 9 to your student.

"You already know that the letter g says /g/. But it also makes another sound, /j/. So the letter g makes two sounds: /g/ and /j/. Repeat after me: /g/–/j/." *Student repeats the sounds.*

Move the letter tiles into the workspace and practice until your student can say the sounds accurately.

 Let your student get creative with these phonograms with the activity "Color It." For instructions, look for this icon in Appendix G.

Complete Activity Sheet

"Are you ready to saddle up?"

<u>**Ride 'em, Cowboy!**</u>
Remove page 305 from the *Blast Off* activity book.

Give your student something fun to use for markers, like raisins, M&Ms, coins, jelly beans, or Cheerios.

Randomly call out the sounds of the letters. As you call each sound or group of sounds, your student should put a marker over the corresponding letter. For instance, for the letter g, ask your student to place a jelly bean over the letter that can say /g/–/j/.

When your student has filled all six saddles, he says "Ride 'em, Cowboy!"

Read a Story or Poem

Read aloud to your student for twenty minutes.

Mark the Progress Chart

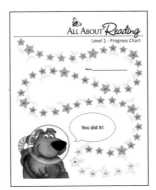

Have your student mark Lesson 46 on the Progress Chart.

Lesson 46: Additional Sounds for O and G

Lesson 47 Read "Pip the Milkman" and "The Duck Egg"

Objective

In this lesson, students read two short stories and learn about character motivation.

You Will Need

☐ *Blast Off to Reading!* pages 307-310

☐ *Cobweb the Cat* book

Before You Begin

Preview the Purpose of the Activity Sheet

An important part of reading comprehension is exploring characters, the role they play in a story, and why they do the things they do. Before reading the first story, your student will complete an activity that will help him understand one of the character's emotions and motives for acting the way he does in the story.

Review

Review the Phonogram Cards that are behind the Review divider in your student's Reading Review Box. Show each card to your student and have him say the sound(s). If necessary, remind your student of the sound(s).

Shuffle and review the Word Cards that are behind the Review divider in your student's Reading Review Box. If your student has difficulty reading a word, build the word with letter tiles and have your student sound it out using the blending procedure shown in Appendix C.

Liven up today's Word Card review with the game "Go Fish." For instructions, look for this icon in Appendix H.

Story 1: "Pip the Milkman"

Complete Activity Sheet

"If you've ever helped make a meal or dessert at home, you know that you need specific ingredients to cook with. Let's help this chef find the ingredients he needs."

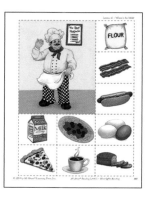

Where's the Milk?
Remove page 307 from the *Blast Off* activity book.

Cut out the nine food cards and place them face up in a pile.

Point to the illustration of the chef. "This is Gil, which is a nickname for Gilbert. Gil is a chef who runs a special kind of restaurant called a pancake house. He needs specific ingredients in order to make his breakfast foods."

Have your student choose one food card at a time. If the food is one that would be used in Gil's restaurant, the student should place the food next to Gil. If the food would not be used to make breakfast food, the student may simply say "No!" and place the card in a pile to one side.

> You may need to explain to your student that pancakes are made with flour, eggs, and milk.

"If you were Gil, how would you feel if the delivery truck brought you hot dogs instead of milk? What would you do?"

<u>Answer Key</u>
Food for Gil's restaurant: flour, bacon, eggs, milk, coffee, bread
Food Gil wouldn't use: hot dog, spaghetti, pizza

New Teaching
(continued)

Read the Warm-Up Sheet for "Pip the Milkman"

Turn to page 309 in the activity book.

Have your student practice reading words and phrases that will be encountered in "Pip the Milkman."

Teach Vocabulary and Activate Prior Knowledge

Point out the illustration of a horse-drawn wagon on the Warm-Up Sheet. "This is a *horse-drawn wagon*. Wagons like this were used a long time ago to deliver goods like milk and ice."

"If you could open a restaurant or shop, what kind would it be? Why?"

"Let's see what happens to the owner of the restaurant in this story."

Read "Pip the Milkman"

"Turn to page 95 in your reader and read 'Pip the Milkman' aloud." Discuss your student's ideas for the questions below as you come to them.

After page 102: "Why is it so important for Gil to have milk?"

After page 104: "Why is Gil angry at the cat?"

After page 106: "Now Gil is grinning. Why do you think his mood changes from angry to happy?"

Story 2: "The Duck Egg"

Read the Warm-Up Sheet for "The Duck Egg"

Turn to page 310 in the activity book.

Have your student practice reading words and phrases that will be encountered in "The Duck Egg."

Teach Vocabulary and Activate Prior Knowledge

Point out the illustration of a duck on the Warm-Up Sheet. "The setting for the next story is a lake and the main character is a duck."

Point out the illustration of a muskrat on the Warm-Up Sheet. "Another animal in this story is a *muskrat*. A muskrat is a large rodent that lives in the water. Muskrats have thick, light-brown fur and a strong odor."

Point out the illustration of a hornet on the Warm-Up Sheet. "This is a *hornet*. A hornet is similar to a wasp. Why do you think some people call hornets *pests*?"

"Have you ever seen a nest with eggs in it? What kind of dangers do unprotected eggs face?" *Possible answers: The nest or eggs could fall and break, another animal could steal the eggs.*

"Let's see what happens to the duck egg in this story."

Read "The Duck Egg"

"Turn to page 109 in your reader and read 'The Duck Egg' aloud." Discuss your student's ideas for the question below when you come to it.

After page 111: "Where do you think the mother duck is? Why would she leave the egg unprotected?" *Possible answers: She is in the water eating; she didn't know the fox was there.*

Read a Story or Poem

Read aloud to your student for twenty minutes.

Read-Aloud Tip!

Practice Predicting

Predicting means making a logical guess about what will happen next in a story. Good readers naturally make predictions while they read based on clues from the story and their own experiences, and this improves comprehension.

You can help your student develop this skill by occasionally stopping at exciting points in the story and asking, "What do you think will happen next?" Share your own predictions with your student, too.

Track Your Progress

Mark the Progress Chart

Have your student mark Lesson 47 on the Progress Chart.

Well, wag my tail! Gil is one
lucky fellow to own a pancake restaurant.
Free pancakes for life!

What kind of restaurant would <u>you</u> have?
If I ever stop blasting through space, the first thing
I'll do is open a biscuit shop called

ROCKET'S BISCUIT GALAXY
Out-of-This-World Biscuits Since Right Now!

Wouldn't that be wooferful?

Lesson 48   Additional Sounds for E, U, Y, and CH

Objective

This lesson teaches additional sounds for the letters e, u, and y and consonant team ch.

You Will Need

☐ Phonogram Cards 12, 23, 24, 29

☐ *Blast Off to Reading!* page 311

☐ raisins, M&Ms, coins, dried beans, or Cheerios

Before You Begin

Preview the Sounds of the Letters

In this lesson, your student will be learning the remaining sounds of e, u, y, and ch. Here's a quick reminder of the sounds of the letters.

e The letter e can say two sounds:

- /ĕ/ as in *echo*, known as the short sound (taught in Lesson 14)
- /ē/ as in *even*, known as the long sound

u The letter u can say three sounds:

- /ŭ/ as in *udder*, known as the short sound (taught in Lesson 12)
- /ū/ as in *unit*, known as the long sound
- /o͝o/ as in *put*

y **y** The letter y can say four sounds:

- /y/ as in *yarn*, a consonant sound (taught in Lesson 4)
- /ĭ/ as in *gym*, a vowel sound
- /ī/ as in *my*, a vowel sound
- /ē/ as in *happy*, a vowel sound

ch The consonant team ch can say three sounds:

- /ch/ as in *child* (taught in Lesson 22)
- /k/ as in *school*
- /sh/ as in *chef*

Refer to the Letter Tiles app or Phonogram Sounds app for a demonstration of the e, u, y, and ch phonogram sounds.

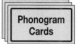

Review the Phonogram Cards that are behind the Review divider in your student's Reading Review Box. Show each card to your student and have him say the sound(s). If necessary, remind your student of the sound(s).

Shuffle and review the Word Cards that are behind the Review divider in your student's Reading Review Box. If your student has difficulty reading a word, build the word with letter tiles and have your student sound it out using the blending procedure shown in Appendix C.

Shuffle the cards behind the Mastered dividers and choose a selection for review.

New Teaching

Teach New Letter Sounds

Show Phonogram Card 24 to your student.

"You already know that the letter e says /ĕ/. But it also makes another sound: /ē/. So the letter e makes two sounds: /ĕ/ and /ē/. Repeat after me: /ĕ/–/ē/." *Student repeats the sounds.*

Show Phonogram Card 23 to your student.

"You already know that the letter u says /ŭ/. But it also makes two other sounds: /ū/ and /o͞o/. So the letter u makes three sounds: /ŭ/, /ū/, and /o͞o/. Repeat after me: /ŭ/–/ū/–/o͞o/." *Student repeats the sounds.*

Show Phonogram Card 12 to your student.

"You already know that the letter y says /y/. But it also makes three other sounds: /ĭ/, /ī/, and /ē/. So the letter y makes four sounds: /y/, /ĭ/, /ī/, and /ē/. Repeat after me: /y/–/ĭ/–/ī/–/ē/." *Student repeats the sounds.*

New Teaching
(continued)

Show Phonogram Card 29 to your student.

"You already know that <u>c-h</u> says /ch/. But it also makes two other sounds: /k/ and /sh/. So the letters <u>ch</u> make three sounds: /ch/, /k/, and /sh/. Repeat after me: /ch/–/k/–/sh/." *Student repeats the sounds.*

Move the letter tiles into the workspace and practice until your student can say the sounds accurately.

e u y ch

> Liven up practice with these phonograms with the game "Phonogram Ball." For instructions, look for this icon in Appendix G.

Complete Activity Sheet

"Let's fill up these dump trucks."

Dump Trucks
Remove page 311 from the *Blast Off* activity book.

Give your student something fun to use for markers, like raisins, M&Ms, coins, jelly beans, or Cheerios.

Randomly call out the sounds of the letters. As you call each sound or group of sounds, your student should put a marker over the corresponding letter. For instance, for the letter y̲, ask your student to place a jelly bean over the letter that can say /y/–/ĭ/–/ī/–/ē/.

When your student has filled all six of the trucks, he can say "Dump it!"

Read a Story or Poem

Read aloud to your student for twenty minutes.

Mark the Progress Chart

Have your student mark Lesson 48 on the Progress Chart.

Lesson 49 Read "The Sled" and "Ducks in a Truck"

Objective

In this lesson, students read two short stories and use the table of contents to locate information.

You Will Need

☐ *Blast Off to Reading!* pages 313-318 ☐ optional: *The Runt Pig* book

☐ *Cobweb the Cat* book

Before You Begin

Preview Table of Contents Discussion

The first story in this lesson includes characters that first appeared in a story from the *The Runt Pig* reader. If you still have that reader handy, you may wish to have your student use the table of contents to locate the story and skim for information. An optional discussion is included for that purpose.

Review

Review the Phonogram Cards that are behind the Review divider in your student's Reading Review Box. Show each card to your student and have him say the sound(s). If necessary, remind your student of the sound(s).

Shuffle and review the Word Cards that are behind the Review divider in your student's Reading Review Box. If your student has difficulty reading a word, build the word with letter tiles and have your student sound it out using the blending procedure shown in Appendix C.

Your student may enjoy practicing Word Cards by typing a selection of them on a computer. This activity is especially good for kids who struggle with handwriting.

Story 1: "The Sled"

Complete Activity Sheet

"Sometimes when you need something but can't get it, you have to be creative and improvise. Let's use our creativity to solve problems."

Make It Work!

Remove pages 313-315 from the *Blast Off* activity book.

Cut out the cards and spread them on the table.

Read the "problem prompts" below to your student one at a time. Each time, your student should look at the cards and find a solution to the problem.

For example, you might ask, "What would you do if you were really thirsty but the water wasn't working at your house?" Your student might choose ice cubes and say, "I would suck on ice cubes," or the bike and say, "I would ride my bike to my friend's house," or the phone and say, "I'd call my grandma." There are no wrong answers as long as the student can defend his choices.

Problem prompts

What would you do if you were really thirsty but the water wasn't working at your house?

What would you do if your friend needed to be cheered up?

What would you do if you were cold?

What could you use if you wanted to make a musical instrument?

What would you do if you got caught in the rain?

What could you use if you wanted to make a fort in the backyard?

What could you use if you wanted to make a costume?

New Teaching
(continued)

Read the Warm-Up Sheet for "The Sled"

Turn to page 317 in the activity book.

Have your student practice reading words and phrases that will be encountered in "The Sled."

Optional: Use the Table of Contents

"Turn to the table of contents in *The Runt Pig* book." Help your student locate the table of contents.

"In the table of contents, find the story called 'Fun at the Pond' that you read several weeks ago, and then turn to that page." *Student turns to page 179.*

"Flip through this story and tell me the names of the three children." *Jill, Dan, and Ben.*

"What season is it in the story?" *Summer (or other reasonable answer).*

"Now, turn to page 121 of *Cobweb the Cat*. The same children appear in this next story, 'The Sled.' Flip through the first few pages. What season is it in this story?" *Winter.*

Teach Vocabulary and Activate Prior Knowledge

Drop a book on the table and ask the student to describe the sound. "When something heavy falls, we often use the word *thud* to describe the sound. What other words could we use to describe the sound?" *Possible answers: smash, boom, crash.*

"In our next story, something—or someone—goes *thud!*"

"Have you ever been sledding in the snow? If you didn't have a real sled, what do you think you could use to slide down a hill?" Discuss your student's ideas.

"Let's see what the children in this story do when they can't find a sled."

New Teaching
(continued)

Read "The Sled"

"Turn to page 121 in your reader and read 'The Sled' aloud." Discuss your student's ideas for the questions below as you come to them.

After page 125: "Look at the illustration. Do you see anything in the picture that could be a sled?"

After page 129: "What do you think will happen if they hit that bump?"

Story 2: "Ducks in a Truck"

Read the Warm-Up Sheet for "Ducks in a Truck"

Turn to page 318 in the activity book.

Have your student practice reading words and phrases that will be encountered in "Ducks in a Truck."

Teach Vocabulary and Activate Prior Knowledge

Point out the illustration of quills on the Warm-Up Sheet. "*Quills* are the hollow, sharp spines of animals like porcupines and hedgehogs. If you threaten a porcupine, he may bristle his quills at you!"

Point out the illustration of a dock on the Warm-Up Sheet. "A *dock* is a platform that juts into the water. People tie their boats to the dock to make it easier to get in and out."

"Have you ever heard the saying *a picture is worth a thousand words*? What do you think it means?" If necessary, explain that it means you can often understand more from a single picture than you can from many words.

New Teaching
(continued)

"In this next story, a flock of ducks gets into all sorts of trouble while out riding in a truck. The text doesn't tell us the whole story. You have to look at the pictures to see what really happens. The pictures are worth a thousand words."

Read "Ducks in a Truck"

"Turn to page 137 in your reader and read 'Ducks in a Truck' aloud." Discuss your student's ideas for the questions below as you come to them.

After page 138: "Where are the ducks going in their truck? Look at the illustration for clues."

After page 139: "Can you tell what happened to the duck with the bump? Look at the illustration for clues." *He fell off the truck and bumped his head when the truck hit a rock.*

After reading: "Although the story doesn't come out and say exactly what happens to each duck, the illustrations give you clues."

Have your student look at the illustrations on the following pages and answer the questions.

"Look at page 141. What happens after the duck gets stuck with quills?" *The truck driver takes all the quills out and puts band-aids on the duck.*

"Look at page 145. What happens to the duck as they pass the snakes?" *A snake wraps itself around his neck like a scarf.*

"Look at page 146. What happens to the duck who goes on the dock?" *He gets a kiss from a duck on the dock.*

Read-Aloud Time

Read a Story or Poem

Read aloud to your student for twenty minutes.

Mark the Progress Chart

Have your student mark Lesson 49 on the Progress Chart.

Lesson 49: Read "The Sled" and "Ducks in a Truck"

Lesson 50   Short Vowels and Counting Syllables

Objective   This lesson teaches the term *short vowel sound* and how to count syllables.

You Will Need   ☐ *Blast Off to Reading!* pages 319-322

Before You Begin

Preview Short Vowels

In this lesson, your student will be introduced to the concept that vowels have a short sound. Very simply, a vowel's short sound is its first sound: /ă/ as in *hat*, /ĕ/ as in *beg*, /ĭ/ as in *sit*, /ŏ/ as in *not*, and /ŭ/ as in *hug*.

So far, your student hasn't needed to know the term *short vowel* to decode words because all the words your student has been asked to decode have contained short vowels. But now we are preparing to decode words in which the vowel appears at the end of a syllable and is therefore long, as in *be*, *hi*, and *go*, which are taught in Lesson 52. Being familiar with the terms *short vowel* and *long vowel* will enable your student to recognize the difference and become a stronger reader.

Preview Counting Syllables

Words are made up of syllables. A word may have one, two, or even more syllables. The number of vowel sounds in a word determines the number of syllables. For example:

- *bat* has one vowel sound and therefore one syllable
- *sticky* has two vowel sounds and therefore two syllables
- *south* has one vowel sound—/ow/—and therefore one syllable

Fortunately, there is an easy way to recognize and count syllables: by clapping. In this lesson, you will demonstrate how to clap syllables and then provide practice for your student. For example:

- *puppy* has two syllables: *pup* [clap]–*py* [clap]
- *tape* has one syllable: *tape* [clap]

The clapping method works well with most students, but see Appendix K if you need alternative methods.

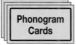 Review the Phonogram Cards that are behind the Review divider in your student's Reading Review Box. Show each card to your student and have him say the sound(s). If necessary, remind your student of the sound(s).

 Shuffle and review the Word Cards that are behind the Review divider in your student's Reading Review Box. If your student has difficulty reading a word, build the word with letter tiles and have your student sound it out using the blending procedure shown in Appendix C.

New Teaching

Teach Short Vowel Sounds

Move the letter tiles a, e, i, o, and u into the workspace.

Point to the a tile.

"Tell me the three sounds of this letter." /ă/–/ā/–/ah/.

"Which of those sounds is the first sound?" /ă/.

"Good. The first sound you said, /ă/, is called the **short sound of a.**"

Point to the e tile. e

"What sounds does this letter make?" /ĕ/–/ē/.

"Good. The first sound you said, /ĕ/, is called the **short sound of e.**"

Repeat this activity with letter tiles i, o, and u so your student can see that the first sound is the short sound.

New Teaching
(continued)

Counting Syllables

In this next exercise, you will demonstrate what a syllable is by clapping your hands as you say the syllables.

"All words have syllables. A word might have one, two, or even more syllables."

"*Swimming* has two syllables: *swim* [clap]–*ing* [clap]."
"*Grass* has one syllable: *grass* [clap]."
"*Reindeer* has two syllables: *rein* [clap]–*deer* [clap]."

"Now you try. Clap your hands for each syllable in the word *dog*."

Have your student practice with the following words.

ham	**telephone**	**sixteen**	**grape**	**table**
butterfly	**ring**	**zipper**	**tent**	**purple**

Complete Activity Sheet

"Let's count some syllables with these animals."

Cute Critters
Remove pages 319-322 from the *Blast Off* activity book.

Cut out all the cards. Mix up the animal cards and lay them on the table with the illustrations facing up.

Lay out the numbers 1, 2, and 3, which represent the possible number of syllables. Have your student sort the cards into three piles according to the number of syllables in the animals' names.

Answer Key
1 syllable: goat, rat, fox, horse, pig
2 syllables: monkey, ostrich, zebra, rabbit, tiger
3 syllables: dinosaur, octopus, kangaroo, flamingo, elephant

Read-Aloud Time

Read a Story or Poem

Read aloud to your student for twenty minutes.

Track Your Progress

Mark the Progress Chart

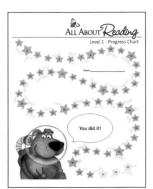

Have your student mark Lesson 50 on the Progress Chart.

Lesson 51 Read "Biff and the Bathtub" and "The Wind on the Hill"

Objective	In this lesson, students read two short stories and draw a picture from oral instructions.
You Will Need	☐ *Blast Off to Reading!* pages 323-326 ☐ a piece of paper to draw on ☐ *Cobweb the Cat* book
Before You Begin	**Preview Purpose of the Activity Sheet** Before reading the first story, your student will complete an activity in which he follows oral instructions to draw the main character of the story. The ability to follow spoken instructions helps develop your student's listening comprehension skills.

Review

 Review the Phonogram Cards that are behind the Review divider in your student's Reading Review Box. Show each card to your student and have him say the sound(s). If necessary, remind your student of the sound(s).

 Shuffle and review the Word Cards that are behind the Review divider in your student's Reading Review Box. If your student has difficulty reading a word, build the word with letter tiles and have your student sound it out using the blending procedure shown in Appendix C.

 Have some fun with today's Word Card review by playing the game "Word Card Slapjack." For instructions, look for this icon in Appendix H.

Story 1: "Biff and the Bathtub"

Complete Activity Sheet

"In our next story, you will meet Biff, a strange-looking creature. Let's see if you can guess what Biff will look like and draw your own version."

Monster Draw

Remove page 323 from the *Blast Off* activity book and set it aside.

Give your student a blank piece of paper to draw on. Read the following descriptions one by one and have your student draw his version of Biff based on these descriptions.

- Biff has a round face.
- Biff has big eyes and a big smile.
- Biff has sharp claws.
- Biff is covered in fur.
- Biff has a long tail.
- Biff has some sharp teeth.

When your student is done with his drawing, have him cut around his monster and place it in the tub illustration provided.

Read the Warm-Up Sheet for "Biff and the Bathtub"

Turn to page 325 in the activity book.

Have your student practice reading words and phrases that will be encountered in "Biff and the Bathtub."

New Teaching
(continued)

Teach Vocabulary and Activate Prior Knowledge

Point out the illustration of a drill on the Warm-Up Sheet. "A *drill* is a tool for making holes in wood, cement, metal, and other materials."

"What would you do if you found Biff in your bathtub? How would you get him out?"

"In the story, the narrator tells us to act gruff with Biff. *Gruff* means rough and firm, so if you act gruff with Biff, you're showing him who's the boss! What is the opposite of gruff?" *Possible answers: friendly, cheerful, polite.*

"Let's see how the child in this story gets Biff out of the bathtub."

Read "Biff and the Bathtub"

"Turn to page 153 in your reader and read 'Biff and the Bathtub' aloud." Discuss your student's ideas for the questions below as you come to them.

After page 155: "How do you think Biff got in the bathtub in the first place? Where do you think he came from?"

After page 161: "Why do you think the narrator grabs a drill? What does he hope will happen?"

After reading: "Does your picture look like Biff? How would you describe Biff?"

New Teaching
(continued)

Read the Warm-Up Sheet for "The Wind on the Hill"

Remove page 326 from the activity book.

Have your student practice reading words and phrases that will be encountered in "The Wind on the Hill."

Point out the name *Mel* in the Names section. "Mel is a nickname for Melanie."

Teach Vocabulary and Activate Prior Knowledge

Point out the illustration of a blob on the Warm-Up Sheet. "A *blob* is a large object that doesn't have a distinct shape. If you say something looks like a blob, it means you can't really tell what it is."

"Sometimes clouds look like big blobs, and other times they make interesting shapes in the sky. Have you ever looked up at the clouds and imagined that they formed an animal shape or something other than a cloud?" Discuss your student's ideas about clouds.

"In this next story, a boy and a girl see lots of things in the clouds."

Read "The Wind on the Hill"

"Turn to page 165 in your reader and read 'The Wind on the Hill' aloud." Discuss your student's ideas for the questions below as you come to them.

After pages 174-175: "What do you see in the clouds on these pages?"

After page 176: "Why do Greg and Mel run away at the end?"

Read a Story or Poem

Read aloud to your student for twenty minutes.

Read-Aloud Tip!

Make Connections to Real Life

Children love to see themselves reflected in the books they read. You can facilitate this by encouraging your student to make connections between his life and the life of the characters. Perhaps he feels the same way as one of the characters or has had a similar experience. Readers who connect with literature in this way are more engaged since they feel more in touch with the people and events in the world of the story. As a result, they are more likely to remember what they have read.

Track Your Progress

Mark the Progress Chart

Have your student mark Lesson 51 on the Progress Chart.

A big, astral woof to you,
space friend!

I was just thinking how far we've come
in these 51 lessons—and we're almost done!
What's been your favorite part?
I like the activity sheets. So far we've ...

fed word bones to a monster
had lunch with a yak
saved a bug from terrible dangers
made a slop pie
ridden trains, trucks, and horses
investigated facts

That's a lot of adventure, but nothing two
SPACEDOGS, MASTERS OF THE UNIVERSE
can't handle!

ONWARD!

Lesson 52   Open and Closed Syllables

Objective

This lesson teaches long vowel sounds, the concept of open and closed syllables, and words containing open syllables.

You Will Need

☐ *Blast Off to Reading!* pages 327-334

☐ Word Cards 186-193

Before You Begin

Preview Long Vowel Sounds

In Lesson 50, your student learned that the first sound of a vowel is its short sound. Today your student will learn that the second sound of a vowel is its long sound. When a vowel says its long sound, it says its name. For example:

- the long sound of <u>a</u> is /ā/
- the long sound of <u>e</u> is /ē/

Preview Open and Closed Syllables

The letter tiles make it easy to teach the difference between open and closed syllables.

`sh` `e` `d`

In the word *shed*, the vowel <u>e</u> is "closed in" by a consonant. When a vowel is in a closed syllable, it usually says its short sound.

Now watch what happens when we remove the consonant from the end of the word.

`sh` `e`

The vowel <u>e</u> is now "open." There is nothing closing it in. When a vowel is in an open syllable, it usually says its long sound. That's why <u>e</u> says /ē/ in this word.

Review the Phonogram Cards that are behind the Review divider in your student's Reading Review Box. Show each card to your student and have him say the sound(s). If necessary, remind your student of the sound(s).

 Shuffle and review the Word Cards that are behind the Review divider in your student's Reading Review Box. If your student has difficulty reading a word, build the word with letter tiles and have your student sound it out using the blending procedure shown in Appendix C.

 One at a time, point to the letter tiles a, e, i, o, and u. Have your student tell you the short vowel sound of each letter.

New Teaching

Teach Long Vowel Sounds

Move the letter tiles a, e, i, o, and u into the workspace.

Point to the a tile.

"Tell me the three sounds of this letter." /ă/–/ā/–/ah/.

"Which of those sounds is the **short** sound?" /ă/ (or the first sound).

"Good. The first sound of a vowel is its short sound. We also have a name for the **second** sound of a vowel. The second sound is called its **long** sound."

"What is the second sound of the letter a?" /ā/.

Point to the e tile.

"What are the two sounds this letter makes?" /ĕ/–/ē/.

"What is the long sound of this letter?" /ē/.

New Teaching
(continued)

Point to the i tile.

"What are the three sounds of this letter?" /ĭ/–/ī/–/ē/.

"What is the long sound of this letter?" /ī/.

Point to the o tile. **o**

Your student can probably see the pattern now.

"And what do you think the long sound of o is?" /ō/.

"And what is the long sound of u?" /ū/. **u**

"Good. The long sound of a letter is the same as its name."

Teach Closed and Open Syllables

Build the word *shed*.

"What is this word?" *Shed.*

"Point to the vowel." *Student points to the e.*

"Is there anything after the e?" *Yes, d.*

"Good. We say that the e is closed in by the d. We call this a **closed** syllable."

"Is the vowel in *shed* short or long?" *Short.*

"Right. When a vowel is in a **closed** syllable, it usually says its **short** sound."

Remove the d tile. **sh e**

"Is there anything after the e now?" *No.*

"We can say that the e is **open**, because there is nothing closing it in."

"When a vowel is in an **open** syllable, it usually says its **long** sound."

New Teaching
(continued)

Point to the e̲. "What does the e̲ say in this word?" /ē/.

"What is this word?" *She.*

Build the following words. Have your student tell you whether the syllable is **open** or **closed**.

he	*Open.*
hem	*Closed.*
so	*Open.*
sock	*Closed.*
got	*Closed.*

For additional practice, use the following words.

go	**wet**	**we**	**no**	**not**
I	**it**	**bed**	**be**	

Practice Reading Words

Have your student practice reading the words on Word Cards 186-193.

File the Word Cards behind the Review divider in the Reading Review Box.

Lesson 52: Open and Closed Syllables

New Teaching
(continued)

Complete Activity Sheet

"Let's help these astronauts get back to their spaceships."

Spaceships
Remove pages 327-331 from the *Blast Off* activity book.

Cut out the spaceships and astronauts.

Lay the spaceships on the table. Mix up the nine astronauts and lay them out in a group with the words facing down.

Have your student select an astronaut, read the word aloud, and then decide whether the syllable is open or closed. If the syllable is open, he can place the astronaut on the spaceship with the open door. If the syllable is closed, he can place the astronaut on the spaceship with the closed door.

Repeat until all the astronauts are correctly placed.

Answer Key
Open: so, she, no, be, we
Closed: not, hem, wet, bed

Practice Fluency

Turn to pages 333-334 in the activity book.

Have your student read from the Practice Sheets.

 To engage your student in the fluency exercises, try breaking up the Practice Sheet. For instructions, look for this icon in Appendix F.

Read a Story or Poem

Read aloud to your student for twenty minutes.

Mark the Progress Chart

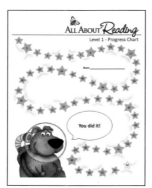

Have your student mark Lesson 52 on the Progress Chart.

Lesson 53   Read "Gus and Hal Go on a Trip" and "The Best Lunch"

Objective	In this lesson, students read two short stories that give them practice with open syllables and complete a story sequencing activity.
You Will Need	☐ *Blast Off to Reading!* pages 335-339 ☐ *Cobweb the Cat* book
Before You Begin	This is the final story lesson! These last two stories pull together all the concepts taught in Level 1, including the newly learned open syllable words. Enjoy the stories—and perhaps plan a little celebration!

Review

Review the Phonogram Cards that are behind the Review divider in your student's Reading Review Box. Show each card to your student and have him say the sound(s). If necessary, remind your student of the sound(s).

Shuffle and review the Word Cards that are behind the Review divider in your student's Reading Review Box. If your student has difficulty reading a word, build the word with letter tiles and have your student sound it out using the blending procedure shown in Appendix C.

Review short and long vowels. One at a time, point to the letter tiles <u>a</u>, <u>e</u>, <u>i</u>, <u>o</u>, and <u>u</u>. Have your student tell you the short sound of each letter. Then have him tell you the long sound of each letter.

Review closed and open syllables. Build the word *met*. "Is this an open or closed syllable?" *Closed*.

Remove the <u>t</u>. "Is this an open or closed syllable?" *Open*.

Repeat with the words *bet, go, not, he, shell, she*.

Story 1: "Gus and Hal Go on a Trip"

Read the Warm-Up Sheet for "Gus and Hal Go on a Trip"

Turn to page 335 in the *Blast Off* activity book.

Have your student practice reading words and phrases that will be encountered in "Gus and Hal Go on a Trip."

Teach Vocabulary and Activate Prior Knowledge

Point out the illustration of chopsticks on the Warm-Up Sheet. "These are *chopsticks*. Chopsticks are thin sticks of wood that are held together in one hand and used as eating utensils, like we use forks. Chopsticks are often used in China and Japan."

"In the next story, the characters go on an adventure. One character calls it a *thrill*. If something is a thrill, it is exciting and gives you a great feeling inside. If you love puppies and you get to babysit for a new litter of puppies, that would be a thrill for you. If you love fast bikes and you get to ride down a steep hill, that would be a thrill for you."

"What is a thrill for one person might not be a thrill for another person. If your friend is afraid of dogs, babysitting for a litter of puppies wouldn't be a thrill. If your sister doesn't like fast bikes, riding down a steep hill wouldn't be a thrill—it would be scary."

"What is something that is a thrill for you?"

"If you could go on an adventure, where would you go and what would you do?"

"If you could only take one thing with you to eat, what would it be?"

"Let's see what happens when the chipmunks in this story go on an adventure."

New Teaching
(continued)

Read "Gus and Hal Go on a Trip"

"Turn to page 179 in your reader and read 'Gus and Hal Go on a Trip' aloud." Discuss your student's ideas for the questions below as you come to them.

After page 184: "Gus and Hal have different reactions to hitting a rock. Why is Gus happy? Why is Hal worried?"

After page 187: "Look at the illustrations on pages 186 and 187. Which pieces of junk did they use to create the Muck Bus?"

After page 190: "How do you think a stick of gum can help?"

After reading: "Do you think these chipmunks have anything in common with the kids in the story 'The Sled'? *Possible answer: They also solve problems by finding ways to use objects in new ways.*"

Complete Activity Sheet

"Gus and Hal made several vehicles out of the lunch box. Let's see if you remember the order in which they made these vehicles."

All Aboard!
Remove pages 337-338 from the activity book.

Cut out the three vehicle cards and mix them up.

Have your student put the cards in the order that they appeared in the story. He may refer to the story if necessary.

Story 2: "The Best Lunch"

Read the Warm-Up Sheet for "The Best Lunch"

Remove page 339 from the activity book.

Have your student practice reading words and phrases that will be encountered in "The Best Lunch."

Teach Vocabulary and Activate Prior Knowledge

Point out the illustration of a giraffe on the Warm-Up Sheet. "This is a *giraffe*. Did you know that giraffes are the tallest living animals?"

Point out the illustration of Swiss cheese on the Warm-Up Sheet. "*Swiss* is a type of yellow cheese that usually has large holes in it. Swiss cheese originally came from Switzerland."

"What is your favorite kind of cheese? What would the best lunch include for you?"

"What if you didn't have one of those ingredients for your best lunch? What would you do?"

"The animals in this story get very creative to make the best lunch. Let's see what they do."

Read "The Best Lunch"

"Turn to page 197 in your reader and read 'The Best Lunch' aloud." Discuss your student's ideas for the questions below as you come to them.

After page 207: "So far, five animals have added to the lunch. Who do you think will end up eating the lunch?"

After reading: "Look at the illustration on page 211. What do you think all the other animals are thinking?"

"Does this sound like a good lunch to you? Why or why not?"

Read a Story or Poem

Read aloud to your student for twenty minutes.

Mark the Progress Chart

Have your student mark Lesson 53 on the Progress Chart.

Celebrate!

Present Your Student with the Certificate of Achievement

SHA-ZAM!
You did it, space buddy! You've taken off
and zoomed to the highest star.
I couldn't be prouder!

Thank you for sharing this space adventure with me.
I know you'll use your new knowledge to explore
the vast galaxies of reading goodness that
stretch before you.

Now it's time to
BLAST OFF
to the next frontier!

3
Appendices

Scope and Sequence of Level 1

Your Student Will:	Lesson
Learn the blending procedure and the sounds of phonograms <u>m</u>, <u>s</u>, <u>p</u>, and <u>a</u>	1
Learn the sounds of phonograms <u>n</u>, <u>t</u>, <u>b</u>, and <u>j</u> and the Leap Word <u>the</u>	2
Read a short story and learn about periods and exclamation points	3
Learn the sounds of phonograms <u>g</u>, <u>d</u>, <u>c</u>, and <u>y</u> and that every word has a vowel	4
Read a short story and learn words with two meanings	5
Learn the sounds of phonograms <u>h</u>, <u>k</u>, and <u>r</u> and the Leap Word <u>a</u>	6
Read two short stories and complete a comprehension activity	7
Learn the sounds of phonograms <u>i</u>, <u>v</u>, <u>f</u>, and <u>z</u>	8
Read two short stories and practice punctuation marks	9
Learn the sounds of phonograms <u>o</u>, <u>l</u>, and <u>w</u> and the Leap Word <u>of</u>	10
Read two short stories and complete a comprehension activity	11
Learn the sound of phonogram <u>u</u> and the second sound of <u>s</u>	12
Read two short stories and discuss a character's point of view	13
Learn the sound of phonogram <u>e</u>	14
Read two short stories and complete a story sequencing activity	15
Learn the sounds of phonograms <u>qu</u> and <u>x</u>	16
Read two short stories and create silly sentences	17
Learn the concept of consonant teams and both sounds of consonant team <u>th</u>	18
Read two short stories and discuss character motivation	19
Learn the sound of consonant team <u>sh</u>	20
Read two short stories and discuss story setting	21
Learn the first sound of consonant team <u>ch</u>	22
Read two short stories and use illustrations to retell a story	23
Learn words with final blends and the Leap Word <u>was</u>	24
Read two short stories and match text with illustrations	25
Learn words with initial blends and the Leap Word <u>to</u>	26
Read two short stories and learn about onomatopoeia	27
Read two short stories and practice reading words with blends	28
Learn words ending in <u>ff</u>, <u>ll</u>, and <u>ss</u> and the Leap Words <u>said</u> and <u>I</u>	29
Read two short stories and follow recipe instructions	30

Your Student Will:	Lesson
Learn the Leap Words or, for, and no	31
Read two short stories and practice previously taught concepts	32
Read two short stories and discuss the main conflict	33
Learn the sound of consonant team ck	34
Read two short stories and discuss character traits	35
Learn the sound of consonant team ng	36
Read two short stories and learn about the five senses in literature	37
Learn the sound of consonant team nk	38
Read two short stories and learn about cause and effect	39
Learn compound words and the Leap Word do	40
Read two short stories and discuss realism vs. fantasy	41
Learn plural words and verbs ending in s and es	42
Read two short stories and learn about rhyme	43
Learn additional sounds for phonograms a, i, and c	44
Read two short stories and skim text to answer questions	45
Learn additional sounds for phonograms o and g	46
Read two short stories and discuss character motivation	47
Learn additional sounds for phonograms e, u, y, and ch	48
Read two short stories and use the table of contents to locate information	49
Learn the term short vowel sound and how to count syllables	50
Read two short stories and draw a picture from oral instructions	51
Learn long vowel sounds and open and closed syllables	52
Read two short stories and complete a story sequencing activity	53

Appendix A: Scope and Sequence of Level 1

Phonograms Taught in Levels 1-4

Phonograms are letters or letter combinations that represent a single sound. For example, the letter b represents the sound /b/ as in *bat*. The letter combination sh represents the sound /sh/ as in *ship*.

Card #	Phonogram	Sound	For the Teacher's Use Only (example of word containing the phonogram)				Lesson/ Level
Phonograms Taught in Level 1							
1	m	/m/	moon				1
2	s	/s/–/z/	sun	has			1, 12
3	p	/p/	pig				1
4	a	/ă/–/ā/–/ah/	apple	acorn	father		1, 44
5	n	/n/	nest				2
6	t	/t/	tent				2
7	b	/b/	bat				2
8	j	/j/	jam				2
9	g	/g/–/j/	goose	gem			4, 46
10	d	/d/	deer				4
11	c	/k/–/s/	cow	city			4, 44
12	y	/y/–/ĭ/–/ī/–/ē/	yarn	gym	my	happy	4, 48
13	h	/h/	hat				6
14	k	/k/	kite				6
15	r	/r/	rake				6
16	i	/ĭ/–/ī/–/ē/	itchy	ivy	radio		8, 44
17	v	/v/	vase				8
18	f	/f/	fish				8
19	z	/z/	zipper				8
20	o	/ŏ/–/ō/–/ōō/–/ŭ/	otter	open	to	oven	10, 46
21	l	/l/	leaf				10
22	w	/w/	wave				10
23	u	/ŭ/–/ū/–/ŏŏ/	udder	unit	put		12, 48
24	e	/ĕ/–/ē/	echo	even			14, 48
25	qu	/kw/	queen				16
26	x	/ks/	ax				16
27	th	/th/–/th̶/	three	then			18

Card #	Phonogram	Sound	For the Teacher's Use Only (example of word containing the phonogram)				Lesson/ Level
28	sh	/sh/	ship				20
29	ch	/ch/–/k/–/sh/	child	school	chef		22, 48
30	ck	/k/, two-letter /k/	duck				34
31	ng	/ng/	king				36
32	nk	/ngk/	thank				38
Phonograms Taught in Level 2							
33	wh	/hw/	while				Level 2
34	ee	/ē/, double e̲	feed				Level 2
35	er	/er/ as in *her*	her				Level 2
36	ar	/ar/	car				Level 2
37	or	/or/–/er/ as in *work*	corn	work			Level 2
38	ed	/ed/–/d/–/t/	wanted	snowed	dropped		Level 2
39	oy	/oy/ that we **may** use at the end of English words	toy				Level 2
40	oi	/oy/ that we may **not** use at the end of English words	oil				Level 2
41	aw	/aw/ that we **may** use at the end of English words	saw				Level 2
42	au	/aw/ that we may **not** use at the end of English words	haul				Level 2
43	ow	/ow/–/ō/	cow	low			Level 2
44	ou	/ow/–/ō/–/o͞o/–/ŭ/	mouse	soul	soup	touch	Level 2
Phonograms Taught in Level 3							
45	ai	/ā/, two-letter /ā/ that we may **not** use at the end of English words	rain				Level 3
46	ay	/ā/, two-letter /ā/ that we **may** use at the end of English words	day				Level 3
47	oa	/ō/, two-letter /ō/ that we may **not** use at the end of English words	boat				Level 3

Appendix B: Phonograms Taught in Levels 1-4

Card #	Phonogram	Sound	For the Teacher's Use Only (example of word containing the phonogram)	Lesson/ Level
48	ir	/er/ as in *first*	first	
49	ur	/er/ as in *nurse*	nurse	
50	oo	/o͞o/–/o͝o/–/ō/	food　　book　　floor	
51	ea	/ē/–/ĕ/–/ā/	leaf　　bread　　great	
52	igh	/ī/, three-letter /ī/	light	
53	tch	/ch/, three-letter /ch/	watch	
54	dge	/j/, three-letter /j/	badge	
55	ew	/o͞o/–/ū/	grew　　few	
56	wr	/r/, two-letter /r/ used **only** at the beginning of a word	write	Level 3
57	kn	/n/, two-letter /n/ used **only** at the beginning of a word	know	
58	eigh	/ā/, four-letter /ā/	eight	
59	oe	/ō/, two-letter /ō/ that we **may** use at the end of English words	toe	
60	ti	/sh/, tall-letter /sh/	nation	
Phonograms Taught in Level 4				
61	ey	/ē/–/ā/	key　　they	
62	ear	/er/ as in *early*	early	
63	ui	/o͞o/	fruit	
64	ie	/ē/–/ī/	field　　pie	
65	ph	/f/, two-letter /f/	phone	
66	gu	/g/, two-letter /g/	guide	
67	gn	/n/, two-letter /n/ used at the beginning or end of a word	gnat	Level 4
68	augh	/aw/, four-letter /aw/	daughter	
69	ei	/ā/–/ē/	vein　　ceiling	
70	ough	/ō/–/o͞o/–/ŭff/– /ŏff/–/aw/–/ow/	though　　through　　rough　　cough　　thought　　bough	
71	si	/sh/–/zh/	mission　　vision	
72	mb	/m/, two-letter /m/	lamb	

Appendix B: Phonograms Taught in Levels 1-4

Card #	Phonogram	Sound	For the Teacher's Use Only (example of word containing the phonogram)	Lesson/Level
73	our	/er/ as in *journey*	journey	Level 4
74	ci	/sh/, short-letter /sh/	special	
75	rh	/r/, two-letter /r/ used in Greek words	rhyme	

Appendix B: Phonograms Taught in Levels 1-4

Blending Procedure

<u>Blending one-syllable words</u>

1. Build the word with letter tiles.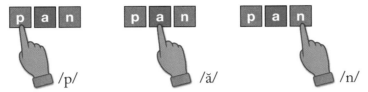

2. Touch under one letter at a time and say the sound of each letter.

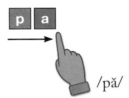

3. Go back to the beginning of the word and blend the first two sounds together.

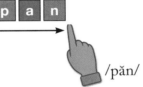

4. Start over at the beginning of the word. Slide your finger under the letters and blend all three sounds together.

/păn/

Starting over at the beginning of the word is optional. Some students need the extra support provided by this step, while others do not.

Whenever you feel that your student is ready, blend all the letters without this additional step.

Tip!

---

5. Finally, say the word at a normal pace as we do when we speak.

Pan!

"Touch the Vowel" Technique

Tip!

Many errors in sounding out words are related to the vowel. If your student says the wrong vowel sound, ask him to touch the vowel and say the vowel sound first. After he says the correct sound for the vowel, he should go back and sound out the word from the beginning.

In Level 2, the blending procedure will be expanded as shown below.

Blending multisyllable words

1. Build the word with letter tiles.

2. Divide the word into syllables using the appropriate syllable division rules.

3. Label the syllable types.

4. Decode one syllable at a time, following the same procedure you would use for a one-syllable word.

5. Start over at the beginning of the word. Slide your finger under each syllable, saying the sound of the syllables.

6. Finally, say the word at a normal pace as we do when we speak.

   If the word has three or more syllables, follow the same procedure:
   1. Divide the word.
   2. Label the syllable types.
   3. Decode one syllable at a time.

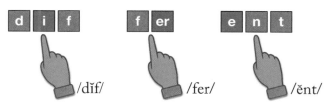

APPENDIX D
Solving Letter Reversal Problems

Most of the letters of the alphabet have unique shapes, so no matter which way you turn them, they can't be confused with any other letters. For example, the letter m looks quite different from the letter x, and f is not likely to be confused with z.

There are a few notorious troublemakers, however, particularly b and d, the letters that students most often have trouble with.

It is easy to see where the confusion comes in: flip the b and it becomes a d. The beginning reader or dyslexic student may not realize that the direction of the letter matters, or he may not be able to remember which letter is which.

Letters and numbers that can be flipped include:

b d   p q   p d   n u   6 9

What is considered normal?

If your student is between the ages of three and seven, is just starting to read, and makes occasional reversal errors when reading or writing, it's perfectly normal. It doesn't mean that your student has dyslexia or a reading disability. Make a gentle correction and move on.

But if your student is eight years or older, has had prior reading instruction, and is making frequent letter reversal errors, it is important to take action to solve the reversal problems.

As reading instructors, we have two jobs to do regarding reversals:

1. Try to prevent confusion.
2. Where confusion exists, resolve it.

Try to prevent letter confusion before it begins.

The *All About Reading* program is carefully structured to minimize the likelihood of letter reversals. We teach the sounds of potentially confusing letters like b and d in separate lessons. The student's task is simplified because he only has to make one new visual discrimination at a time.

When your student is learning to print, be sure to teach correct letter formation. Doing so is critical to prevent confusion.

When forming the letter <u>b</u>, start with the stick first, followed by the circle. To write the letter <u>d</u>, start with the circle first, followed by the stick.

Have your student use lined paper so it is clear where the circle is in relation to the stick. Also be sure your student does not lift the pencil from the paper when writing any of the confusable letters.

What to do if your student already reverses letters.

If you are working with older learners, it may be too late to prevent confusion. They may have had a few false starts in reading and may have already confused these troublemakers. They may encounter the letter <u>b</u> and misinterpret it as the letter <u>d</u>. They may read the word *bad* as *dab*, or *fad* as *fab*. You might give a gentle correction, pull out the corresponding Phonogram Cards, and re-teach the letters separately, but your student still mixes them up.

Below are four effective methods to clear up tough reversal problems.

The demonstrations are for correcting <u>b</u> and <u>d</u> reversals, but the same concepts can be applied to any letter or number. You may only need to use one of these methods, but for really resistant cases, you will need to use all four methods.

Please note that it's important to concentrate on just one letter per session. Wait until that letter is completely mastered before teaching another letter.

Method 1: Teach the letters <u>b</u> and <u>d</u> using tactile surfaces.

Have a variety of tactile surfaces for your student to choose from. Possibilities include flannel fabric, corrugated cardboard, very fine sandpaper, fluffy fur fabric, or a carpet square. Ask your student which surface reminds him of the letter <u>b</u>, and then cut a large lowercase <u>b</u> out of the chosen tactile surface.

Using the pointer finger of his dominant hand, have your student trace the letter <u>b</u> on the textured surface. Be sure he starts and ends in the correct place. Practice until he can easily write the letter <u>b</u>.

When your student is ready to go on to a new letter, choose a different textured surface. If fine sandpaper was used for the letter <u>b</u>, perhaps furry fabric can be used for the letter <u>d</u>.

Method 2: Use "air writing" to reinforce proper letter formation.

Another simple but powerful method for correcting reversals is "air writing." Using the dominant hand, the student uses his entire arm to write letters in the air as he says the sound of the letter. The whole arm should be involved, and the student should pretend that his pointer finger is a pen.

Brain research shows that two ideas practiced at the same time can permanently bond the ideas together. In this case, the large movements of the arm combined with saying the sound of the letter helps link these two concepts together in your student's brain. Additionally, this multisensory activity takes advantage of the fact that the muscles in the shoulder and in the jaw have muscle memory, and this makes it easier for your student to recall the shape and sound of the letter.

Method #3: Teach the letters b and d using analogies.

Explain that the letter b is made up of two shapes: a bat and a ball. Using the tactile surface, demonstrate how you write the bat part of the letter first, followed by the ball.

As you write the letter b, say "bat-ball-/b/," like this:

To further clarify which side of the letter the straight line is on, tell your student that *first you grab the bat, and then you hit the ball.*

Have your student practice this motion and chant many times over a two-minute time period. Repeat the exercise several times a day.

Show your student that when you are reading from left to right, you encounter the bat part of the letter first. If he is ever unsure of the sound this letter makes when he sees it, he should think to himself, "bat-ball-/b/." This will help him recall the sound of the letter b.

To teach the letter d, you can use the analogy of a doorknob and a door. The doorknob represents the circle part of the letter, and the door represents the straight line, like this:

To clarify which side of the letter the straight line is on, tell your student that *first you grab the doorknob, and then you open the door.*

Again, practice the motion and chant many times over a two-minute period. Repeat the exercise several times a day.

Show your student that when you are reading from left to right, you encounter the doorknob part of the letter first. If he is ever unsure of the sound this letter makes when he sees it, he should think to himself, "doorknob-door-/d/." He will now be able to recall the sound of the letter d.

Another common analogy to help with b and d is a bed. Though this analogy may help some kids, for others it may require more thought, and for many kids it may not become automatic.

The letter *b* forms the head of the bed and makes the first sound in the word *bed* ...

Form sticks with your pointer fingers and circles with your thumbs and fingers to make *b* and *d* with your hands.

... and the letter *d* forms the foot of the bed and makes the last sound in the word *bed*.

Method #4: Help your student notice the shape of the mouth while saying the letter sounds.

When we say /b/, our lips come together in a straight line. Point out that the straight line comes first when you write the letter b.

When we say /d/, our lips are open. Coincidentally, the circle comes first when you write the letter d.

If your student misreads a b as a d, refer back to the tactile surface activity and air writing that you did together. Point to the misread letter and say, *If you wrote this letter, what would this letter say?*

If your student can't answer easily, ask him to draw the letter b using air writing. The sound of the letter (/b/–bat) should come more easily this way. Then have your student read the word again.

APPENDIX E
How to Assemble Word Flippers

Word Flippers are a fun way for your student to practice fluency. Follow these steps to assemble and use them in your lessons.

1. Remove the appropriate pages from the activity book. Cut apart the pages on the dotted lines.

2. Put the larger pieces of paper on the bottom. Stack the smaller pieces on top. Note that some Word Flippers will be stacked on the left side and some on the right side.

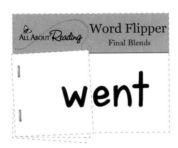

3. Staple the Word Flipper along the left or right side as indicated.

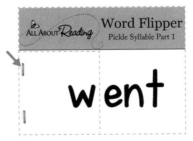

4. Have your student turn the pages and read the words that are formed.

APPENDIX F
Tips and Activities for Using the Practice Sh

Fluency is the ability to read smoothly, accurately, and with expression, and the P
an important part of developing your student's fluency. But students don't always ..
Sheets as exciting as the other hands-on activities in the lessons.

If working on Practice Sheets becomes a chore for you and your student, try some of the following games and creative activities to make them fun again.

Be sure to photocopy the Practice Sheets before playing games that require the pages to be cut into strips or single words.

Games and Activities

 Feed the monster. Cut out the monster on page 375. Cut the Practice Sheets into strips. Have your student feed the strips to the monster as he reads them. For a fun alternative, go to blog.allaboutlearningpress.com/feed-the-puppy-alphabet-game to download our Feed the Puppy printable.

 Number the rows of words and sentences on the Practice Sheet from 1 to 6, repeating those numbers as necessary. Have the student roll a die and read the words or sentences in the row of the number he rolled. For example, if he rolls a 2, he must read the words in row 2.

 Read with a buddy. Take turns reading lines with your student, or let her read with a favorite stuffed animal or toy.

 Use sticker dots. Break up the assignment and reduce your student's frustration by creating a "starting dot" and a "stopping dot."

 Play hide and seek with words and sentences. Cut up the Practice Sheets and hide the pieces around the room. When the student finds a piece, he must read it before searching for the next piece.

 Use an online word search puzzle maker to create your own word search puzzle using your student's fluency words. Have the student read the words as she finds them.

 Choose a letter and have your student search for and read only words that begin with that particular letter.

Play Swat the Words. Cut out the splat graphic on page 377. Attach it to an object to use as a swatter, such as a new flyswatter, a plastic ruler, or even just your student's hand. Cut out words from the Practice Sheet and lay them on the table. Have your student find and swat each word as you read it out loud. Then switch—you swat while your student reads.

Break up the Practice Sheet by covering it with a piece of paper. Slide the paper down to uncover one line or section at a time.

Make progress more concrete. Allow your student to track progress using colored highlighters or fun stickers.

Play Fluency Hopscotch. Write fluency words in each square of a hopscotch grid. Gather a different marker for each student, such as a beanbag, stone, or bottle cap. Follow the standard rules, but when the student stops to pick up his marker, he reads the word(s).

Play Fluency Snowball Fight. Cut up the Practice Sheets into strips and tape them to the wall. Have your student read the fluency words. After each strip is read correctly, have him stand back and throw a snowball at it! Use Ping-Pong balls, Nerf balls, styrofoam balls, or even crumpled paper for snowballs.

Art and Creative Play

Let your student use the Ziggy puppet from the Pre-reading program to read the words and sentences on the Practice Sheets.

Make a word road. Cut the rows of words into long strips. Place the strips on a long table or on the floor to make a road. Have your student drive a matchbox car over the words as he reads them.

Illustrate the words. Select a few words and have your student draw a picture for each one. She may then make a collage of the words and pictures.

Silly sentences. Have your student read a word and then make up a silly sentence using the word.

Have fun with emotions! Cut out the emoticons on page 379. Put the faces in a hat. Cut out the words and sentences from the Practice Sheet and put those in another hat. Have your student pick a word/sentence from one hat, pick a face from the other hat, and then ham it up by reading the word with the selected emotion.

Snacks and Rewards

 Eat your words! Motivate your student to read each row of the Practice Sheet by putting a chocolate chip, marshmallow, M&M, popcorn, granola, fruit, or other favorite treat at the end of a section or row. At the end of the practice session, snuggle up with a story and munch on the rest of the snack.

 Set up a points system in the corner of your white board or on a separate chart and give your student a small prize when she reaches 100 points. For example, you might give your student one point for every correct word she can read in five minutes. You might combine the points system with Phonogram Card and Word Card review as well so your student has more chances to rack up points. There are many point variations, so use what works best for you.

Positive Words

Fluent reading is hard work for your student! Catch him working hard and give him a few words of encouragement. Try positive words like these:

"Very good! You are a quick learner!"
"Hey, you got that the first time!"
"You are doing great!"
"That was a tough one, and you got it!"
"You remembered that from yesterday—great!"
"I can tell that you tried hard to figure that out."

Many of the tips and activities in Appendices F, G, and H can be mixed and matched to review Practice Sheets, Phonogram Cards, or Word Cards. **Tip!**

Appendix F: Tips and Activities for Using the Practice Sheets

Feed the Monster

Instructions: Cut out the monster and cut a slit in its mouth. Cut your Practice Sheet into strips. Have your student read each strip aloud and "feed" it to the monster as it is completed.

Appendix F: Tips and Activities for Using the Practice Sheets

Swat the Words

Instructions: Cut out the splat graphic and attach it to an object to use as a swatter. Cut out words from the Practice Sheet and lay them on the table. Have your student find and swat each word as you read it out loud.

Appendix F: Tips and Activities for Using the Practice Sheets

Fun with Emotions

Instructions: Cut out the emoticons and place them in a hat. Cut out the words and sentences from the Practice Sheet and put those in another hat. Have your student pick a word/sentence from one hat, pick a face from the other hat, and then ham it up by reading the word with the selected emotion.

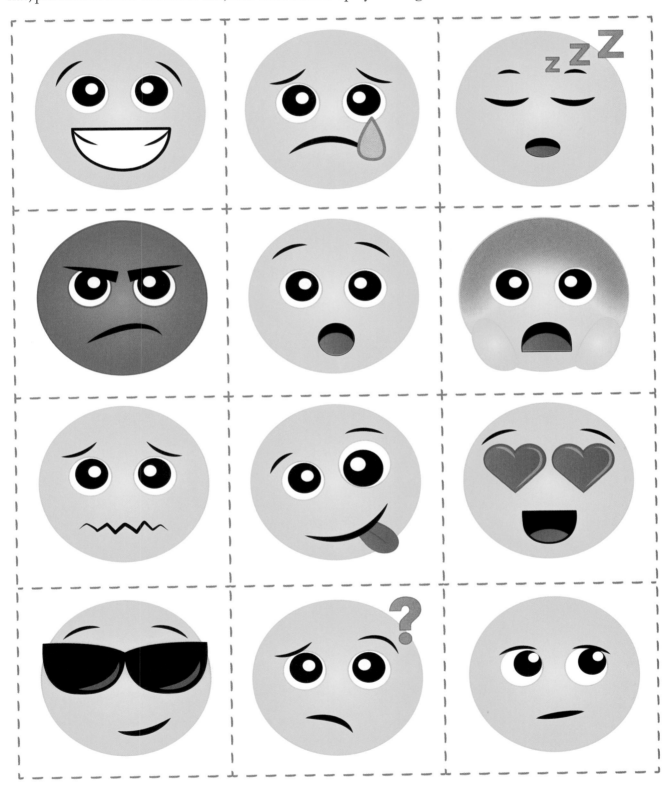

Appendix F: Tips and Activities for Using the Practice Sheets

Activities for Review

Games and Activities

 Play Fun with Phonograms. Go to info.a[l] to download five free folder games to use fo[r]

 Play Swat the Phonograms. Cut out the s[ ] to use as a swatter, such as a new flyswatte[r] Choose a selection of Phonogram Cards a[s] and swat each phonogram as you say the s[ounds] says the sounds.

 Play Phonogram Bingo. Download our Phonogram Bingo [ ] press.com/phonogram-bingo, or make your own bingo cards with a selection of review phonograms.

 Play Phonogram Go Fish. Choose ten to fifteen phonograms to practice. Use index cards to make up two identical sets of cards. Play according to the regular rules.

 Play Phonogram Snowball Fight. Write a selection of review phonograms on index cards and tape them to the wall. As you call out phonograms, have your student locate the phonogram on the wall, say the sound(s), and throw a snowball at it. Use Ping-Pong balls, Nerf balls, styrofoam balls, or even crumpled paper for snowballs.

 Jump on it! Write a selection of review phonograms on index cards and spread them around the floor. Have your student locate and jump to the correct phonogram as you call out the sound(s).

 Play Phonogram Hopscotch. Write a different phonogram in each square of a hopscotch grid. Gather a different marker for each student, such as a beanbag, stone, or bottle cap. Follow the standard rules, but when the student stops to pick up his marker, he says the sound(s) of the phonogram in that square.

 Play Phonogram Ball. Use a marker to write phonograms on a large beach ball. Have the student throw the ball in the air, catch it, and then say the sound(s) of the phonograms closest to his thumbs.

...ave letter stamps, use them to reinforce the phonogram of the day. After ...nogram, use the stamps to stamp the phonogram on the back of your student's ...to it throughout the day, asking what the phonogram is, what sound(s) it makes,

...or it. Look for coloring book pages with big spaces and write review phonograms in ...hose spaces. Have the student say the sound(s) of each phonogram. If she says the sound(s) correctly, she may color that space. Continue until the picture is complete.

Build a Phonogram Card city. Create a city in your living room by arranging the Phonogram Cards face up on the floor and furniture so that every Phonogram Card is a building. Have your student drive around the city, saying the sound(s) of the phonograms as he arrives at each building. If he says the sound(s) correctly, turn that card face down. The game continues until all the cards have been turned face down.

Make a salt tray. Fill a baking pan, jelly roll pan, or other shallow container with salt or sand. Have your student write phonograms in the salt tray with the pointer finger of the dominant hand. Gently shake the salt tray to "erase" phonograms. For added fun, experiment with different colors and scents. Go to blog.allaboutlearningpress.com/salt-trays for recipes.

Create a race track. Line up the Phonogram Cards to form a "track." Place a toy car on the first card. Have your student say the sound(s) of the Phonogram Card. If he says it correctly, he can drive his car to the next Phonogram Card, and so on until he arrives at the finish line.

Snacks and Rewards

Play Phonogram Cup Hunt. Choose five to seven review phonograms, write them on mailing labels, and attach the labels to plastic cups. Under one of the cups, place a small wrapped treat, like a few raisins or chocolate chips in plastic wrap, and then have your student close her eyes as you mix up the cups. Have your student open her eyes, choose a cup, say the sound(s) of the phonogram on the cup, and lift the cup. Continue playing until she finds the treat.

Play Snack Track. Use the Phonogram Cards to make a snack track on your floor. Place a small snack next to each card. Starting at the beginning of the track, have your student hop forward one space and say the sound(s) of the phonogram. If he says the sound(s) correctly, he gets to eat the snack and advance to the next card. If incorrect, he must move back two spaces and try again.

Make an ABC Snack. Go to abc-snacks.com, the home of all our ABC Snacks recipes. Choose the phonogram you are working on and make a yummy snack for it.

Activities for Reviewing Word Cards

Games and Activities

 Play Swat the Words. Cut out the splat graphic on page 377. Attach it to an object to use as a swatter, such as a new flyswatter, a plastic ruler, or even just your student's hand. Choose a selection of Word Cards and lay them on the table. Have your student find and swat each word as you read it out loud. Then switch—you swat while your student reads.

 Have your student type a selection of words on the computer. This activity is especially good for kids who struggle with handwriting.

 Play Word Card Slapjack. Designate one word as the "jack" and then deal out a stack of cards to two players. Play as you would Slapjack, slapping the "jack" as it comes up. Play several times, changing the "jack" card each time. To make it more challenging, have the student say the word every time he lays down a card.

 Guess the Word. Lay down two Word Cards at a time and have your student read one of the cards. You then "guess" which one she read. Be sure to guess wrong now and then! Switch sides and let your student guess which word you read.

 Use favorite family board games for Word Card review. Pull out games like Sorry! or Candy Land and have each player read a word before his or her turn.

 Play Word Card Concentration. Choose ten to fifteen review words. Use index cards to make two identical sets of cards, and then play according to the regular rules.

 Play Fun with Word Cards. Go to info.allaboutlearningpress.com/fun-with-phonograms to download five free folder games. Instead of Phonogram Cards, use Word Cards for review.

 Play Bingo. Download our Phonogram Bingo cards at blog.allaboutlearningpress.com/phonogram-bingo, but use Word Cards instead of phonograms. Or make your own bingo cards with a selection of review words.

 Play Go Fish. Choose ten to fifteen Word Cards to practice. Use index cards to make up two identical sets of cards. Play according to the regular rules.

Art and Creative Play

 Tell a story. Lay out a selection of review words and have your student make up a silly story using all the words. It's okay if it doesn't make sense; in fact, it probably won't!

 Illustrate the words. Select a few words and have your student draw a picture for each one. She may then make a collage of the words and pictures.

 Color it. Look for coloring book pages with big spaces and write review words in those spaces. Have the student read each word. If read correctly, she may color that space. Continue until the picture is complete.

 Create a racetrack. Line up the Word Cards to form a "track." Place a toy car on the first card. Have your student read the Word Card. If he reads it correctly, he can drive his car to the next Word Card, and so on until he arrives at the finish line.

 Use Ziggy activities from the *All About Reading* Pre-reading program, such as having Ziggy read the words incorrectly so your student can correct him, or having Ziggy read the first sound and the student read the second sound.

 Glue the Feed the Monster graphic on page 375 to an empty cereal box and cut a hole where the mouth is. Have your student read the Word Cards and feed them to the monster. You might also use the monster box as an alternative storage place for the mastered cards. Or go to blog.allaboutlearningpress.com/feed-the-puppy-alphabet-game to download our Feed the Puppy printable.

 Create a colorful word cloud. Choose a selection of review words and have your student write each one several times, each time using a different color marker. Create the cloud on a light-colored piece of construction paper. Encourage your student to vary the direction and size of each word.

Snacks and Rewards

 Snack stacks. Select fifteen review words and place them in five piles of three in front of your student. Place some chocolate chips, marshmallows, M&Ms, popcorn, granola, fruit, or other favorite treat behind each stack of cards. Have your student choose a stack and read the words. If she reads them correctly, she may enjoy the snack from that stack. Continue until all the words have been read correctly, and all the snacks eaten!

 Play Yucky Snacks. Select fifteen review words and have your student use them to make up "Silly Recipes for Yucky Snacks." For example, the recipe might be to add three cups of *grass*, mix in a tablespoon of *rat*, and garnish with some *bells*. Don't forget to have your student name her creation at the end—and then go make a *real* snack to celebrate.

APPENDIX I
List of Comprehension Activities

Pre- and post-reading comprehension activities are included in every story-related lesson in Level 1. Depending on your student's needs and interests, you may choose to use additional activities.

Pre-Reading Discussions and Activities

- Before your student reads, skim the story and note possible **vocabulary** words your student may not know. Introduce them briefly before your student reads the story.

- Activate prior knowledge by asking one or two questions related to the story. For example, a question for "Fox in a Box" might be: Have you ever played with or made something out of an empty box? Follow the questions with a brief discussion of your student's experiences.

- Show the title page. Based on the title and any illustration that appears there, discuss what the story might be about.

- Make predictions about the story by asking a story-specific question. For example, questions for "The Bat and King Sam" might include: What do you think might happen if a lonely king met a bat in his castle? Do you think they would be friends?

- Discuss the **setting** of the story. If the story is set in a new or unusual place, use a globe or map to introduce the place to your student.

- Relate the story to your student's experience. Questions you might ask include: Have you ever helped a friend solve a problem? Has anyone ever told you that you're too young or too small to do something? Questions may also be story-specific: What are some reasons you might not want an ox in your house? What would you do if it happened?

- Introduce any **literary devices** used in the story, such as onomatopoeia, alliteration, and rhyme. Have your student watch for these devices while reading the story.

Post-Reading Discussions and Activities

- Discuss the **main character** of the story. Who is the main character in this story? Why? What is the character's problem? How does he feel about it? What does he do about it? How does he feel by the end of the story? How has he changed?

- Discuss the main **conflict** of the story. What problem does the main character face? What does the character do to solve the conflict? Does the character's solution work? What would you have done if you were the character?

- Practice meaningful expression. When reading **dialogue**, demonstrate for your student how you can change your tone of voice to reflect how the character is feeling. For example, if the character is scared, you could read "Yuck! I am not fond of cobwebs!" in a scared voice. Then let the student give it a try.

- Skim through the story and ask comprehension questions that require more than a yes or no answer. Types of questions you might ask include: Why do you think the character said that? Does the character look upset or happy? What does your face look like when you're upset? Why do you think the character did that? What happened after the character left home?

- Have your student skim the story for information about a question you ask. For example, a question for "Yuck!" might be: What are the things that Tam is not fond of?

- Relate the story to your student's experience. Questions you might ask include: What would you do if you were this character? How would you solve the problem? What are some things you could do to cheer up a friend (or help someone in danger, or make a nice lunch, and so on)?

- Connect the story to other literature the student has read. Talk about similarities in **theme**, conflict, setting, or character between stories.

- Imagine an alternate ending for the story. For example, questions for "No Mud for Max" might include: What would have happened if Max's friends hadn't come to help him? How would that have changed the outcome of the story?

- Practice story **sequencing**. Choose three action sentences from the story and write them on separate slips of paper. Have your student read the sentences and place them in the correct order as they happened in the story.

- List similarities and differences between characters or settings in the story. For setting, the student could also compare the story setting to his own location.

- Discuss how authors often use the five senses of sight, hearing, touch, smell, and taste in their writing. Encourage your student to go back through the story and point out places that appeal to any of the senses.

- Talk about realism and fantasy. Which parts of the story could have happened? Which parts could not have happened? Why?

Appendix I: List of Comprehension Activities

APPENDIX J
If Your Student Struggles with the Stories

Do any of these situations sound familiar?

- Your student has trouble reading an entire story in one sitting.
- Your student sees how many pages a story is and feels discouraged before he begins.
- Your student has a decoding special need.

If so, it's important to be proactive and tackle the problem head-on so you can maintain your student's motivation to read. Here are some suggestions.

- **Review.** Spend more time reviewing with the flashcards, activities, and Practice Sheets before reading the story. The more familiar the student is with the words, the easier it will be to read the story.

- **Set a timer.** Have your student read until the timer goes off. Choose the length of time according to your student's ability. You may need to start with a short time, such as three minutes, and then gradually build up to ten minutes.

- **Divide the story into two or three parts.** Have your student read just one section in a sitting. Bookmark the page. At the next reading session, have your student listen as you reread the part he has already read, and then have him continue reading on his own.

- **Reread.** Rereading stories from previous lessons will help your student gain fluency.

- **Try buddy reading.** Split up the reading duties by reading with your student. Alternate pages by reading a page yourself and then having your student read the next. For even more practice, you might read the story three times by buddy reading twice, switching the pages you each read, and having your student read the story on his own the third time.

  Younger students may enjoy buddy reading with Ziggy the Zebra puppet or another favorite puppet or stuffed animal.

- **Practice blending to eliminate word guessing.** Sometimes students struggle because they guess at words rather than try to decode them. The best solution for word guessing is to use the blending (or decoding) procedure in Appendix C.

- **Check for vision problems.** Be alert to vision problems that may be interfering with your student's ability to read fluently. Some signs to watch for include:
  - frequent eye rubbing, blinking, or squinting
  - short attention span
  - avoiding reading and other close activities
  - frequent headaches
  - covering one eye
  - tilting the head to one side
  - holding reading materials close to the face
  - an eye turning in or out
  - seeing double
  - losing place when reading
  - difficulty remembering what he or she read

Methods for Counting Syllables

Knowing how to recognize and count syllables is an important part of your student's reading progress and is immensely useful when it comes to decoding words.

If your student needs help with counting syllables, choose one of the engaging methods below.

	Method	What to Say	What to Do	Example
	The Hum Method	Say the word.	Hum each syllable.	el – e – phant (hum) (hum) (hum)
	The Clap Method	Say the word.	Clap each syllable.	win – dow (clap) (clap)
	The Robot Method	Say the word in a robotic tone.	Listen to the separation of the word chunks.	pres – i – dent (pause) (pause)
	The Jump Method	Say the word.	Jump on each syllable.	mon – key (jump) (jump)
	The Name Method	Say your student's name.	Emphasize each syllable.	Em – i – ly Cae – den Mad – i – son Bryce

Tip! Download our free Help the Monkeys game at blog.allaboutlearningpress.com/count-syllables and use any of the five methods above to practice counting syllables.

Magnet Board Setup at the End of Level 1

In Level 1, your student will learn the twenty-six alphabet phonograms as well as six consonant team phonograms. If you are using a magnetic white board instead of the Letter Tiles app, you will add the letter tiles to your board as they are taught and as indicated in the lessons.

At the end of Level 1, your white board will look like the illustration below. This is also how your white board will be set up when you begin Level 2.

In future levels, more letter tiles will be added to the board, organized under the following categories:

APPENDIX M
Leap Words Taught in Level 1

Leap Words are high-frequency words that either don't follow the normal rules or contain phonograms that your student hasn't practiced yet. Your student will be "leaping ahead" to learn these words as sight words. They are indicated on the Word Cards by the leaping frog.

Leap Words comprise a small percentage of the words taught in Level 1. Out of 193 words taught, only eleven are Leap Words.

Leap Word	Lesson	Why Taught as a Leap Word	True Rule Breaker?
the	2	The most common pronunciation, /thŭ/, is not phonetic.	Yes
a	6	The most common pronunciation, /ŭ/, is not phonetic.	Yes
of	10	The o says its fourth sound, which hasn't been taught yet. The f says /v/ instead of /f/ like we would expect.	Yes
was	24	The a says /ŭ/, which isn't one of its typical sounds.	Yes
to	26	The o says its third sound, which hasn't been taught yet.	No
said	29	The ai says /ĕ/, which isn't one of its typical sounds.	Yes
I	29	The long i sound hasn't been taught yet.	No
or	31	Phonogram or hasn't been taught yet.	No
for	31	Phonogram or hasn't been taught yet.	No
no	31	The o says its second sound, which hasn't been taught yet.	No
do	40	The o says its third sound, which hasn't been taught yet.	No

APPENDIX N
Words Taught in Level 1

The number listed corresponds with the lesson in which the word is first introduced.

A

a 6
act 24
ad 4
add 29
Alps 42
am 1
an 2
and 24
Ann 29
ant 24
anthill 40
anthills 42
as 12
Ash 20
ash 20
ask 24
at 2
ax 16

B

back 34
backdrop 40
backlog 40
backpack 40
bad 4
bag 4
bam 2
ban 2
band 24
bang 36
bank 38
banks 42
bash 20
bask 24
bat 2
bath 18
bathtub 40
bathtubs 42
be 52
bed 14
bedbug 40
beg 14
bell 29
bells 42
belt 24
belts 42
Ben 14
bench 24
benches 42
bend 24
bent 24
Bess 29
best 24
bet 14
Beth 18

Bev 14
bid 8
big 8
Bill 29
bill 29
bin 8
bit 8
black 34
blacktop 40
blank 38
blink 38
bliss 29
blob 26
block 34
blot 26
bluff 29
blush 26
Bob 10
bobcat 40
bobcats 42
bog 10
bond 24
bop 10
boss 29
box 16
boxes 42
Brad 26
brag 26
bran 26
brass 29
Bret 26
brick 34
bricks 42
brim 26
bring 36
broth 26
brush 26
brushes 42
buck 34
buckskin 40
bud 12
Bud 12
bug 12
bulk 24
bump 24
bumps 42
bun 12
bunch 24
bunk 38
bunkbed 40
bus 12
but 12
buzz 29
buzzes 42

C

cab 4
Cal 10
camp 24
can 4
cannot 40
Cap 4
cap 4
cash 20
cashbox 40
cast 24
castoff 40
cat 4
cats 42
catfish 40
catnip 40
Chad 22
chaff 29
champ 24
chap 22
chat 22
check 34
checklist 40
checks 42
chess 29
Chet 22
chick 34
chill 29
chills 42
chimp 24
chin 22
Chip 22
chip 22
chips 42
chomp 24
chop 22
chopstick 40
chopsticks 42
chuck 34
chug 22
chum 22
chunk 38
clad 26
clam 26
clamshell 40
clang 36
clank 38
clap 26
clash 26
class 29
classes 42
Clem 26
click 34
cliff 29
Cliff 29
cling 36

clink 38
clip 26
clock 34
clocks 42
clop 26
cloth 26
club 26
cluck 34
clung 36
clunk 38
cobweb 40
cobwebs 42
cod 10
codfish 40
cop 10
cost 24
cot 10
crab 26
crack 34
cram 26
crank 38
crash 26
crashes 42
cress 29
crib 26
crop 26
cross 29
crosswind 40
crush 26
cub 12
cud 12
cuff 29
cup 12
cups 42
cut 12

D

dab 4
dad 4
damp 24
Dan 4
dash 20
Deb 14
deck 34
Del 14
den 14
dent 24
desk 24
desktop 40
Dex 16
did 8
dig 8
dim 8
ding 36
dip 8
dish 20

dishes. 42
dishcloth 40
dishpan 40
disk 24
do. 40
Doc 10
dock. 34
dog. 10
doll. 29
Don 10
dot 10
Dot 10
drab 26
drag 26
drank 38
dress. 29
drill 29
drink 38
drip 26
drop 26
drug 26
drum 26
drumstick. 40
duck. 34
duct 24
dug. 12
dump 24
dunk 38
dusk 24
dust 24
dustbin. 40
dustpan 40

E
Ed 14
egg. 29
eggs 42
eggnog. 40
eggshell 40
elf. 24
elk 24
elm 24
end. 24

F
fact. 24
fad 8
fan 8
fang 36
fast 24
fat 8
fax 16
fed 14
fell 29
felt 24
fend 24
fest. 24
fig 8
figs. 42
fill 29
film 24
filth 24
fin 8

finch 24
Finn 29
fish. 20
fist 24
fit. 8
fix 16
fixes 42
fizz 29
flag. 26
flags 42
flank 38
flap 26
flapjack 40
flash. 26
flashes 42
flat 26
fleck. 34
fled 26
flick 34
fling 36
flip 26
flit 26
flock. 34
flop 26
floss 29
fluff 29
flung 36
flunk 38
flush. 26
flushes 42
fog 10
fond 24
for 31
fox 16
Fran 26
Frank 38
Fred 26
fresh. 26
frog 26
fun 12
fund 24
fuss. 29
fuzz 29

G
gal 10
gang 36
gap. 4
gas 4
gash 20
gasp 24
get 14
gift 24
Gil 8
glad 26
glass. 29
glasses 42
Glen. 26
glob 26
glop 26
glum 26
go 52
gob. 10

gong. 36
got 10
grab 26
gram 26
grass. 29
grasses 42
Greg 26
grid 26
grim 26
grin 26
grip 26
grit 26
grub 26
gruff. 29
gull. 29
gulp 24
gum 12
gumdrop 40
Gump 24
gun. 12
gunshot 40
Gus 12
gush 20
gust 24

H
had. 6
ham 6
hand. 24
handbag. 40
handcuff 40
handgun. 40
handheld 40
hang. 36
Hank 38
has 12
hash 20
hat 6
he. 52
held 24
help 24
hem 14
hen. 14
hi 52
hid 8
hill 29
hilltop 40
him 8
himself. 40
hint 24
hip 8
his 12
hiss. 29
hisses 42
hit 8
hog. 10
honk 38
honks 42
hop 10
hops 42
hot. 10
hotspot. 40
huff 29

hug. 12
hugs 42
hum 12
hump 24
humpback 40
hung 36
hunk 38
hunt 24
hush. 20
husk. 24
hut 12

I
I. 29
ick 34
if 8
ill 29
in 8
inch 24
ink 38
inkblots 42
inkjet 40
inkwell. 40
inn 29
into 40
is 12
it 8
itself. 40

J
jab 2
Jack 34
jam. 2
Jan 2
Jax 16
jazz 29
Jeb 14
Jed 14
Jeff. 29
Jen 14
Jess. 29
jest 24
jet. 14
jig. 8
Jill 29
Jim 8
job 10
jog 10
Jon 10
Josh 20
jug 12
jump 24
jumps. 42
junk 38
just. 24
jut 12

K
Ken. 14
Kent. 24
kept. 24
kick 34
kid 8

kill 29
Kim 8
king 36
kings 42
Kip 8
kiss 29
kisses 42

L

lack 34
lad 10
lamp 24
land 24
lap 10
laptop 40
lash 20
last 24
lax 16
led 14
left 24
leg 14
lend 24
lent 24
less 29
let 14
lick 34
lid 10
lift 24
Lill 29
limp 24
Ling 36
lint 24
lip 10
lipstick 40
lisp 24
list 24
lit 10
Liv 10
Liz 10
lock 34
locks 42
locksmith 40
loft 24
log 10
long 36
loss 29
lost 24
lot 10
luck 34
lug 12
lump 24
lunch 24
lung 36

M

Mac 4
mad 4
man 2
map 1
maps 42
mash 20
mask 24
mast 24

mat 2
math 18
Matt 29
Max 16
me 52
Meg 14
Mel 14
meld 24
melt 24
men 14
mend 24
mess 29
messes 42
met 14
milk 24
milkman 40
mill 29
Ming 36
mint 24
miss 29
Miss 29
mist 24
mix 16
mixes 42
mob 10
mock 34
mom 10
mop 10
moss 29
moth 18
much 22
muck 34
mud 12
muff 29
mug 12
mulch 24
mum 12
munch 24
mush 20
musk 24
muskrat 40
must 24

N

nab 2
Nan 2
nap 2
naps 42
Nat 2
neck 34
Ned 14
Nell 29
nest 24
nests 42
net 14
next 24
Nick 34
nip 8
no 31
nod 10
not 10
nut 12
nutshell 40

O

odd 29
of 10
off 29
offset 40
on 10
onto 40
or 31
ox 16

P

pack 34
pad 4
padlock 40
pal 10
Pam 1
pan 2
panfish 40
pang 36
pant 24
pass 29
passes 42
past 24
pat 2
Pat 2
path 18
paths 42
peck 34
Peg 14
pen 14
pens 42
pest 24
pet 14
pets 42
pick 34
pig 8
pigpen 40
pill 29
pin 8
pinch 24
ping 36
pink 38
Pip 8
pit 8
plan 26
plank 38
plod 26
plop 26
plot 26
pluck 34
plug 26
plum 26
plunk 38
plus 26
pod 10
pond 24
pop 10
popgun 40
pot 10
prank 38
press 29
prick 34
prim 26

prop 26
puff 29
pug 12
pump 24
pun 12
punch 24
punt 24
pup 12

Q

quack 34
quest 24
quick 34
quicksand 40
quill 29
quills 42
quilt 24
Quinn 29
quit 16
quiz 16

R

rack 34
raft 24
rag 6
ram 6
ramp 24
ran 6
ranch 24
rang 36
rank 38
rant 24
rap 6
rash 20
rashes 42
rasp 24
rat 6
red 14
rent 24
rest 24
rib 8
rich 22
riches 42
Rick 34
rid 8
rig 8
rim 8
ring 36
rink 38
rip 8
risk 24
rob 10
Rob 10
rock 34
rod 10
romp 24
Ron 10
Ross 29
rot 10
rub 12
rug 12
run 12
runt 24

rush 20
Russ 29
rust 24
rut 12

S
sack 34
sad 4
sag 4
said 29
Sam 1
sand 24
sandbox 40
sandboxes 42
sang 36
sank 38
sap 1
sash 20
sat 2
scab 26
scam 26
scan 26
sell 29
send 24
sent 24
set 14
Seth 18
sh! 20
shack 34
shaft 24
shall 29
she 52
shed 20
shelf 24
shell 29
shells 42
shellfish 40
shift 24
shin 20
ship 20
ships 42
shock 34
shop 20
shot 20
shotgun 40
shrank 38
shred 26
shrill 29
shrink 38
shrub 26
shrug 26
shrunk 38
shuck 34
shut 20
sick 34
Sid 8
sift 24
silk 24
silt 24
sing 36
sink 38
sinks 42
sip 8

sis 8
sit 8
six 16
skid 26
skill 29
skim 26
skin 26
Skip 26
skip 26
skit 26
skull 29
skunk 38
slack 34
slam 26
slang 36
slap 26
slash 26
slat 26
sled 26
slick 34
slid 26
slim 26
sling 36
slingshot 40
slink 38
slip 26
slit 26
slop 26
slosh 26
slung 36
slunk 38
slush 26
smack 34
smash 26
smashes 42
smell 29
smock 34
smug 26
snack 34
snacks 42
snag 26
snap 26
snapshot 40
sniff 29
snip 26
snuck 34
snug 26
so 52
sob 10
sock 34
sod 10
soft 24
song 36
songs 42
speck 34
sped 26
spell 29
spill 29
spills 42
spin 26
spit 26
spot 26
spun 26

squish 26
stack 34
staff 29
stag 26
Stan 26
stash 26
stem 26
stems 42
step 26
stick 34
sticks 42
stiff 29
still 29
sting 36
stink 38
stinkbug 40
stop 26
stub 26
stuck 34
stuff 29
stun 26
stung 36
stunk 38
such 22
suck 34
sun 12
sundress 40
sundresses 42
sunk 38
sunlamp 40
sunlit 40
sunset 40
sunsets 42
sunspot 40
suntan 40
swam 26
swell 29
swim 26
swims 42
swing 36
swish 26
Swiss 29
swung 36

T
tab 2
tack 34
tad 4
tag 4
tamp 24
tan 2
tang 36
tank 38
tap 2
task 24
tax 16
taxes 42
Ted 14
tell 29
ten 14
tend 24
tent 24
tenth 24

Tess 29
test 24
Tex 16
text 24
than 18
thank 38
thanks 42
that 18
the 2
theft 24
them 18
then 18
thick 34
thin 18
thing 36
think 38
this 18
thresh 26
thrill 29
throb 26
thud 18
thump 24
thumps 42
tick 34
tilt 24
tilts 42
Tim 8
tin 8
tint 24
tip 8
to 26
tock 34
Tod 10
Tom 10
top 10
toss 29
tot 10
track 34
trap 26
trash 26
trick 34
trim 26
trip 26
Trish 26
trot 26
truck 34
trucks 42
trunk 38
tub 12
tuck 34
tuft 24
tug 12
twig 26
twin 26

U
up 12
uphill 40
upon 40
upset 40
upwind 40
us 12

Appendix N: Words Taught in Level 1

V

Val 10
van 8
vast 24
vent 24
vest 24
vet 14
Vic 8
Viv 8

W

was 24
wax 16
we 52
web 14
wed 14
weld 24
well 29
went 24
wept 24
Wes 14
west 24
wet 14
wetland 40
wig 10
Will 29
will 29
wilt 24
win 10
wind 24
windmill 40
windsock 40
wing 36
wings 42
wink 38
wish 20
wishes 42
wisp 24
wit 10
with 18
within 40

Y

yak 6
yam 4
yank 38
yell 29
yells 42
yelp 24
yes 14
yet 14
yip 8
yuck 34
yum 12

Z

Zack 34
zag 8
zest 24
zig 8
zip 8